THE ORIGINS OF ANTI-SEMITISM

THE ORIGINS
OF ANTI-SEMITISM

Attitudes Toward Judaism
in Pagan and Christian Antiquity

JOHN G. GAGER

New York   Oxford
OXFORD UNIVERSITY PRESS
1983

Copyright © 1983 by Oxford University Press, Inc.

Library of Congress Cataloging in Publication Data
Gager, John G.
The origins of Christian anti-semitism.
Includes bibliographical references and index.
1. Christianity and antisemitism.   2. Judaism—
Relations—Christianity.   3. Christianity and other
religions—Judaism.   4. Philosemitism—Rome.
5. Paul, the Apostle, Saint—Attitude towards
Judaism.   I. Title.
BM535.G33   1983   296.3'872   82–24523
ISBN 0–19–503316–7

Printing (last digit): 9 8 7 6 5 4 3 2 1

Printed in the United States of America

PREFACE

This book originated in a grandiose dream for a doctoral dissertation. Instead, I settled for a much more manageable project on pagan views of Moses. (*Moses in Greco-Roman Paganism* [Nashville, 1972]). The question of manageability aside, the present book simply could not have been written at that time. The work of Rosemary Ruether, Lloyd Gaston, and Menahem Stern has been utterly indispensable to my own. This assertion reflects my strong belief in the corporate character of all humanistic scholarship. Our labor is part of an unbroken conversation—inherited from our predecessors, transmitted through and sometimes modified by ourselves, and passed on to our successors. But our enterprise is corporate in yet another sense, for the ultimate concern of all humanistic scholarship is what it means to be human. At its most fundamental level, this book is intended to address the question of what it means to be human by examining reactions to Jews and Judaism in Western antiquity. The undertaking as a whole rests on the contention that certain conversations, begun in antiquity, continue to shape our lives today. Particular voices in these conversations—the dominant ones I fear—have repeatedly represented our common humanity in the meanest and narrowest terms. At times they have threatened civilization itself. Other voices, potent in the beginning but eventually lost or garbled in the disquieting triumph of Christianity, hold a promise of preserving our common humanity without sacrificing particularity.

My own work, it should be obvious, is heavily indebted to both predecessors and contemporaries. My debt to the former is acknowledged primarily in the footnotes of this work. Among contemporaries, special mention must be made of Lloyd Gaston, of the Vancouver School of Theology; and my former teacher, Krister Stendahl, of the Harvard Divinity School. My editor, Cynthia Read, provided me with invaluable assistance at various points in the completion of the manuscript.

A final note about the use of ancient sources. In dealing with pagan texts, I have tried to be exhaustive. In general I have relied on Menahem Stern's monumental two-volume compendium, *Greek and Latin Authors on Jews and Judaism* (Jerusalem, 1974 and 1980; a third and final volume is projected). In treating Christian materials, the same procedure is neither possible nor desirable. Here I have striven to be judiciously selective rather than comprehensive. Some very recent publications, most notably H. Conzelmann's *Heiden-Juden-Christen. Auseinandersetzungen in der Literatur der hellenistisch-römischen Zeit* (Tübingen, 1981), receive no attention here. The bearing of my own work on such publications will be clear to any who care to read them. Conzelmann's work makes it painfully clear just how difficult it is to change the course of long-established conversations.

CONTENTS

THE ORIGINS OF ANTI-SEMITISM

INTRODUCTION

Let us imagine a conversation involving a Jew, a Christian, and two Gentiles, one a Roman and the other a Greek from Alexandria. The time is 138 C.E., the Romans have just decisively crushed the final Jewish revolt in Palestine, a revolt inspired by messianic hopes surrounding its leader, Bar Cochba.

"This Jesus whom you worship," says the Jew. "How can you expect us to take your claims about him seriously? Equal to God? A crucified messiah? Your own writings tell the truth about him—a man of dubious parentage, untutored in the traditions of the fathers, a violator of the Sabbath, and a friend of tax collectors and prostitutes. Where does his authority come from, this man you proclaim the chosen one of God? Why, your Gentile converts not only fail to observe the commandments but are actually *forbidden* to do so! And in support of your claims you offer the most ridiculous and implausible interpretations of scripture imaginable."

"The Jews are a rebellious and a stiff-necked people," the Christian retorts. "The Pharisees and Sadducees have led you away from the paths of righteousness. You killed the ancient prophets sent to you by God and now you have killed Jesus, whom God has made Lord and Christ for all nations. You have closed your ears to his call to repentance. If you were not deaf and blind to the truth you would know that everything that has happened is in accordance with the law and the prophets. Now God has abandoned you, and your city lies in ruins. The old covenant and commandments are no more. God has established a new

3

covenant for a new people. *We* are the new Israel. The promises are ours. Repent and be baptized in the name of Jesus Christ for the forgiveness of your sins."

The Greek now joins in. "What foolishness! All this nonsense about messiahs, divine covenants with the Jews, and commandments! I say, a plague on *all* religious fanatics! The Jewish writings are nothing but a collection of foolish myths and degrading stories about the deity, most of which were pilfered from the ancients in any case.

Let us consider for a moment the Jewish contribution to civilization. Your founder was a charlatan and magician, and his followers a motley and infected rabble of runaway slaves. Throughout history you have been subject to other nations. Today you live in our cities but refuse to worship our gods or honor our customs. It is no surprise that you should be a rebellious people—you despise the rest of mankind. But you Christians are worse, if anything. Your gospels are a hopeless tangle of wild exaggerations and blatant contradictions. You have thrown away the one thing that gives respectability to the Jews—their ancestral customs. Silly and useless as they are, at least they are ancient. In rejecting even these, you Christians leave yourselves with nothing at all."

The Roman takes a different view. "My Alexandrian friend, in Rome we have heard these stories about the Jews. One must of course be repelled by their rebellious actions. But after all, the revolt has now been crushed and their city captured. With us they have always made good neighbors and citizens. None of the Jews in Rome wanted any part of this uprising—this Bar Cochba was nothing to them. You know, the Jews have really made quite an impression in Rome. Many of our people are attracted to their cult and choose to take up this or that Jewish custom. Some have even embraced the cult completely. There are converts in the highest circles—one or two even in the emperor's family, or so I hear. But the emperor doesn't approve one bit, I can tell you. Several prominent individuals have paid with their lives. It's caused quite a sensation. There's no objection to Jews following their own customs, you understand, but the emperor won't hear of it for Romans. I'm sure I don't know what to think. The Jews' monotheism and unshakeable loyalty to their god, the great antiquity of their scriptures—you can't fault them there. And you know some of their customs are really not at all unlike our own. But others are really *quite* peculiar—I'm referring to circumcision, of course. I just can't help wondering what will happen to Rome itself if the Jews continue to make such inroads. I'm not all that pious myself, actually, but I simply can't imagine Rome without the Roman gods and rituals."

Up to this point, a fifth man has listened in silence. Now he is moved to speak. He identifies himself as *both* a Jew *and* a Christian, throwing the others into a state of confusion compounded by the fact that all present know him as the son of a local pagan family. "Look here," he begins, "there's no doubt at all about who Jesus is. In addition to his ciracles and resurrection, who can fail to be convinced by the extraordinary number of prophecies that have found their fulfillment in him? The number of correspondences is simply staggering. You Jews must be blind not to see them. And now you have made matters worse for yourselves by ruling out of your synagogues those of us who follow God's chosen messiah. But as for you, sir, who call yourself a 'Christian,' whence is this absurd notion that you represent the true Israel? Why, you reject the very things that have always defined what it means to be a Jew. How can you deny the Mosaic covenant and yet claim to be Israel? And as the crowning absurdity you brand *us* as heretics! The very words of Jesus condemn you: 'Think not that I have come to abolish the law and the prophets. I have come not to abolish them but to fulfil them. . . . Whoever then relaxes one of the least of these commandments and teaches men so, shall be called least in the kingdom of heaven!' I know that you call upon the great apostle Paul as witness for your position. And Paul has indeed written that Christ is the end of the law. Many of those who believe as I do have repudiated Paul as an apostate from the law who urged other Jews to apostatize as well. But as the apostle Peter has rightly said, some things in Paul's writings are very difficult to understand. I wonder if we have really understood Paul's teaching."

Although this conversation is fictional, the views expressed herein were widely held and expressed by many pagans and Christians in antiquity. This book represents an attempt to understand the facts that underlie this conversation and to correct the basic misunderstandings that persist in the literature concerned with it. Prominent among these misunderstandings are the following:

    • the study of relations between Jews and Gentiles in antiquity is synonymous with the study of ancient anti-Semitism;

    • at the very moment when Christianity began to spread in the Roman world Judaism was at its lowest ebb of religious vitality; Judaism was ripe for replacement by Christianity because of intrinsic limitations which were as evident to inhabitants of the Roman world as they are to modern Christian scholarship;

    • early Christianity was unanimous in believing that the old covenant, its laws and rituals, had been annulled, and in declaring the Jews to have been supplanted by Gentile Christians as God's chosen people;

    • those early Christian remarks concerning Jews that are most offensive to modern sensibilities can be traced to the pervasive anti-Semitism of pagan antiquity;

    • modern anti-Semitism merely recapitulates the feelings and opinions of pagan and Christian antiquity.

These propositions not only reinforce one another but are mutually dependent. If we begin to have doubts about any one of them, the entire structure starts to collapse. If, for example, we find that in Roman society Judaism competed vigorously and often successfully for the religious sympathies of Gentiles, it will no longer be possible to attribute intemperate anti-Jewish Christian outbursts exclusively to pagan influences. If we find that Gentile converts brought with them to Christianity a sympathetic understanding of Judaism, then we must look elsewhere for the sources of Christian anti-Judaism. We may further speculate that those Christians who insisted on observing Jewish ritual practices in the face of repeated warnings from their leaders reflect an ongoing debate in Roman society at large, concerning the status and value of Judaism. Such a conclusion would be of fundamental significance for our understanding of the story of Christianity. The possibility arises that Christianity was forced to regard Judaism as a serious rival for the allegiance of pagans and committed Christians alike, and reacted accordingly.

    Why, despite significant evidence to the contrary, has the belief in a uniformly anti-Semitic pagan antiquity persisted so tenaciously? One answer is that this belief has in different ways served the needs of both Christians and Jews. For Christians, it has supported the contention that Judaism could not have succeeded as a religion for the Roman world (and its historical successors) and it has served to absolve Christianity of full responsibility for anti-Semitism in the West. Some Jews, on the other hand, have seen it as one explanation for the very survival of Judaism. Pagan persecution is held to have greatly strengthened the cohesiveness which has enabled Judaism to survive.

The bulk of early Christian literature and certainly of the New Testament does in truth deal harshly with Judaism. But this undoubted fact must be interpreted in light of the strong likelihood that the surviving Christian writings comprise a deliberately selective sample. The voice of the Judaizing Christians—those who saw no need to tie their acceptance of Christianity to a repudiation of Judaism—is scarcely heard at all. The conception of early Christian history as governed by a progressive de-Judaization is true only for the victorious minority whose position is reflected in the surviving literature. The New Testament and other extant Christian writings represent and reinforce the views of the ultimate winners. Like other retrospective, value-laden assessments endorsed by history's winners, these writings are intended to create an image of earlier centuries that accords with their idea of what *should* have been. This artificial image must now give way to a richer and more variegated picture that is only now beginning to emerge.

Present circumstances inevitably influence historical judgments about earlier times. As we shall see in our extended treatment of Paul's views on Judaism and Torah, the status of the New Testament as Christian scripture creates a tendency to read it as if it were directed not to the specific issues of a particular time and place but rather to every time, every problem, and every human situation. Krister Stendahl has shown that such a "timeless" reading can have a radical effect on interpretation. For as Stendahl contends, "[i]n the common interpretation of Western Christianity . . . Paul's argument has been reversed into saying the opposite to his original intention."[1]

Serious discussion of the issues I shall address has been hampered by confusion surrounding important terms, including "anti-Semitism," "anti-Judaism," and even "Christianity" and "Judaism." Some efforts to dispel the confusion have been useful, but others have devolved into mere nit-picking or served to create even greater confusion. The search for a pure and unbiased vocabulary is probably doomed from the start. It is important, however, that we make clear how we use the terms we select.

I shall retain *anti-Semitism* as the term to designate hostile statements about Jews and Judaism on the part of Gentiles. Such statements show certain basic similarities to what we call anti-Semitism today. They are expressed by complete outsiders, betray very little knowledge of Jews or Judaism, and tend to be sweeping generalizations.

Early Christian judgments against Judaism are, by and large, of a different order. For these I shall adopt the term *anti-Judaism.* Unlike pagan anti-Semitism, Christian anti-Judaism is primarily a matter of religious and theological disagreement. This is not to deny that Christian statements about Judaism sometimes manifest strong negative feelings, at times even hatred. Nonetheless, the undeniable family ties between Judaism in a way that was never true for pagans.

Beyond this general distinction, D. R. A. Hare has proposed a refinement within the category of Christian anti-Judaism:[2]

(a) *prophetic anti-Judaism,* which is the sort of intra-Jewish critique characteristic of the biblical prophets and of later sectarian and reformist movements within Judaism. This attitude is embodied in Jesus' negative reaction to the Jewish leadership of his time;

(b) *Jewish Christian anti-Judaism,* which reflects the belief that the decisive act God's involvement with Israel is the death and resurrection of Jesus. In this view, these events not only fulfill the promises of the old covenant but actually negate the primary characteristics of that covenant, namely, Temple, Torah, and ritual commandments. Faithful Gentiles now stand alongside faithful Jews as the new Israel. The path to repentance and redemption is still open for the "old" Israel, but only through faith in Jesus Christ. This attitude appears in passages like Luke 23:28–31 ("Daughters of Jerusalem . . . weep for yourselves and for your children");

(c) *Gentilizing anti-Judaism,* which emphasizes the newness of the "new" Israel, the Gentile character of Christianity, and God's final rejection of the "old" Israel. Richardson finds this attitude throughout Matthew.

While Hare's categories do overlap to some extent, they are useful in distinguishing among various kinds of early interactions between Christians and Jews in antiquity. I shall make only one further modification in these categories. The term "prophetic anti-Judaism" is misleading in that it implies a negative attitude toward Judaism as such, although it is actually meant to describe an internal debate in which, though the meaning and control of the central symbols—Temple, Torah, ritual commandments—are in dispute, the symbols themselves are not. Therefore I shall substitute the phrase "*intra-Jewish polemic.*"

These definitional matters lead me to a fundamental observation about terminology. Put simply, the real problem lies not in these or any other distinctions but in the tendency, noted earlier, to use terms like anti-Semitism and anti-Judaism in a global manner, as if they encompassed the full range of interactions between Jews and non-Jews in antiquity. However understood, anti-Semitism and anti-Judaism tell only part of the story, and therein lies the basic issue. Only in a highly restricted sense can Western anti-Semitism be said to originate in pagan and Christian antiquity. The presumption of a universal anti-Semitism in antiquity, pagan or Christian, has been made possible only by suppressing, ignoring, or misinterpreting the mass of non-conforming evidence.

My point of view is unlike that of most scholars in this area in that my interests cannot be described as either religious or theological. But I do not thereby pretend to absolute objectivity or dispassion—traits that to me seem undesirable as well as unattainable. Even a cursory reading of works in this area, whether popular or academic, reveals great depths of passion and personal involvement. I remain convinced, however, that sound scholarship is possible even when we deal with issues which matter a great deal to us. The goal is not to silence our passions but to challenge them. I believe that my disinterestedness does not detract from the relevance of this study for those whose interests *are* primarily religious and theological whether Christian or Jewish. Like the fifth participant in our imaginary conversation, an outsider is sometimes in a better position to challenge and redirect the discussion surrounding a particular area of controversy.

The fact that I am not a direct participant in this conversation does not mean that I am not touched by its deepest concerns. No twentieth-century child of Western civilization is unaffected by the issues raised here. I hardly intend to claim that a revisionist reading of early Christian anti-Judaism can provide the means to eradicate religious anti-Semitism in the modern world. Yet the images of the past that we carry within us do help to shape both our present and our future. A new set of images may have a liberating effect not only on scholars, with their specialized concerns, but also on the culture of which they are a part.

PART I

Anti-Semitism and Anti-Judaism: The Modern Debate

A Christian Church with an antisemitic New Testament is abominable, but a Christian Church without a New Testament is inconceivable. Many would add that a New Testament without the Christ-event as its material center and the Pauline corpus as its formal center would not be the New Testament at all. And yet, whatever the general effect of the gospels, it is Paul who has provided the theoretical structure for Christian anti-Judaism, from Marcion through Luther and F. C. Baur down to Bultmann, in a manner even more serious than Ruether indicates in her brief discussion of Paul. Here then is the dilemma.

Lloyd Gaston, "Paul and the Torah"

I

From Jules Isaac to Rosemary Ruether

The study of relations between Judaism and early Christianity, perhaps more than any other area of modern scholarship, has felt the impact of World War II and its aftermath. The experience of the Holocaust re-introduced with unprecedented urgency the question of Christianity's responsibility for anti-Semitism: not simply whether individual Christians had added fuel to modern European anti-Semitism, but whether Christianity itself was, in its essence and from its beginnings, the primary source of anti-Semitism in Western culture.

Formulated thus, as it was in the years immediately following the war, the question quickly drew attention to three further problems: first, the relationship between pagan and Christian attitudes toward Judaism in the Greco-Roman World; second, the extent to which Judaism was a cultural force in Roman society at the time of Christianity's birth and early development; and third, the precise character and extent of both pagan and Christian anti-Semitism in the ancient world.

The formulation of these issues clearly reflects the historical setting of Europe in the late 1940s. Preoccupation with the Holocaust and the question of its historical sources was so overwhelming that anti-Semitism itself has only recently come to be seen as but one among a number of important factors, rather than the single overriding concern in the study of pagan and Christian views of Judaism in the ancient world. The question of anti-Semitism in pagan or Christian circles has not now been forgotten, but it no longer represents the sole starting point or the only framework for scholarly inquiry. Instead of treating the study of pagan and Christian attitudes toward Judaism as more or less equivalent to the study of anti-Semitism in antiquity—and treating nonconforming data as

13

insignificant exceptions—recent approaches have concentrated on careful studies of particular authors;[1] on specific geographical regions and historical periods;[2] on the broader social, political, and religious context within which Jews, Christians, and pagans interacted;[3] and finally, though to a lesser extent, on studies of modern attitudes toward Judaism as they shed light on earlier periods.[4]

This survey will concentrate heavily on work produced since the end of World War II and will argue that the trauma of the war is largely responsible both for bringing the study of pagan and Christian views of ancient Judaism into the mainstream of scholarship and for determining the direction which that study has taken. It is nonetheless true that virtually all of the concerns of recent scholarship find their antecedents in earlier works. Jean Juster's magisterial work on Jews in the Roman Empire approaches the subject in the broadest possible terms, while at the same time seeking to pay scrupulous attention to matters of detail.[5] Although new discoveries in the fields of archaeology and papyrology have added important new information to our knowledge of Judaism in the Roman Empire, recent studies are still very much in Juster's debt. Theodore Reinach's pioneering attempt to collect all references to Judaism in ancient Greek and Latin authors occupies a similar position.[6] Though Reinach missed a few texts along the way and gave little space to analysis of the materials, his collection remained unchallenged until a new edition of the texts was undertaken by Hans Lewy.[7] Lewy's early death in 1945 left the project well short of being finished, and it was only in 1974 and 1980 that Menahem Stern brought the project to virtual completion with his *Greek and Latin Authors on Jews and Judaism.*

On the Christian side, the works of G. F. Moore,[8] James Parkes,[9] and A. Lukyn Williams[10] first drew attention to the systematic anti-Judaism of early Christian literature, to the origins of this anti-Judaism in a bitter ideological conflict between "the Church and the Synagogue," and to the disastrous consequences of anti-Judaism in later history. As Moore says in his survey of Christian writers on Judaism, "Christian interest in Jewish literature has always been apologetic or polemic rather than historical."[11] These scholars were among the first to challenge the traditional image, rooted in the very earliest Christian literature, of ancient Judaism as desiccated, legalistic, and altogether without appeal to outsiders. They were the first to demonstrate that this image was very much the product of the polemical framework within which early Christian attitudes toward Judaism first took shape.

These concerns have remained constant throughout the period reaching from the early twentieth century to the present. But between them and more recent scholarship stands the experience of World War II. That experience brought these topics into the mainstream of modern scholarship. As a consequence, they have benefited from unprecedented scholarly attention.

With the publication in 1948 of *Jesus and Israel*,[12] the French historian Jules Isaac inaugurated a new era in the study of pagan and Christian views of Judaism. In 1943, at the age of sixty-six, Isaac could look back on a distinguished career as a historian of modern Europe, the author of a standard seven-volume *Cours d'histoire* and Inspector General of Education in the French government. But in that year his wife, his daughter, and several other members of his family were arrested and murdered by the Nazis. From that moment until his death in 1963, Isaac wrote exclusively on the Christian origins of anti-Semitism and worked for cooperation and understanding between Jews and Christians.

Jesus and Israel, written between 1943 and 1946 while Isaac was himself fleeing arrest, consists of twenty-one propositions. Propositions 1–10 refute the traditional view that Judaism was a moribund religion at the time of Jesus and demonstrate the fundamentally Jewish character of primitive Christianity; 11–13, by the use of contrasting passages from the canonical gospels and modern Christian interpretations, drawn from liturgical, exegetical, and catechetical sources, argue that Jews have been wrongly blamed for the rejection and crucifixion of Jesus; 16–20 demonstrate that these modern Christian texts reflect a long-standing indictment of all Jews for the crime of deicide; and 21 states that the Jews of Jesus' time neither rejected nor crucified Jesus, that Jesus did not reject Israel, and that the people of Israel are totally innocent of the crimes of which Christian tradition has accused them. Somewhat later, in *Genèse de l'anti-sémitisme*, Isaac added the premise that anti-Semitism was not prevalent among pagans in pre-Christian times and characterized pre-Christian anti-Semitism as trivial and vulgar in comparison with later Christian anti-Semitism.

The net effect of Isaac's work has been twofold: (1) to lay the blame for anti-Semitism squarely at the door of Christianity; and (2) to buttress the argument that anti-Semitism, while exclusively a Christian product, results from a misinterpretation by Christians of their own scriptures and founder, and stands in fundamental opposition to the historical origins and basic tenets of Christianity. Consequently, the ensuing debate was focused almost exclusively on the topic of anti-Semitism and its Christian sources.

If Isaac's *Jesus and Israel* inaugurated a new era in the study of pagan and Christian views of Judaism, Marcel Simon's *Verus Israel* has dominated that era until quite recently.[13] This is not the place to attempt a summary of Simon's work. Suffice it to say that he has covered every facet of nascent Christianity and its interactions with Judaism in the Roman Empire. In his treatment of Christian anti-Jewish polemic, Simon insists on the importance of distinguishing between: (1) *anti-Jewish polemic*, which represents an ideological conflict in which Christianity seeks to define its originality and to defend its legitimacy against the claims of Judaism; and (2) *Christian anti-Semitism*, which is born of the Jewish refusal of Christian claims and expresses itself increasingly as hostility toward Jews in general. Though Christian anti-Semitism draws in part on pagan traditions, it is finally to be distinguished from them by virtue of its religious and theological basis. Christian anti-Semitism goes back as far as the Gospel of John—but not to the letters of Paul—and attains its fullest expression in the fourth century. From that time forward, within the context of a Christian Empire, anti-Semitism ceased to be merely a matter of popular resentment and theological-exegetical debate. It became the ideological justification for anti-Jewish legislation and for the destruction of synagogues.

Discussing the sources of these attitudes, Simon recognizes the traditional factors: Jewish anti-Christian polemic; tensions produced by the Jewish revolts of 70 and 135 C.E.; the charge of deicide; and the traditional image of the Jews as persecutors of Christians. But he argues that underlying all of these specific factors, and causally prior to them, was the enduring religious vitality and appeal of Judaism in the later Roman Empire. The traditional view of Judaism in late antiquity as isolated, introverted, and generally unappealing has been stood on its head:

The caricature of the Pharisees in the gospels translates . . . the disappointment and resentment of nascent Christianity. Similarly, ecclesiastical anti-Semitism in its original and specific aspect translates the irritation of the church at this same Israel which, far from converting or collapsing, continued to exert itself even among the ranks of the faithful. . . .[14]

In the extensive *Post-Scriptum* which Simon appended to the second edition of *Verus Israel* in 1964, he responds to a variety of critics and reflects further on specific issues. Of particular interest are his remarks about the writings of Jules Isaac. Simon is critical of Isaac's view that pagan anti-Semitism was intrinsically trivial and without significant impact on Christian attitudes. We should not, however, exaggerate the distance between Simon and Isaac on this issue. For Simon himself argues persuasively that pagan anti-Semitism makes a significant impact on Christian attitudes only toward the end of the fourth century C.E., and, while such views did become increasingly prominent thereafter, they remained fundamentally different from Christian anti-Semitism, whose basis was and remained theological.

Simon endorses Isaac's criticism of the widely held view that hostility toward Jews appeared wherever and whenever pagans encountered Jews in the Greco-Roman world. He contends that Isaac sometimes fails to distinguish adequately between anti-Semitism—which Simon defines as a fundamental and systematic hostility toward Jews—and anti-Jewish apologetic—which is part and parcel of Christianity's effort to define itself vis-à-vis Judaism. Once again, however, the distance between the two is not great. Just as Isaac admits that anti-Semitism is a perversion of true Christianity, so Simon recognizes that there is no clear line of separation between anti-Jewish polemic and anti-Semitism and that systematic hostility toward Jews is to be found from the very beginnings of Christianity. On this point, there is fundamental agreement between Simon the historian and Isaac the prophet.

Following Simon, the most significant responses to Isaac's challenge came from the French scholar F. Lovsky[15] and Gregory Baum, a Christian convert from Judaism.[16] While deeply affected by Isaac's work, Baum speaks of being "shattered" by *Jesus and Israel*[17]—both challenge him on important historical issues. Lovsky's argument is twofold: first, that Isaac seriously underestimated the depth and the extent of pre-Christian, pagan anti-Semitism and had completely ignored its impact in Christian circles from the second century onward; and second, that there is a significant difference between the theological anti-Judaism of the early decades, when Christians sought to differentiate themselves from Judaism, and later anti-Semitism which was manifested as enmity towards the Jews as people, their culture, and their religion. With the possible exception of the Gospel of John, anti-Semitism as such is not to be found in the New Testament. Lovsky's argument thus isolates and protects the New Testament from the charge of anti-Semitism, attributing the increase of anti-Semitic views in Christian circles of the second, third, and fourth centuries to the impact of popular anti-Semitism throughout the Greco-Roman world.

Baum's earliest treatment in *The Jews and the Gospels* deals exclusively with the New Testament and bypasses entirely the issue of pagan anti-Semitism. Like Lovsky, Baum distinguishes sharply between the legitimate, theological anti-Judaism of the New Testament and modern, racial anti-Semitism. The passionate anti-Semitism of later catechisms, sermons, and ecclesiastical documents was able to make use of the New Testament passages only by distorting them. Its real sources lie in secular political and social tensions within the Christian Empire of the early middle ages. In short, while admitting a degree of historical continuity between early Christian anti-Judaism and later Christian anti-Semitism, Baum and Lovsky contend that the New Testament, properly understood, cannot be characterized as in any way anti-Semitic.

For all of these authors, the distinction between anti-Judaism and anti-Semitism is all-important. This distinction became a standard apologetic device for refuting the charge that the New Testament contains the seeds of anti-Semitism. It is important to note, however, that while criticizing Isaac on specific issues, his critics have been in accord with him on some fundamental points: first, that Isaac's work represents a serious theological challenge for Christians; and second, that anti-Semitism cannot be found in the pure and original form of the Christian faith. The issue that remained was when and why anti-Semitism came to pervert, as Baum puts it, "the purity of the gospel."[18] Indeed, the subsequent development of Baum's own thinking can be seen as a barometer of the continuing pressure exerted by Isaac's work. In 1961 Baum confessed that Isaac had forced him to modify his earlier uncritical approach to the theological problem of Israel.[19] Later still, in 1974, in his introduction to Rosemary Ruether's *Faith and Fraticide*, he cited Ruether's work as one among several factors that had forced him to abandon his earlier attempts to defend the New Testament against the charge that its writings reflect a fundamental hostility toward Jews and Judaism.[20]

Like all of the scholars cited thus far in the discussion, Rosemary Ruether's *motivation* for her study of Christian anti-Semitism is primarily theological. Also like them, she chooses the *method* of literary and historical analysis of Jewish-Christian relations, primarily in the first four centuries. Unlike Isaac's earlier critics, Ruether not only embraces his basic position on the Christian sources of modern anti-Semitism but moves beyond it on the issue of the inseparability of anti-Semitism and early Christianity. Her argument is centered on two familiar themes: first, the effect of pagan attitudes on Christian views; and second, the distinction between anti-Judaism and anti-Semitism.

Ruether follows Isaac and Simon in maintaining that Christian attitudes toward the Jews are fundamentally different from and independent of pagan sources, despite occasional borrowings. Unlike its Christian counterpart, pagan polemic against the Jews was rooted "in the special social consequences of the Jewish religious law,"[21] that is, religious exclusivism and social separateness. She makes the telling observation that early Christianity shared with Judaism a fundamental antipathy toward pagan culture. Conversely, those elements that Gentiles found offensive in Judaism were equally offensive in Christianity. This not only makes it possible to account for the striking similarities in pagan criticisms of Jews and Christians in the early centuries but it also heightens the implausibility of deriving Christian anti-Judaism from pagan sources. In late Hellenistic and early Roman times, especially in the aftermath of the Jewish revolts of 70, 115, and 135, the political interests of various power blocks—including the Greek anti-Roman faction in Alexandria, the Empire itself, and pro-Roman Jewish groups in local centers—produced riots, rebellions, and violent retaliations. But the overall attitude toward Judaism was by no means hostile and the rapid return to normal relations after the revolt in 135 suggests that the normal situation, far from being one of unbroken tension and hostility, was one of "mutual cooperation that would respect Jewish religious distinctiveness."[22]

Christian attitudes, Ruether argues, arise from wholly different sources. These she characterizes variously as "the theological dispute between Christianity and Judaism over the messiahship of Jesus,"[23] "hatred between groups whose relations express a religious form of 'sibling rivalry,' "[24] and finally a fear that "as long as 'the Jews,' that is, the Jewish religious tradition itself, continues to reject this [Christian] interpretation, the validity of the Christian view is in question."[25] Each of these tensions was exacerbated, as Simon had earlier noted, by the continued existence "of a lively and proselytizing Judaism"[26] which threatened the Church by offering a viable alternative to the New Testament and presenting itself as the true and legitimate successor to and fulfillment of the Hebrew Scriptures. Ruether traces the development of Christian attitudes from the anti-Pharisaic polemic of the synoptic gospels, into the philosophical or mythological reformulation of anti-Judaism by Paul, Hebrews, and the Gospel of John, and finally to the literary and theological negation of the Jews and Judaism in the Church Fathers.

Two further insights may be drawn from Ruether's analysis. She has shed new light on the much-debated terminological distinction between anti-Judaism and anti-Semitism. On the one hand, she recognizes the formal distinction between anti-Judaism as a set of beliefs regarding the inauthenticity of the religious and theological claims of Judaism, and anti-Semitism as a combination of hostile beliefs and actions regarding Jews. On the other hand, she passes well beyond her predecessors both in her assertion that anti-Judaism "constantly takes social expression in anti-Semitism"[27] and in her denial that anti-Judaism is an accidental by-product of historical circumstances. She rejects the possibility of separating anti-Judaism from historical Christianity. "For Christianity, anti-Judaism was not merely a defense against attack, but an intrinsic need of Christian self-affirmation. Anti-Judaism is a part of Christian exegesis."[28]

These are bold claims, but that should not blind us to their continuity with a tradition of scholarship reaching back to Simon and Isaac, and behind them to figures like Moore and Parkes. In addition, Ruether's two central claims receive support from quite a different quarter. In

weighing the interrelatedness of anti-Judaism and anti-Semitism, it may
be useful to reflect on the extensive sociological study of modern American attitudes in *Christian Beliefs and Anti-Semitism* by Charles Y. Glock
and Rodney Stark.[29] Glock and Stark used extensive survey data to test
the hypothesis that anti-Semitism in modern America has clear religious
roots within Christianity. They posit three components in the dynamics
of anti-Semitism: beliefs → feelings → actions. They argue that given
negative images of historic Jews as, say, malevolent Christ-killers, and
a high level of "religious particularism," that is, the belief that only a
narrow sphere of persons qualify as properly religious, and that other
persons and groups are religiously illegitimate, the model "overwhelmingly predicted a hostile *religious* image of the contemporary Jew."[30]
They conclude that

> not only is anti-Semitism very characteristic of Christian church mem-
> bers, but all of these aspects [beliefs, feelings, actions] of anti-Semitism
> were found to be strongly correlated with our model of the religious
> sources of anti-Semitism.[31]

These comments about specific conditions which give rise to religious particularism point to the second of Ruether's results, which, like
the issue of terminology, requires further elaboration. At one point she
speaks of a sibling rivalry between Judaism and Christianity and adds
that "hatred between groups who have no stake in a common stock of
religiously sanctioned identity symbols can scarcely be as virulent as
hatred between groups whose relations express a religious form of 'sibling
rivalry.' "[32] In *The Functions of Social Conflict*, Lewis Coser has formulated several propositions which bear on early relationships between
Christianity and Judaism.[33] Proposition 6 in particular reads: "The closer
the relationship, the more intense the conflict." Coser speaks of the renegade as one whose "attack on the values of his previous group does not
cease with his departure, but continues long after the rupture has been
completed."[34] This will be all the more true if, as in the present case,
both groups appeal to and depend on an identical set of symbols, that is,
the Hebrew Bible, for their religious existence and legitimacy. For
Christianity the threat has been "symbolically, if not in fact, its existence

as an ongoing concern."[35] Or as Uriel Tal has put it in his *Christians and Jews in Germany*, "racial anti-Semitism and traditional Christianity . . . were moved by a common impulse directed either to the conversion or to the extermination of Jews."[36]

Much the same point is made by Peter Berger and Thomas Luckmann in *The Social Construction of Reality*.[37] The force of their approach lies in its heightened appreciation of the indispensable role played by symbols in the life of any social institution. The mechanisms used to maintain and legitimate a symbolic universe include mythology, theology, philosophy, and exegesis. And in the case of early Christianity, we must add the New Testament itself. But for all of these efforts, such mechanisms never fully succeed in creating a symbolic universe which is beyond doubt (internal) or question (external). Specifically, the appearance or existence "of an alternative symbolic universe poses a threat because its very existence demonstrates empirically that one's own universe is less than inevitable."[38] The threat will be even more perilous, of course, if it comes not just from outside the institution but from inside as well.

At such times, the institution will seek to maintain its legitimacy through the process of ideological nihilation, that is, the conceptual liquidation of everything in opposition to its own universe. While the appearance of heretics or renegades represents one type of situation that evokes the need for ideological nihilation, conversion or the transfer of identities is another. Citing the example of Paul's conversion, the authors remark that what needs legitimation "is not only the new reality, but . . . the abandonment or repudiation of all alternative realities. The nihilating side of the conceptual machinery is particularly important in view of the dismantling problem that must be solved."[39]

In short, *if* we are dealing with a religious community whose view of its own legitimacy is fundamentally dependent on a set of symbols, viz., the Hebrew Scriptures, which are simultaneously claimed by another religious community; *if*, in addition, this other religious community is able to present arguments which appear at least initially to establish the priority of its claims (continuity of ritual observance, use of scriptures in the original language, and so forth); and *if* this other community not only continues to flourish but exercises an appeal among the faithful of the new religion, then, under these circumstances, the task of conceptual nihilation will appear all the more urgent and continuous. Or, as the psychoanalyst Rudolph Loewenstein puts it in *Christians and Jews. A Psychoanalytic Study*, the negative image of Jews and Judaism within the Christian tradition are indicative of "the Christian reaction to their moral debt to the Jews. All reflect also Christianity's incomplete victory over Israel."[40] This, presumably, is what Ruether means in stating that "for Christianity, anti-Judaism was not merely a defense against attack, but an intrinsic need of Christian self-affirmation."[41]

2

Consensus and Crisis
in the
Response to Ruether

The views of Ruether and of the tradition behind her have not gone unchallenged.[1] Baum's change of heart is indicative of a broad consensus that anti-Jewish elements are to be found at many levels of the New Testament, but various critics have contested Ruether's claim that the writings of the New Testament, as a whole, reveal a systematic connection between anti-Judaism and all forms of early Christian messianic theology.

These critics have focused on five issues: (A) Ruether's monocausal view of Christian anti-Judaism as rooted exclusively in Christian messianic theology; (B) the figure of Jesus; (C) her interpretation of the canonical gospels and of (D) Paul's views of Israel, the Torah and Judaism; (E) the influence of pre-Christian, pagan anti-Semitism in Christian circles; and (F) the treatment of Judaism in ancient and modern literature.

(A) Among Ruether's critics a persistent theme has been that messianic christology does not necessarily entail, nor can it alone account for, anti-Judaism. Some stress the impact of anti-Jewish sentiments introduced into Christianity at a later date by pagan converts. Others argue that christological reflections do not inevitably lead to anti-Judaism, or that other factors such as the growth of Gentile Christianity,[2] the rejection of the Christian message by Judaism, and the increasing hostility between local Christian and Jewish communities during the late first and early second centuries were necessary to turn messianic christology, and Christian theology in general, in an anti-Jewish direction.[3]

Some of these are familiar themes, present in the debate long before Ruether and merely brought into sharper focus by her claims. It must also be said that the distance between Ruether and her critics is not great. Ruether concedes that "initially, of course, the early Church did not think of the message of the crucified and risen messiah as putting them outside or against Judaism."[4] This is an important concession, for it brings the first Christians close to what D.R.A. Hare calls the "hallowed tradition" in Israel itself of prophetic anti-Judaism.[5] In light of this, Ruether's statement that "the difference between prophetic self-critique and anti-Judaism lies in the relation of the critic to the covenant and the Torah of Israel,"[6] can only mean that, by itself, allegiance to Jesus does not explain Christian anti-Judaism in its strong sense. Furthermore, when she adds that local tensions between individual Christian and Jewish communities—such as clearly lie behind the gospels of Matthew and John—account for the "vehemence of these authors,"[7] she stands much closer to the view that some additional factor is necessary to transmute loyalty to Jesus into Christian anti-Judaism.

Here our earlier discussion of terminology is directly relevant. In discussing the gospels and their sources, Paul, or later Christian writers, we will need to determine with care how they view their relationship with contemporaneous Judaism. Do they see themselves as carrying out a debate and dialogue within Judaism or do they view it from the outside? It will not be easy to make such distinctions in every case. Some figures will prove intractably ambiguous or ambivalent. Still, we need to be able to make one important distinction: between those for whom loyalty to Jesus placed them outside Judaism, whether in their own thinking or in the judgment of other Jews; and those whose criticisms of Jewish beliefs and practices came from within the circle of Judaism.

From here it follows that yet another apparent disagreement quickly subsides. Against Ruether's attempt to link christology with anti-Judaism, Hare objects that *messianic claims as such* could never have brought about the complete separation of church and synagogue, particularly from the Jewish side. Messianic claims about individual Jews were often greeted by other Jews with skepticism or even scorn but never with excommunication.[8] Beneath the messianic claim and far more serious in Jewish eyes was the subordination of "the primary symbols of Jewish identity—Torah, temple, circumcision, Sabbath, food laws—to a rank below the central Christian symbol of the crucified and risen Jesus. . . ."[9] In her response to Hare, Ruether has modified her position on two important points: first, in her remark that at least some among the earliest Christians did not think of this message of the crucified and risen messiah as putting them outside or against Judaism; and second, in her recognition that "ceasing to practice the Torah is the critical moment when Christians pass outside Judaism."[10] While making these concessions, however, Ruether insists that messianic claims about Jesus and a decision to turn away from observance of Torah are more closely connected than her critics have recognized. We will deal with this question extensively at a later point. For the time being it will suffice to comment that for some Jewish Christians and for a number of Gentile Christians it was precisely messianic claims about Jesus which, respectively, reinforced and induced observance of Torah. In other words, christology alone does not lead inevitably to anti-Judaism.

As to whether loyalty to Jesus plays any essential role in generating anti-Judaism, once again the differences between Hare and Ruether are not great. On the one hand, she is prepared to agree that the vehement anti-Judaism of Matthew and John arises at a time when Jewish communities had begun to take a strong stand against followers of Jesus; on the other, Hare recognizes that there will always be an essential, if limited anti-Judaism in Christianity "as long as Christians insist that hopes and expectations articulated in the Hebrew Scriptures find some kind of fulfillment in Jesus of Nazareth. . . ."[11] And in this context it matters little whether the christology in question understands Jesus as crucified messiah, prophet, or teacher of divine wisdom.

One final issue raised by Ruether, and earlier by Isaac, deserves mention. Several critics have argued that she has underestimated the role played by the Jewish rejection of Christianity. In response, Ruether has called attention to the fact that the theme of the Jewish rejection of the Christian message is itself part and parcel of the ideology of Christian anti-Judaism and must therefore be used with restraint in any effort to explain that phenomenon. We know that many Jews embraced Christianity. Whether or not one accepts Ruether's further proposal that "the vehement projection by the early Church of blame upon the Jewish authorities for his rejection has something to do with the exculpation of the disciples' own rejection of him,"[12] it seems clear that the theme of rejection cannot be more than one minor factor in the rise of Christian anti-Judaism.

(B) The modern quest for the historical Jesus has engendered a powerful reluctance among students of early Christianity to speak with assurance, if at all, about Jesus' acts and pronouncements, let alone his beliefs, feelings, or intentions. Still those hoping to discover a moment in Christian history that is free of Christian anti-Judaism often start with the figure of Jesus. Here, it has been argued, the critique of Judaism takes place entirely from within. Isaac adopts this position in several of his propositions.[13] Ruether follows the same line in her statement that "within the teachings of Jesus himself I would find nothing of what I would call Christian anti-Judaism."[14] And John Koenig speaks of Jesus and the Jerusalem church as directing criticisms at fellow Jews and re-quiring repentance of them. "Yet," he adds, "the new salvation they proclaimed was a salvation of and within Judaism. Its images of redemp-tion came directly from Jewish Scripture and tradition. The validity of Torah, the election of the Jewish people, and (generally) the sanctity of the Temple were upheld."[15]

The primary difficulty here is that any argument based on claims about "the real Jesus" is unlikely to persuade in the present climate of skepticism about our ability to discriminate between authentic Jesus material and the expansions and additions gleaned from the pre-gospel traditions or generated by the gospel writers themselves. The enormous variety of Jesus-images in modern scholarship suggests that we should limit ourselves to speaking of sayings and stories in circulation before the written gospels, some of which may well go back to the figure of Jesus. It is of the greatest interest, however, that certain of these traditions reflect attitudes toward Judaism that differ sharply from those of the gospels in which they come finally to be embedded. Thus we must be prepared to dis-tinguish between Matthew's overall view of Christianity as a Gentile movement (for example, Matt. 22:7; 24:1–3; 28:19) and certain non- or even anti-Gentile passages (for example, Matt. 10:6) which clearly represent pre-Matthean traditions, and to recognize modifications of inherited materials which result in drastic reinterpretations, many of which enhance or even create for the first time an anti-Jewish thrust.

(C) Several recent studies have argued that the canonical gospels

preserved traditions from early Christian communities that require significant modifications in Ruether's views. Hare in particular insists that there
exist several types of anti-Judaism in early Christian literature and that
the synoptic gospels and Acts in particular require a more nuanced
treatment than Ruether and others have been able to provide.

The pre-gospel traditions reveal other important differences which
also bear directly on Ruether's argument. For her, it will be recalled, the
crucifixion of Jesus and the consequent interpretation of him as the
crucified messiah led early Christians to develop anti-Judaism as a necessary
corollary—"the Jews crucified the messiah." But there is evidence that at
least some of the pre-gospel traditions placed little or no emphasis on the
cross as the key to understanding Jesus and his mission.[16] Images of Jesus
as prophet and teacher of heavenly wisdom were central to a number of
traditions later incorporated by Mark and the other gospel writers. These
divergent images are discernible precisely because they clearly stand apart
from Mark's own view of Jesus as crucified messiah. The non-canonical
Gospel of Thomas, which derives ultimately from very early gospel
traditions, presents us with an image of Jesus in which cross and messiah
play no role at all.[17]

We have noted that the distinction between the written gospels and
their earlier sources requires certain modification in Ruether's treatment
of anti-Judaism in the canonical gospels. Quite apart from the problems
raised by her reference to "Jesus' own messianic identity,"[18] we can no
longer credit a simple contrast between Jesus on the one hand, as standing
within Judaism, and the early church on the other, as appropriating the
figure of Jesus so as to reject the "old covenant" in his name. Nor can we
assume that all criticisms of Judaism in these early traditions necessarily
arise outside the circle of Judaism. The point here is not just, as the
Israeli scholar David Flusser has put it, that "all the motifs of Jesus' famous
invective against the Pharisees in Matthew xxiii are also found in rabbinical
literature."[19] Beyond this, we must learn to distinguish between early
material and its use in later settings. In its present setting within the
overall framework of the Gospel of Matthew and more broadly in the
total collection known as the New Testament, the anti-Pharisaic invective
of Matt. 23 clearly presents us with a situation in which Judaism is under

attack from the outside. But once we imagine this and similar sayings in their original, pre-gospel form, we will almost certainly find ourselves in the presence of debates and arguments within rather than outside Judaism.

(D) We will deal at length with Paul in Part IV. For the moment, we may simply take note of the fact that the view of Paul reflected by Ruether has remained unchallenged in Christian and Jewish circles from the very beginning. Briefly, the traditional and still dominant view holds that Torah and Christ are mutually exclusive categories for Paul, that with the coming of Christ the Torah no longer represents God's path of salvation, and that Israel thus stands condemned and rejected by God for its refusal to have faith in Christ. The fact that there are enormous difficulties in reconciling such a view with the texts of Paul has not prevented it from holding sway over more than nineteen hundred years. Quite recently, however, this view has come under attack from a variety of quarters. Lloyd Gaston has responded directly to Ruether in a manner that breaks completely with the traditional view.[20]

Gaston's radical reappraisal challenges Ruether on every major issue, including the linkage of christology and anti-Judaism.[21] If, as he argues, there is no trace of anti-Judaism in Paul, what are we to make of the claim that christology leads always and inevitably to anti-Judaism? Here at least is one christology, indeed a christology whose central feature is the crucifixion and resurrection of Jesus, which may not lead to a pre-occupation with Jesus' opponents or to a view of Israel's rejection. Once again we must ask whether it is christology as such, or rather particular kinds of christology or christologies in combination with other factors, such as the rapid gentilization of Christianity in the late first and early second centuries, and the succession of Jewish revolts in 70, 112, and 135 C.E., that moved Christians outside the circle of Judaism.

(E) Along with Isaac and others, Ruether has insisted that the allegedly widespread hostility of Gentiles toward Judaism had little impact on Christian attitudes. Her argument is twofold: first, that pagan anti-Semitism has been widely misunderstood and overestimated by modern scholars; and second, that in nature and origins Christian anti-Judaism is something altogether unlike such expressions of pagan antipathy as do occur.

One article by John Meagher and another by R. B. Ward and T. Idinopulos, have sought to overturn Ruether's position. Meagher has written that "antiquity, on the whole, disliked Jews."[22] He reasons that once Christianity achieved a position of preeminence in the Roman world, it had nothing to fear from Judaism and simply used its anti-Jewish theology to cover up the underlying antagonisms toward Judaism introduced into Christianity by Gentile converts. Much of this antagonism, notes Meagher, arose from an understandable reaction of Gentiles to Jewish exclusiveness and separation on the one side and to the successes of Jewish proselytism on the other.[23] Ward and Idinopulos follow much the same line of attack, adding only that "the principle of the ghetto in the dynamic of separation-isolation-ostracism-oppression was operative several hundred years before the triumph of the church over both pagans and Jews in the fourth century. . . ."[24]

There is much to say about the views of Ruether's critics on these issues. In fact, Part II of this book will be devoted exclusively to them. For the moment, we may be content with a few brief observations. First, we cannot fail to perceive the implicitly apologetic element in the concerns of Ruether's critics. To the extent that the blame for Christian antipathy toward Judaism can be shifted from Christian to Gentile shoulders, to that same extent will Christianity itself be partially exonerated. Meagher is a paradigm case, for he turns the tables completely, arguing that Christian theological anti-Judaism is a mere cover for pagan anti-Jewish sentiments.

If bias and prejudice characterize much traditional scholarship on relations between Christians and Jews in antiquity, it must be said that ignorance seems to dominate much of what has been written about relations between Jews and Gentiles. Meagher's documentation and argumentation are woefully inadequate, while Ward and Idinopulos cite no pagan texts at all. This inattention to the sources helps us to understand a seeming contradiction in the claim put forward in both articles to the effect that pagan antipathy toward Judaism arose both from Jewish separatism and from successful Jewish proselytism. As our examination of pagan texts will demonstrate, the only way around the contradiction is to suppose that one group of Gentiles was offended by the conversion to and/or sympathy toward Judaism of a different group of Gentiles.

Even so, unless we presume that Gentile converts to Christianity came primarily from the former, hostile faction—an unlikely hypothesis—it is difficult to see how pagan dislike for Jews could have made its way into Christianity largely via pagan converts.

Finally, we look briefly at treatments of Jewish "separateness" in recent studies of pagan anti-Semitism. The alleged separatism of Jews in the Greco-Roman world has served as the most frequent explanation of pagan antipathy to Judaism, most recently in a work by J. N. Sevenster.[25] This view is mistaken in every respect. Like those scholars who fail to perceive the extent to which early Christian judgments about Judaism as a religion are deeply embedded in anti-Judaism, Sevenster and others fail to hear the polemical undertones in the complaints about Jewish separateness in authors like Apion and Tacitus. Allegations of Jewish separateness are at least as much a pretext as a cause of local tensions between Jews in the Diaspora and their Gentile neighbors—indeed most Jews were not separate at all. This initial error is then compounded, first by the assumption that Jewish communities were in fact aloof and separate, and then by the use of this separateness as an explanation of anti-Semitism. Here we have a classic case of question begging, in this case by assuming that Jewish customs, whether practiced by Jews or pagans, separated adherents from the mainstream of Greco-Roman culture. Once we lift the veil of polemics, we find not "a people apart, with their own customs and religion which admitted little intermingling with their Greek neighbors,"[26] but a people both in and of their world. We do not find a self-confident paganism aggressively and unanimously set against Judaism as a "barbaric superstition," but a prolonged debate *within* an increasingly anxious culture over the status of Judaism as a religion of universal humanity.[27]

(F) There remains one final issue that has emerged from the recent debate, though not directly in response to Ruether. I refer to the "discovery" that much of Christian scholarship on ancient Judaism has been shaped by the legacy of early Christian anti-Judaism. Despite G. F. Moore's warning in 1921 that "Christian interest in Jewish literature has always been apologetic or polemic rather than historical,"[28] his words appear to have gone unheeded until very recent times. Isaac's protest against the distorted image of early Judaism in the Christian tradition has been largely without effect. Simon was one of the first and for a long time one of the few to treat Judaism as an attractive and lively competitor of Christianity, particularly in the later Roman Empire.[29]

By and large, however, the image of Judaism described by Moore and Isaac has shown a powerful reluctance to disappear. Throughout her *Anti-Judaism in Christian Theology*,[30] Charlotte Klein notes with dismay that the presentation of Judaism in general introductions and specialized studies has remained essentially unchanged since Emil Schürer and Wilhelm Bousset, the latest authors cited by Moore. Her analysis of modern Christian—mostly, but not exclusively German—scholarship on early Judaism yields a disheartening picture. This tradition of scholarship is incomprehensible unless we presuppose that it has been shaped by a systematic anti-Judaism: first, by taking the image of Judaism in early Christian writings at face value and failing to recognize the anti-Judaism behind that image; and second, by perpetuating the anti-Judaism of later Christianity which required a negative image of Judaism for its own theological legitimacy.

Shortly after the appearance of Klein's book, E. P. Sanders published his *Paul and Palestinian Judaism*,[31] together with an extended section entitled "The persistence of the view of Rabbinic religion as one of legalistic works—righteousness." To read this section is a disheartening experience. The works surveyed there are influential and representative. The optimistic judgment of several Jewish and Christian scholars to the effect that Christian scholarship on Judaism has finally been purged of its anti-Jewish bias would seem to be somewhat premature.[32] More recent publications do nothing to encourage such optimism.

The titles and authors surveyed by Moore, Klein, and Sanders will be immediately familiar to anyone with training in modern biblical studies. They are standard reading: Schürer, Bousset, Strack-Billerbeck, Charles, Bornkamm, Bultmann, Käsemann, and Conzelmann. Recent discussion has suggested some underlying causes for the remarkable resistance of this image to repeated exposure to the truth. Apart from the general theological usefulness of the view that Judaism had degenerated to such a state that it deserved to be replaced by the true Israel, Moore pointed out that Protestant scholarship in particular engaged in a covert polemic against Roman Catholicism by projecting distasteful aspects of Catholic belief and practice onto Judaism and attacking them in that guise.[33] This process appears to be at work in specifically Lutheran scholarship.[34] For when Luther's antithesis between Law and Gospel is applied to the relationship between Judaism and Christianity, the result is a conglomeration of falsities in which the "facts" of history disappear altogether behind a cloud of religious polemic.

Before concluding this discussion of modern scholarship, we must emphasize once again the presence of recurrent themes in the more recent phases of the debate. By and large, the process of returning to and re-evaluating the ancient sources has taken place within a traditional, that is, Christian and theological framework. This has meant that many of the studies have followed the division of early Christian literature into canonical and non-canonical books. Simon begins his study at 135 C.E. Blumenkranz's survey of Augustine's predecessors reaches back only as far as Tertullian; and Ruether entitles the relevant chapters in *Faith and Fratricide*, "The Rejection of the Jews in the NT" and "The Negation of the Jews in the Church Fathers."

Some authors have chosen to steer clear of the New Testament altogether, and until quite recently later Christian literature has received more attention than canonical writings. One underlying reason for this is no doubt the fact that for Western Christianity the New Testament stands as the foundation of the faith. Thus at the deepest level, the new consensus represented by figures like Baum, Ruether, and others indicates not just a historiographic problem of how to interpret ancient documents but a profound theological crisis in which nothing less than faith itself is at stake.

Nowhere is the crisis depicted more sharply than in Lloyd Gaston's essay, "Paul and the Torah":

> It may be that the Church will survive if we fail to deal adequately with that question, but more serious is the question whether the Church ought to survive. A Christian Church with an antisemitic New Testament is abominable, but a Christian Church without a New Testament is inconceivable.[35]

The problem is most acute for those theologians who acknowledge anti-Jewish themes within the New Testament itself. Among them, the theological solution has been to seek a point within the canon—usually Jesus, sometimes Paul—from which to develop a more acceptable Christian view of Israel and Judaism. All share a commitment (perhaps more of a hope) that true Christianity must be entirely free of anti-Semitism. Authentic Christianity cannot serve to justify later anti-Semitism. Instead it must allow for the full religious autonomy and authenticity of Judaism alongside Christianity. This commitment has taken shape in efforts to reinterpret various New Testament texts so as to demonstrate that traditional interpretations, not just within classical Western Christianity but among modern biblical scholars as well, are profoundly mistaken. Obviously this is an enormously difficult task. At the very least, assumptions about the meaning of New Testament texts have been challenged, and it has been demonstrated that new approaches inevitably produce new meanings.

Whatever the long-term theological results of these efforts—and we should not forget that the real issue for most of these scholars is theological—we must remember that the hermeneutical problems are fundamentally the same whether we are dealing with Christian or pagan texts. The experience of World War II has engendered a new appreciation of how these texts have influenced subsequent Western history and has caused scholars to return to the texts themselves with a new set of questions.

PART II

Judaism and Judaizing Among Gentiles
Attractions and Reactions

Whenever we see a man halting between two faiths, we are in the habit of saying, "He is not a Jew, he is only acting the part." But when he adopts the attitude of mind of the man who has been baptized and has made his choice, then he both is a Jew in fact and is also called one.

Epictetus, *Discourses* 2.9.20

The first known contacts between Greeks and Jews date back as far as the sixth century B.C.E., when refugees from the Babylonian conquest of Judea settled in Sepharad (Sardis) in Asia Minor, then known as Lydia. The first literary evidence does not appear until more than two hundred and fifty years later, still some three hundred years before the birth of Christianity.

For reasons quite independent of the Christian movement, relations between Jews and Gentiles reached their nadir in the one hundred years between the death of Jesus (30 C.E.) and the final Jewish revolt against Rome (132–135 C.E.). This is also the period during which Christian attitudes toward Judaism moved toward their classic formulation. Students of early Christianity, many of whom are unfamiliar with pagan-Jewish relations in preceding centuries, have tended not only to suppose that the circumstances of the first century prevailed in earlier times, but to project them onto later times as well.

Students of Christian anti-Judaism have given little attention to pagan

35

attitudes in the Hellenistic era (the third through first centuries B.C.E.). It
has been customary to assume that this earlier period differs little from
the first century C.E., and since many of these same students have been
unfamiliar with the background and setting of the encounter between
Judaism and Greco-Roman civilization, they have tended to take certain
famous authors—Cicero, Apion, Tacitus, Seneca, and Juvenal—as typical
for the period as a whole. Consequently the study of pagan views of
Judaism is commonly thought of as tantamount to the study of ancient
anti-Semitism.

Only on the basis of this assumption is it possible to contend that
early Christian attitudes toward Judaism were influenced negatively by
the pagan environment. Only so is it possible to account for such a statement, written in response to Ruether, as "Antiquity, on the whole, disliked Jews."[1] This remark does a disservice to its intended apologetic aim
and is untrue to the facts. For all of this, however, it reflects a widespread
point of view among scholars whose primary focus is early Christianity.
More recently, J. N. Sevenster, in *The Roots of Pagan Anti-Semitism in
the Ancient World*, defines the subject as "anti-Semitism" and treats non-
conforming evidence only briefly in a final chapter entitled "Diversity
of opinions regarding Jewry."[2]

The following chapters will offer a different hypothesis regarding the
period most directly relevant to early Christianity, the first century C.E.
This hypothesis, which has its origins with the Israeli scholars, Menahem
Stern and Shimon Applebaum, has directly challenged the inherited view
of this century as a time of unprecedented and unmitigated animosity
toward Jews and Judaism. Their work has shown that there existed
among many Greeks and Romans of this period a remarkable degree of
sympathy for Judaism. The relevance of this work for students of early
Christianity can no longer go unnoticed.

We will divide the topic along chronological lines, paying attention
to geographical and cultural variations along the way. The first period
reaches from the late fourth century to the mid-first century B.C.E., that
is, the Hellenistic era. The second era begins with the arrival of Rome
as the new political force and ends around 140 C.E. This period is punctuated by a series of riots and wars involving Jews and pagans in Alexandria,

Judea, Cyrene, and Cyprus. By this time Christianity has also entered the scene. The third and final period extends through the reign of the Christian emperor Constantine (306–337), the brief revival of pagan hopes under Julian (360–363), and concludes around 430 during the reign of Theodosius II.

3

The Greek and Roman Encounter
with Judaism *Philosophy and Politics*

THE HELLENISTIC ERA (to 50 B.C.E.)

In the Greco-Roman world, the earliest and most abiding view of the
Jews was as a nation of philosophers. Theophrastus (c. 300 B.C.E.), Megasthenes (c. 300 B.C.E.), Clearchus of Soli (c. 300 B.C.E.), Hermippus of
Smyrna (c. 200 B.C.E.), and Ocellus Lucanus (second century B.C.E.) all
associate Judaism with the traditions of ancient philosophy.[1] A similar
image appears among Hellenistic ethnographers. Hecataeus of Abdera (c.
300 B.C.E.) as well as numerous authors cited by Josephus in his *Against
Apion* indicate a strong and appreciative interest in Jewish history and
culture throughout the Hellenistic period. In short, there is considerable
evidence to substantiate Martin Hengel's observation that "down to
Posidonius [c. 50 B.C.E.] . . . the earliest Greek witnesses, for all their
variety, present a relatively uniform picture: they portray the Jews as a
people of philosophers."[2]

Beyond these authors, mention must be made of various other writers
on Jewish history and culture who are known only by name—for ex-
ample, Hieronymus of Cardia, Eratosthenes, Polybius, Timachares, and
Agatharcides of Cnidus. Undoubtedly the most significant of these was
Alexander Polyhistor, whose work *On the Jews*, preserved in Eusebius's
Praeparatio Evangelica, was an anthology of Jewish Hellenistic writings.[3]

Palestine

During the period of Seleucid control in Palestine, under Antiochus IV
Epiphanes and the successful Jewish revolt under the Maccabees (c. 168–

140 B.C.E.), the tradition of good relations was interrupted. Nonetheless, the traditional view that Antiochus's invasion of Jerusalem was prompted by his own anti-Semitic sentiments has been called into question.[4] Although it seems almost certain that Antiochus himself was not motivated by anything but political factors, there is evidence to suggest that these conflicts mark the beginnings of pagan anti-Semitism. Diodorus of Sicily portrays certain advisors of the later Antiochus VII Sidetes as urging the king to punish the Jews for their "misanthropic and impious customs."[5] Although Antiochus rejects their advice, the speech of the advisors reads like a script for much of the subsequent anti-Semitism in Greek and Latin authors. The specific anti-Semitic accusations in the speech are not unrelated to the accounts of the earlier Hellenistic ethnographers. Hecataeus in particular, following the conventions of ancient historiography and ethnography, had noted certain distinctive and peculiar elements of Jewish culture, including a way of life he described as "somewhat unsocial and hostile to foreigners." As I have argued elsewhere, such comments presuppose no negative judgment whatsoever and must be read as part of Hecataeus's overall presentation of Moses' legislation as a political and religious utopia.[6] But when enmity later arose between Jewish revolutionaries and various political and military opponents, these originally disinterested observations served as the starting point for unmistakably anti-Semitic statements.

There is no better illustration of this transformation than the many pagan stories about the Jews' departure from Egypt under Moses. Versions which in Hecataeus and even later writers like Strabo are reported in a straightforward and noncondemnatory fashion are appropriated by others —Apion, Lysimachus, the advisors of Antiochus VII, and Tacitus—to vilify the Jews by depicting their ignominious origins as polluted Egyptian exiles.

Apart from this period of Jewish-Seleucid conflict in the mid-second century B.C., there is little information on pagan views of Judaism in Palestine before the Roman occupation. The sole exceptions are Mnaseas of Patara (c. 200 B.C.E.)[7] and Poseidonius (c. 100 B.C.E.).[8] Mnaseas, who is the first to record the story that the Jews worshipped the head of an ass in the Jerusalem temple, reports this libel in the context of a military struggle between the Jews and the Idumeans—a typical occasion for the invention or transmission of slanders about one's enemy. Poseidonius remains a shadowy figure, although much has been written about him. Some are inclined to credit Josephus's words about "the authors who supplied him [Apion] with his materials, I mean Poseidonius and Molon"[9] and to conclude that he was unfriendly towards Judaism.[10] Others have argued that because of the imprecision of Josephus's reference as well as the more general difficulty of ascertaining Poseidonius's views on any matter, "we must pronounce a *non liquet* on the question of Poseidonius' real views on the Jews and their religion."[11] In fact, there is no text anywhere that can be taken as reflecting Poseidonius's knowledge or opinion of Judaism.

Rome

The Maccabean struggle marks the beginning of official dealings between Rome and Judea as the Jewish leaders sought and found support for their cause in Rome. From this point onward, Roman attitudes toward Judaism flow in three separate channels: (1) the official policy of the Roman government; (2) the views of Roman *literati*; and (3) the popular attitudes in Rome and other cities and towns of the Empire.

(1) Recent studies have indicated that official Roman policy toward Judaism was laid down as early as the mid second century B.C.E. and continued in effect, with occasional exceptions, until the early fifth century C.E.[12] This policy applied everywhere in the Empire. Its basic premise was the right of Jews to live according to their ancestral customs. It gave them the privilege of making annual donations to the temple in Jerusalem, of settling most disputes within the community, and of freedom from civic obligations on the Sabbath. It did not, as a matter of course, grant them citizenship. In return, the community was expected to maintain its own internal order and not to engage in proselytism among non-Jews.

(2) It has been customary to assert that Roman literary circles were uniformly hostile toward Jews and Judaism. In large part this is due to the writings of Cicero. Cicero's unfriendly remarks and the incorrect assumption that they remained normative for later times have been the point of departure for surveying later Roman views of Judaism. The case of Cicero's contemporary Varro (c. 50 B.C.E.) is instructive.[13] In his work on ancient religious customs, Varro sought to identify the god

of the Jews with Jupiter and praised the Jewish cult for its prohibition of images. In his effort to fit the Jewish deity into the pagan pantheon, he is but one among many—pagans and Jews—to use the technique of *theokrasia*, that is, the identification of different national deities as a single, universal god.

(3) What little evidence there is for popular attitudes toward Judaism suggests that some felt an attraction to Judaism and showed a willingness to embrace certain Jewish practices. This pattern of Judaizing emerges strongly during the Empire and will play an important role in Christianity.

Egypt

In many respects, the reception of Judaism in Ptolemaic Egypt is reminiscent of Hellenistic Palestine and Syria. Jewish settlers and mercenaries figured prominently in the affairs of the early Ptolemies, particularly during the reign of Ptolemy Philometor (181–145 B.C.E.).[14] From that time onward, the ambiguities and potential dangers of this involvement became increasingly apparent in the internal dynastic struggles of the Ptolemies and later still with the intervention of Rome. For by making friends with one side, the Jewish mercenaries automatically made enemies of the other. In particular, the Greek population seems to have resented the role played by Jewish military advisors. This resentment exploded into violence when the Jews of Alexandria later placed their full weight behind the Romans.

There is general agreement, however, that in Egypt "during the whole Hellenistic period anti-Semitism does not pass beyond the limits of the literary."[15] Simply put, anti-Semitism is a minor theme. Nonetheless, the sudden turn of events in the 30s of the first century C.E. was not entirely without antecedent causes. The much-debated texts attributed by Josephus to Manetho, a Greco-Egyptian priest of high standing in early Ptolemaic Egypt (c. 300 B.C.E.), are relevant here.[16] Whether these texts are authentic or later fabrications, their hostile version of the Jewish exodus from Egypt demonstrates the potential for an anti-Semitism whose form and roots are religious as well as political. In any case, whether the sentiments attributed to Manetho go back to his time or were created at a later date, this literary expression of hostility toward Judaism could have exercised little influence outside priestly circles. Only in the early decades of the first century c.e., with important public figures like Lysimachus, Chaeremon, and Apion does it begin to exert a broader influence. Beyond this, tensions between Jews and Gentiles in Egypt before the arrival of Christianity provide the essential background for understanding later tensions between Jews and Christians in Egypt in the fourth century c.e. and after.

We may now speak of a new consensus on the nature of relations between Jews and Gentiles during most of the Hellenistic period. As Hengel comments, not even the bitterness arising from the Maccabean revolt failed to dampen the sense of "amazement at the founder of the Jewish religion and the original teaching of Moses."[17] When contrasted with the years 30 b.c.e. to 135 c.e., the Hellenistic period is striking not just for the absence of anti-Semitic actions and the low level of anti-Semitic beliefs but for the indications of active interest in Jewish history and religion. Those who would assess this period differently must do so on shaky grounds. The cultural exchange between Jews and Greeks from the Hellenistic side was, by and large, open and appreciative. As we shall see, the images and traditions established in the Hellenistic era will persist to the very end of pagan culture and continue to manifest themselves even during the turbulence of the Roman Empire.

THE EARLY ROMAN EMPIRE: 30 B.C.E.–140 C.E.

Anti-Semitism and Anti-Romanism in Egypt[18]

The emperor Augustus changed the course of history for all nations and peoples in the ancient world. His consolidation of power reached its climax with the defeat of Antony in 31 b.c.e. and his immediate annexation of Egypt. From that moment on, Roman power was the basic fact for all inhabitants of the Mediterranean basin. Ironically, it was precisely this Roman power, together with the policy of protecting the special status of Judaism, that created the conditions in which Alexandrian anti-Semitism came to life.

The Jews of Egypt were quick to embrace the Roman cause. As non-citizens (non-Greek) and non-indigenous (non-Egyptian), their well-being must have seemed best assured by a strong Roman government. On the Roman side, there are strong indications that Augustus officially confirmed the rights and privileges of all Jewish communities. In line with past practice, Rome established herself as a protector of the Jewish community in Egypt.

At this point, however, the Roman policy toward Judaism began to reveal its fragile and contradictory character. Shortly after gaining control of the country, Augustus imposed a new tax, the *laographia*, on all non-citizens in Egypt. Full exemptions were granted only to full Greek citizens of Alexandria. The tax fell not only on the native Egyptian population but on all non-citizen residents, including the large majority of Jews. The impact on certain segments of the Jewish community in Alexandria was considerable. While the imposition of the *laographia* was entirely consistent with Rome's earlier support for the Jewish community, it meant not only that Jews—including those who were wealthy, well-educated, and long-established in the city—were subject to a heavy tax, but that they were classified publicly with native Egyptians. This new set of circumstances led to new efforts by individual Jews to obtain full Greek citizenship.

These two Roman actions, the one designed to protect Jewish privileges and the other to raise taxes among non-citizens, set the scene for the wave of anti-Semitism that was to engulf Roman Egypt beginning with the riots of 38–41 C.E. In other words, the two basic sources of the violence were (1) the fervent anti-Romanism of a group described by Tcherikover as "hot-headed Alexandrian patriots,"[19] a group which could hardly confront Rome directly but which "could make indirect attacks on Rome through her protégés the Jews, who were at hand and far more vulnerable";[20] and (2) the efforts of numerous Jews to obtain citizenship by enrolling as students in the gymnasium, efforts which met with strenuous resistance from Alexandrians as well as Roman officials. The radical Alexandrians made use of Judaism's special status to attack the Jews and through them to express their resentment of Rome's presence in Egypt.

While there can be no doubt that the events of 38–41 were preceded by a period of mutual frustration, there is little evidence for incidents of any kind during the early years of Roman control. Apart from Lysimachus, whose dates are unknown, the only direct testimonies derive from participants in the riots themselves. Chaeremon, whom Josephus cites in his *Against Apion*, was a Greco-Egyptian priest (*hierogramma-teus*), a member of the rabidly anti-Semitic faction, a teacher of Nero, and the author of a *History of Egypt*. In all likelihood he is identical with the Chaeremon mentioned in the emperor Claudius's *Letter to the Alexandrians* as a member of the Alexandrian delegation to Rome in 41 C.E. In the course of his *History*, Chaeremon included an anti-Jewish account of the exodus:[21] the Jews, numbering 250,000 polluted persons, were driven from Egypt together with their leaders, Moses and Joseph, who were renegade Egyptian priests; with help from allies, they returned to Egypt; finally, they were driven into Syria by Ramses. Lysimachus's story is altogether different, showing no dependence on Chaeremon:[22] in response to an oracle, the King (Bocchoris) purified the land by expelling all unclean persons; one group was under the sole leadership of Moses; Moses exhorted them to show kindness to no one, to offer the worst rather than the best advice and to overthrow the temples and altars of the gods; after crossing the desert, they reached Judea where they maltreated the population and plundered and set fire to the temples; the town where they settled was originally called Hierosyla ("sacrilege"), after the people themselves, but later changed to Hierosolyma in order to cover up this disgrace.

Apion the grammarian, at whose provocation Josephus produced his apologetic treatise *Against Apion*, was also a Greco-Egyptian who achieved citizenship in Alexandria and came to occupy an important academic post in the city, probably as head of the great Alexandrian library. Like Chaeremon, he was also a member of the delegation which pleaded its anti-Jewish case before the emperor Gaius Caligula. He also authored a history of Egypt (*Aegyptiaca*), in the course of which he incorporated numerous pieces of anti-Semitic polemic.

Josephus divides Apion's material into several categories: (1) passages relating to the departure of the Jews from Egypt; (2) those in which he deals with the civic status of Jews in Alexandria; (3) slanderous remarks about Jewish religious practices; and (4) references to the role of Jews in Ptolemaic Egypt. Throughout Apion manifests the implacable hostility that filled the air in the late 30s and early 40s of the first century C.E. His account of the ancient exodus drew on a variety of sources. One of them derived the Jewish Sabbath from the Egyptian word for a disease of the groin, stating that the Jews developed this disease during their flight from Egypt. But unlike his predecessors, Apion may well have possessed first-hand knowledge of the Jewish Scriptures, for he notes that Moses went up into the mountain called Sinai, which lies between Egypt and Arabia, remained in concealment there for forty days, and then descended in order to give the Jews their laws.[23] When it came to Jewish religious observances, however, Apion was dependent on traditional material: Jewish laws are unjust and their religious ceremonies mistaken; circumcision and abstention from pork are ridiculous. He repeats the earlier tale of Mnaseas about the golden head of an ass in the Jerusalem temple and adds that Jews worship that animal. As if this were not enough, he reports that when Antiochus IV Epiphanes entered the temple in Jerusalem he discovered a Greek man whom the attendants were fattening in preparation for their annual sacrifice of a Gentile![24]

On the matter of the Jews' civic status in Alexandria, he used a variety of arguments to buttress his contention that the Jews held no legitimate claim to citizenship: the Jews are outsiders from Syria and occupied an undesirable part of the city;[25] he rejects the Jews' designation of themselves as Alexandrians, that is, citizens;[26] he points to actions taken against the Jews by various Ptolemaic rulers;[27] he points to the exclusion of the Jews from the grain dole under Cleopatra and Germanicus as proof that they were not citizens;[28] and finally he objects that the Jews fail to erect statues of the emperors or to worship the same gods as the Alexandrians.[29]

In Apion and his compatriots the intensity of the situation in Alexandria before, during or after the riots of 38 can be clearly seen. Given their beliefs and feelings, it is not difficult to comprehend the actions that arose from them. Apion and Chaeremon were prominent leaders in Alexandria. Their words would have carried considerable weight, particularly among the Greco-Egyptian population of non-citizens. But beneath all of their inflammatory rhetoric about religion and history, there is good reason to believe that the issue of citizenship was the primary irritant.[30] In his famous letter to the Alexandrians, the emperor Claudius makes this quite explicit when he warns the Jews "not to aim at more than they have previously had . . . and not to intrude themselves into the games presided over by the *gymnasiarchoi*. . . ." For Apion, opposition to Jewish attempts to obtain full civic status was clearly an important matter, not least because he had had to earn the honor himself. As for his followers among the Greco-Egyptian populace, their opposition was undoubtedly founded on their own ineligibility. Once emotions reached a fever pitch, however, the question of citizenship quickly blended into the mass of inflammatory words and actions.

At the center of this inflammatory rhetoric, it will be remembered, stood anti-Semitic accounts of the exodus. In the past the purpose of these stories has never been quite clear. Perhaps these too should be interpreted with reference to the issue of citizenship. Just as Apion used the Jews' Syrian origins as proof that they could not be citizens, so one function of the exodus stories may have been to demonstrate that the Jews, whose ancestors had been expelled from Egypt as sacrilegious and polluted renegades, were even less deserving of full civic status than the native Egyptian population.

Philo, the Acts of the Pagan Martyrs, and the Events of 38–41

The causes behind the outbreak of violence in 38 C.E.—"the disturbances and rioting, or rather, to speak the truth, the war, against the Jews" as Claudius himself puts it—were numerous. Some of them had little to do with local matters, for example, the Roman governor Flaccus's fear that the new emperor, Gaius Caligula, would retaliate for Flaccus's open support of his rivals. What makes this important for us is that the governor's fear for his position made him more susceptible to the Alexandrian anti-Semitic lobby. There were also other factors. At about this time, Herod's grandson, Julius Agrippa I, passed through Alexandria on his way to his new kingdom in northern Galilee. His public appearances in Alexandria as a defender of the Jewish cause and a favorite of the Roman emperor further inflamed the anti-Roman, anti-Semitic sentiment of the nationalist political clubs.

Under these circumstances, according to Philo's account, the anti-Semitic lobby persuaded Flaccus to issue a series of rulings regarding the civic status of the Jews.[31] Most of his subsequent actions are to be seen as consistent with efforts to redefine that status in a restrictive manner: the seizure of the synagogues; the declaration that the Jews were "aliens and strangers," no doubt based on the anti-Semitic exodus stories; the resettlement of the Jewish population in a single section of one residential quarter; the arrest of members of the Jewish council of elders; and the administration of punishments normally reserved for non-citizen Egyptians.[32] In other words, the issue of citizenship was foremost in the program of the anti-Semitic leaders, and it was in order to "clarify" this issue, at the urging of these leaders, that Flaccus seized the initiative. Simultaneously, and perhaps with his blessing, the anti-Semitic clubs undertook a campaign of pillaging, destruction, beatings, torture, and murder. Eventually, after a period of perhaps two or three months, order was restored, and Flaccus was arrested and returned to Rome for trial. Rival delegations from the Greeks and Jews of Alexandria went to plead their case before the emperor Caligula. Fortunately for the Jewish side, Caligula was murdered in January of 41 and succeeded by Claudius, whose disposition of the outstanding issues is contained in his letter of 41, in which he cautions the Alexandrians "to behave gently and kindly toward the Jews . . . and not to dishonor any of their customs in their worship of their god."[33] To the Jews he restored the privileges guaranteed earlier by Augustus but warned them "not to aim at more than they have previously had" and not "to bring in or invite Jews coming from Syria or Egypt."

In discussing the attitudes and motives of the Alexandrian rioters, we must distinguish at least three separate categories: Flaccus himself, the leaders of the riots and later of the delegation, and finally the "mob" as Philo calls them. Flaccus had governed Egypt peaceably for several years before the difficulties of 38. There is no reason to believe that he was an anti-Semite before that date—or after. Certainly Philo gives no indication that this was the case. His change of heart was motivated instead by his fear of the new emperor Caligula, for Flaccus had earlier played an active role in opposing Caligula and in having his mother sent into exile. Thus when Caligula suddenly and unexpectedly came to power in Rome, Flaccus's fear of reprisal created a situation which Dionysius and Lampo were quick to exploit for their own ends. They offered to intercede with Caligula on Flaccus's behalf in return for a change of policy on the status of Jews in the city. When Flaccus accepted their offer, the Roman barrier was removed and the troubles began.

It is clear from all of the accounts—Philo as well as the notorious *Acts of the Alexandrian Martyrs*—that the key forces were Dionysius, Lampo, and Isidorus. To them Flaccus delegated the task of implementing his new policies regarding the Jews. Apion and Chaeremon were also involved, as members of the Alexandrian delegation to Claudius, but almost certainly at a higher level. Indeed, Philo mentions neither of them in the *Against Flaccus* or the *Embassy to Gaius*. Of the others, however, Philo presents a vivid, though not altogether unbiased portrait—"demagogues like Dionysius, record-porers like Lampo, sedition-leaders like Isidorus, busy bodies, devisers of evil, city troublers."[34] We know little of their particular attitudes—though they are not difficult to imagine— but what we know of their social and political roles suggests that their own anti-Semitism had its roots not in hatred of Jews as such but in nationalistic and violent anti-Romanism. Thus the Jews were not the direct targets but rather the immediate victims. Isidorus and Lampo were both leaders of the Alexandrian gymnasium. Since the gymnasium was the central institution in determining citizenship, it is hardly coincidental that its leaders should turn out to be the primary opponents of Jewish attempts to secure citizenship.

In one of the fragments of the *Acts of the Alexandrian Martyrs*, Isidorus argues against Agrippa that the Jews are not qualified for citizenship because they pay the same poll-tax as the Egyptians.[35] For the most part, Isidorus and Lampo were notorious in the city for their anti-Roman activities. Lampo, reports Philo, had been put on trial for disloyalty to the emperor Tiberius.[36] Isidorus had mounted an unsuccessful campaign against Flaccus during his early years as governor. A similar picture of Isidorus and Lampo emerges elsewhere in the *Acts of the Alexandrian Martyrs*. In a series of fictitious hearings before various emperors (Caligula, Claudius, Trajan, Hadrian, and Commodus), Isidorus, Lampo, and others are depicted as heroes and martyrs for defending the cause of Alexandria against Rome. In the course of their defense, they reveal the anti-Roman thrust of their anti-Semitism, for the basic and recurrent charge against the emperors was that they were friends of the Jews. In one fragment, dealing with a case of Isidorus against Agrippa, Claudius warns Isidorus to say nothing against his friend. The same fragment has Isidorus refer to Agrippa as "a two-penny-halfpenny Jew," to Claudius as "the cast-off son of the Jewess Salome" and, in an aside of Lampo, to the emperor himself as crazy.[37] The embassy to Trajan which included a number of *gymnasiarchs* arrives in Rome only to find that the emperor's wife, Plotina, had turned the senate and the emperor against the Alexandrians. This leads one of their spokesmen to complain to the emperor that his council is filled with "impious Jews."[38] Ultimately, Claudius executed both Lampo and Isidorus for their role as enemies of Agrippa.

A final element in the picture concerns the role played by local political clubs, the *thiasoi*, *synodai* or *klinai* as Philo calls them. Isidorus in particular appears to have served as their spokesman and was able to muster their support whenever it was needed. In contrast to his customary references to Isidorus's followers as a disorganized mob, Philo is probably closer to the truth when he states that Isidorus organized them "into sections after the fashion of committees."[39] Thus, Philo continues, "whenever he wants them to perpetrate some unprofitable act, at one signal they come together in a body and say and do what they are bidden."[40] These clubs had already carried out an unsuccessful campaign early in Flaccus's prefectureship. They were undoubtedly behind the insulting parody of Agrippa's newly acquired kingship during the latter's disastrous visit to Alexandria in 38. And they must have taken a leading hand in the riots themselves. To what extent these clubs and their members were motivated by the anti-Semitic sentiments of their leaders is impossible to determine. In all likelihood, however, they must have heard and rehearsed the catalogue of calumnies created by Apion and others. Their anti-Semitism, like Apion's, took its origins in local political conditions peculiar to Alexandria.

In Alexandria and Egypt following the "war" of 38–41, one fact of utmost importance emerges: from that point on, we begin to hear different voices from both sides. The period of cordial relations between Rome and the Jews of Alexandria was over. On the pagan side, there is no more Apion or Manetho. On the Jewish side, the voice of Philo is heard no more. Instead we hear from Josephus that "the Jews" greeted the news of Caligula's death by taking arms against the Alexandrians.[41] Josephus omits to say, whether or not intentionally, who among the Jews of Alexandria took arms, but they would surely have represented groups and interests different from those of Philo and his social class.

Were these insurgents newcomers to Alexandria? This seems unlikely, although both Philo's report that Flaccus's people found no arms in their search of Jewish homes and Claudius's warning, written after the event, against inviting Jews from Syria or Egypt might be taken as evidence to the contrary. More likely, Philo's account of the events in the 30s quite deliberately ignored all other voices. There is much evidence to support Tcherikover's claim that a new group "captured the leadership of the Jewish community in Alexandria."[42] In all likelihood, these new leaders rejected Alexandrian citizenship as undesirable, abhorred the pagan cults, and were not reluctant to take arms to defend their cause. In any case, from this time forward, relations between Jews and pagans in Alexandria and Egypt were punctuated by a series of bloody conflicts.

Josephus's statement that there had been incessant strife between the native inhabitants and the Jewish settlers since the time of Alexander,[43] while overstated for the Hellenistic period, is not inaccurate for the remainder of the first century and the early decades of the second. The uprising in 41 was quickly put down and a period of quiet followed under Claudius's reign. In 66 C.E. a riot again broke out between Greeks and Jews. When the Roman prefect failed to pacify the rioters by peaceful means, he unleashed two Roman legions to do the job. According to Josephus, who is the sole source for the events, the soldiers, aided by the Alexandrian populace, fell upon the Jews in order to teach them a "severe lesson." These reprisals resulted in a significant number of casualties, though Josephus's figure of 50,000 dead is perhaps exaggerated.[44]

Little is heard from Egypt in connection with the revolt in Palestine of 66–73. Of far greater significance was the influx of Jewish radicals— Josephus's *sicarii*—from Palestine following the collapse of the revolt and their attempts to generate support for their cause among the Jews of Egypt and Cyrene. According to Josephus, whose account terminates shortly after 73 C.E., they met with but limited success. But the outbreak of a new revolt, with centers in Egypt, Cyrene, and Cyprus, merely indicates the degree to which Josephus's own interests as a member of the political and social establishment blinded him to what was happening at other levels of Jewish society in the Diaspora.

The revolt of 115–117 was, if anything, the most violent and costly of all.[45] A battle (*machē*) between Jews and Romans broke out in the city in 115—perhaps inspired by an earlier uprising in Cyrene—and was quickly put down by the prefect. Sometime thereafter the struggle expanded to the Egyptian countryside and intensified. The various sources speak of violent confrontations, numerous atrocities on both sides, and widespread disruption of normal activities in a variety of Egyptian locations—not to mention Cyprus and Cyrene. By the time the revolts were finally put down in 117, the results were calamitous: the Jewish revolutionaries, in their messianic fervor, destroyed several pagan temples, including the Temple of Nemesis and the Sanctuary of Serapis in Alexandria; the great synagogue of Alexandria was itself destroyed; Dio Cassius, no doubt exaggerating, reports that the Jewish forces killed 220,000 persons in Cyrene and 240,000 in Cyprus; and the eventual suppression of the revolt by the Roman army "amounted to the almost total extermination of the Egyptian Jews."[46]

Numerous questions arise in connection with the recurrent conflicts between 66 and 117 C.E. For our purposes the relevant ones are the extent to which they were prompted by, or in turn contributed to the tradition of Greek anti-Semitism in Egypt, and whether the reactions of successive Roman emperors, governors, and generals betray a systematic enmity toward Judaism, that is, whether the cultural environment in Egypt brought about fundamental changes in the traditional Roman policy regarding Judaism.

On the matter of Roman policy, it is difficult to find any major shifts from the time of Claudius onward. His letter to the Alexandrians clearly treats the riots under Flaccus and Gaius Caligula as aberrations. At the same time, the events which preceded Claudius's letter just as clearly led the emperor to issue a harsh warning against Jewish revolutionary activities: "If they disobey, I shall proceed against them as fomenting a common plague for the whole world." This warning, and the suspicions which underlay it, no doubt explain the extreme measures taken in the process of suppressing the later uprisings.

As to the views of non-Roman circles, we are reasonably well-informed. Josephus remarks, almost in passing, that in 66 C.E. the Roman troops pulled back as soon as the general issued the order to desist. "But," he continues, "the Alexandrian populace in the intensity of their hate were not easily called off and were with difficulty torn from the corpses."[47] Here, once again, we are almost certainly dealing with the same base of opposition, rooted in the political clubs, as earlier in 38–41. Beyond this, however, the influx of Jewish messianic revolutionaries from Palestine added a new element to the struggle. Not only did they bring a willingness to take arms, but they added a strong religious dimension. The destruction of pagan temples was part of their messianic campaign. Their assaults on religious sites gave rise in turn to the widespread use of the phrase "impious (*anosios*) Jews" throughout this period. In one of the *Acts of Alexandrian Martyrs*, placed under the reign of Trajan, a certain Hermaiskos twice accuses Trajan of favoring the "impious Jews."[48] A second fragment, this one placed under Hadrian and depicting a discussion between rival delegations during the revolt in 115–117, again refers to the "impious Jews." One of the references occurs in a speech protesting the prefect's decision to settle the Jews of Alexandria in a new location from which "they could easily attack and ravage our well-named city."[49]

Even if we cannot accept the view put forward by the *Acts* that the emperors were consistently pro-Jewish in their attitudes, there is no concrete evidence to suggest that Rome ever abandoned its fundamental policy, that is, to protect the rights and privileges of Jewish communities as long as they lived peaceably amongst themselves and with their Gentile neighbors. At the same time, there is no reason to imagine a basic change in the conditions that precipitated the events of 38–41, viz., that the leaders of the Alexandrian anti-Semitic movement sought every opportunity to influence local Roman officials against the Jews. Throughout this period anti-Semitism was firmly embedded in the structure of anti-Romanism; both were hallmarks of Alexandrian patriotism.

The fact that the *Acts of the Alexandrian Martyrs* were still being copied in the third century C.E. indicates not only that these sentiments remained alive long after Judaism had been eliminated as a meaningful social and religious force in Roman Egypt, but also that their primary and enduring motivation lay on the anti-Roman rather than the anti-Jewish side. Apart from the continued transcription of the *Acts*, we hear nothing further of pagan anti-Semitism in Egypt. Not coincidentally the voice of Judaism itself fades out after 117. It is important to realize, however, that it does not disappear altogether. As noted earlier, a new settlement of Jews is attested at the outskirts of Alexandria; and isolated Jewish names appear in scattered villages and towns in the countryside. Only at the end of the third century do Jewish names begin to occur with greater frequency.

But this gradual reawakening took place within a significantly changed cultural context. To the extent that Judaism once again encountered hostility from the religious and political establishment, the source of that hostility was now Christian rather than pagan. While even in Alexandria the basis of Christian hostility was fundamentally different from that of earlier paganism, there is no mistaking certain lines of continuity, especially in Alexandria. As pagan Alexandrians began to embrace Christianity, they brought with them the residue of traditional Alexandrian anti-Semitism.

The other important change in the cultural environment was Judaism itself. Tcherikover speaks of the period after 117 as a time in which Egyptian Jewry sought "to accommodate itself to the new epoch."[50] A prominent feature of this process was cultural assimilation. Of course, this element had long been present in figures like Artapanus, Tiberius Julius Alexander, and the extreme allegorists attacked by Philo, not to mention Philo himself. What is different about this later period is that the voice of assimilation grows louder and that we hear of no Philo rising to challenge it. The evidence for the process of assimilation lies not just in names—the use of Egyptian names by Jews and the more unusual occurrence among non-Jews of Jewish names—but the active participation of Jews in the syncretistic circles of Greco-Egyptian magic, alchemy, and astrology. This, too, may have been present all along, but it comes to light for the first time in the papyri of the third, fourth, and fifth centuries.

4

The Later Roman
Encounter with Judaism
The Politics of Sympathy and Conversion

Our examination of Judaism in Roman Egypt has emphasized the importance of making a distinction between official policy and personal attitudes: on the one hand, the generally protective policy of Rome sprang not from any sympathy with Judaism, but from policy considerations relating to Roman self-interest. This policy appears as pro-Jewish only in the anti-Roman *Acts of the Alexandrian Martyrs* where it was used to defame Rome herself. In reality, it is no more appropriate to designate official Roman policy as pro-Jewish than it is for Isidorus in the *Acts* to call the emperor Claudius "the cast-off son of the Jewess Salome."[1] On the other hand, the policy did have the effect of setting limits to anti-Semitic words and actions wherever they might arise. Until the Jewish revolutionaries sought to repudiate this policy with force, Rome saw the protection of Jewish rights and privileges as important to its own well-being. And even here, once the revolutionaries were removed from the stage, the traditional policies were quickly re-established.

Cicero's passing jibes against the Jewish people cannot be taken to represent widely held views in the first century B.C.E. Nor does he reveal any special knowledge of Judaism. Still, the very fact that he was able to borrow or invent phrases like "barbaric superstition" and "a nation born to slavery" shows the potential for the enmity that would materialize in later writers. In Rome as in Alexandria and elsewhere, this potential resided in two closely related factors: the peculiarity of certain Jewish observances *and* Rome's policy of protecting these observances. Under certain conditions a combination of these factors might give rise to anti-

55

Semitic feelings, beliefs, and actions. The precipitating conditions themselves might vary widely according to time and place: petty jealousy
between individuals; political disputes in which Jews were caught in the
cross-fire between the primary antagonists; armed resistance to Roman
rule by revolutionary Jews; and negative reactions prompted by the full
or partial conversion of "natives" to Jewish beliefs and practices.

The Greek ethnographers had from the beginning recorded the
peculiarity of certain Jewish religious observances. Cicero, perhaps
echoing his teacher Apollonius Molon, says "the practice of their sacred
rites was at variance with the glory of our empire, the dignity of our
name, and the customs of our ancestors."[2] After Cicero, Roman authors
concentrated on circumcision, the Sabbath, and abstention from pork.

Circumcision received particular attention from the Romans, especially
the Roman satirists. Throughout the first century, it would appear that
circumcision came to be seen as a synonym for Judaism itself. Horace
uses the phrase "circumcised Jews" as though it were common parlance.[3]
Persius, in describing various aspects of Sabbath observance, dispenses
with the term "Jewish" altogether and speaks simply of "the Sabbath of
the circumcised."[4] One of the characters in Petronius's *Satyricon* describes
a servant as perfect but for two faults—his snoring and his circumcision.[5]
Later in the same story, two of the characters find themselves threatened
while on a voyage and propose various disguises to elude their enemy.
Eumolpus suggests that they use ink to dye themselves like Aethiopian
slaves. To this his companion Giton adds, "please circumcise us too, so
that we will look like Jews and bore our ears to imitate Arabians, and
chalk our faces till Gaul takes us for her sons."[6] A fragment of Petronius
goes even further in making circumcision the central feature of Judaism:
"The Jew may worship his pig-god and clamour in the ears of high heaven,
but unless he also cuts back his foreskin with the knife, he shall go forth
from the people. . . ."[7] So, too, Juvenal, in his bitter portrait of a Roman
proselyte, treats circumcision as the final and decisive stage in conversion
to Judaism. Finally, in the later part of the first century, Martial reflects
the commonplace use of the phrase "circumcised Jews." In one of his
epigrams he complains that a Roman woman, Caelia, bestows her favors
on men of every nation except Rome, failing to shun even "the lecheries of
'circumcised Jews' ";[8] he mentions that his own slave was circumcised[9]

and describes a Jewish actor whose identity was revealed when his cloak fell off while he was exercising in public—"lo, he was circumcised."[10] In another epigram, he uses *verpe* ("circumcised") four times in berating a rival poet. Martial is able, he writes, to forgive his rival's criticisms and plagiarisms, but what troubles him most is his suspicion that he has been seducing Martial's favorite boy![11]

Much the same picture emerges regarding the Sabbath—a distinctive custom of Judaism which deeply impressed Roman observers.[12] A variety of theories were in circulation regarding its origins. Because it invoked a prohibition of labor, it was widely misunderstood by observers as a day of fasting.[13] Others correctly saw it as a day of rest.[14] A character in a satire of Horace refuses to discuss business with Horace because "today is the thirteenth day, a Sabbath."[15] Ovid mentions the seventh day in three places and in two of them he alludes to it as a time of refraining from normal activities.[16] Persius even mentions authentic details associated with the Sabbath—the lighting of lamps and the preparation of fish.[17]

On the question of Jewish dietary regulations, abstention from pork was widely noted. Romans were intrigued by this requirement because the pig was treasured by them both as good eating and as a sacrificial animal. Here again, the peculiarity of a Jewish custom prompted a wide variety of comments. Philo reports that the emperor Gaius Caligula suddenly turned on the members of the Jewish embassy and demanded to know why they abstained from pork.[18] A certain amount of misunderstanding and speculation also surrounded the origins of this practice. Petronius imagined that the Jews worshipped the pig,[19] while Plutarch's friends debated whether abstention from pork derived from appreciation or abhorrence of the animal.[20]

The traditional view that anti-Semitism was widespread among Romans relies heavily on these satirists. By its very nature, however, the task of satire is to isolate and ridicule unusual behavior. Thus Jewish customs were natural targets for Roman satirists, but no more so than other religious traditions. Circumcision in particular lent itself to exploitation because of its obvious associations with the erotic aspects of Roman satire. In short, it is a serious mistake to infer from these texts that their individual authors or Roman literary circles in general harbored strong negative feelings about Judaism.

We need not leave these circles, however, to discover sentiments of a different kind. In Juvenal, the last of the traditional Roman satirists, we cross the line between literary sport and personal animus. Born near the middle of the first century, he experienced the Jewish revolt in Palestine of 66–73 as well as the later uprisings of 115–117. Several of his references to Judaism are simple rehearsals of the themes established by earlier satirists. But others reveal a new spirit. In his third satire, he complains of the degenerate state into which Rome has fallen. "I cannot abide," he comments, "a Rome of Greeks; and yet what fraction of our dregs comes from Greece? The Syrian Orontes has long since poured into the Tiber bringing with it its lingo and manners. . . ."[21]

As part of his xenophobic reaction to the cosmopolitan character of his city, he mentions the Jews as one among many foreign elements. "Here Numa once held his nightly assignations with his mistress; but now the holy fount and grave and shrine are let out to Jews, who possess a basket and a truss of hay for all their belongings."[22] Later in the same satire, he complains of rowdy drunkards in the vicinity of a synagogue (*proseucha*).[23] Here, at least, his irritation has nothing to do with Judaism itself, but rather with poverty-stricken foreigners who have sullied his beloved city. In his sixth satire, on women, he once again rails against the corruption of foreign ways (*mores peregrini*). He speaks of a palsied Jewess as "an interpreter of the laws of Jerusalem, a high priestess of the tree, a trusty go-between of highest heaven!"[24] She sells dreams, but charges less for her services than do others. But in his fourteenth satire, dealing with the corruption of Roman youth by the degenerate ways of their elders, Juvenal's tone becomes harsher. As one example he cites the father who observes the Sabbath and abstains from pork, while the son undergoes circumcision and assumes the full burden of Jewish custom.[25]

At one level, what bothers Juvenal about Judaism can be summed up in Cicero's phrase—*barbara superstitio*: it is both foreign (*barbara*) and anti-Roman (*superstitio*). On specific details, he simply follows the views then current in Roman literary circles: abstinence from pork makes no sense; Jews are forbidden to show the way to any except co-religionists; and the Sabbath derives from laziness. At a deeper level, however, what troubles Juvenal most deeply is the appeal of Judaism among Romans of his time. Indeed, it seems likely that the increasingly negative view of

Judaism among certain Roman authors in the late first century stems largely from two factors, the Jewish war of 66–73 and the successes of Jewish proselytism.

What is of interest here is not just that Roman attitudes undergo an unmistakable change at the end of the first century, from benign satire to real aversion, but that the change was precipitated not by any new information or policy regarding Judaism but by events which altered the status of Judaism in the eyes of certain influential Romans. Proselytism in particular, or rather the appeal of Judaism among Romans of all classes, became the focus of a prolonged and lively debate.[26]

From the very first reports of Jews in Rome, it would appear that Roman attitudes toward Judaism were sharply divided: some were drawn to it and made it part of their religion, while others—including some who shaped official policy—saw it as essentially un-Roman. The view now being advanced is that these opposed points of view are in some way related. In particular, I would argue that Roman officials were especially prone to enforce the restrictive side of their policy precisely because they saw Judaism as a persistent "threat" among their own people. Not unlike later Christians—Ignatius, John Chrysostom, and others—whose negative reactions to Judaism can be plotted as a function of Judaizing tendencies among their own faithful, Roman political and intellectual leaders responded negatively to pagan Judaizers for essentially the same reasons. Roman converts and sympathizers to Judaism made it painfully apparent that the confident "Romanism" of the established classes was less inevitable or eternal than they wished to believe. As noted earlier, converts from an established religious tradition represent the worst possible threat to that tradition.

In order to give some sense of how serious this "crisis" was, let me mention a list of texts from Roman sources relating to proselytism:

(1) 139 B.C.E. Two epitomators of Valerius Maximus report the expulsion of Jews from Rome following an edict of the praetor Cornelius Hispanus. According to one epitome, the Jews had attempted "to introduce their own rites to the Romans"; the other describes the offense as being an effort "to infect Roman morals with the cult of Jupiter Sabazius."[27]

(2) Late in the first century B.C.E. the *Suda* lexicon describes Caecilius

of Calacte, the well-known rhetor of servile origin, as a convert to Judaism (*tēn doxan Ioudaios*). Plutarch, in his *Life of Cicero* (7.5) refers to the Roman quaestor, Quintus Caecilius Niger, in such a way as to suggest that he may have been Jewish. There is good reason to believe that Plutarch has confused the two Caecilii.[28]

(3) 19 c.e. Josephus,[29] Tacitus,[30] and Suetonius[31] record Tiberius's decision to expel the Jews from Rome. Neither Tacitus nor Suetonius gives a reason. Josephus says that the order came about when the husband of an aristocratic Roman convert to Judaism told the emperor of a plot by four Jewish men to defraud his wife of her wealth. In her analysis of the evidence, Smallwood concludes that the order of expulsion cannot have been based on this single episode.[32] A brief mention of these events by Dio Cassius indicates that the underlying cause lay in the fact that "they were converting many of the natives to their ways."[33]

(4) 90 c.e. According to Suetonius, the emperor Domitian widened the category of those subject to the *fiscus Judaicus*—a special tax imposed by Vespasian immediately after the Jewish revolt of 66–73—to include not just those born Jews and full proselytes but to Judaizers as well, people who followed the Jewish way of life without formally professing Judaism.[34]

(5) 95 c.e. Flavius Clemens, Domitian's cousin and his wife Flavia were convicted of atheism. Flavius was executed and Flavia sent into exile. Dio Cassius, who reports the events, states further that Glabrio, consul in 91, was also executed on the same charges. Dio's text makes it clear that the "atheism" was Judaism and that the three named individuals were not alone: "the charge against them was atheism, a charge on which many others who were drifting into Jewish ways were condemned, some to death and others to the confiscation of their property."[35]

(6) Late first century b.c.e. Horace speaks of the forceful company of poets in Rome and likens them to the Jews: "we, like the Jews, will compel you to make one of our throng."[36]

(7) Mid-first century c.e. Seneca, in a fragment preserved by Augustine, speaks of the widespread popularity of Judaism: "the customs of this accursed race have gained such influence that they are now received throughout all the world. The vanquished have given their laws to their victors."[37]

(8) 109 C.E. Juvenal in the fourteenth satire, cited earlier, complains of a partially observant Roman father whose son becomes a full convert. Juvenal treats the situation as fairly common.

(9) The *Digest* of Justinian reports that the emperor Antoninus Puis (c. 140 C.E.) modified an earlier ruling of Hadrian by allowing Jews only to practice circumcision.[38] At the same time, he maintained several penalties for circumcision of Gentiles. Speaking of the same period, the *Historia Augusta* states that the Jews revolted under Bar Cochba because circumcision was prohibited.[39] The return to earlier policies under Antoninus, despite the ban against circumcising Gentiles, had the effect of promoting proselytism once again. As Smallwood puts it, "this indirect attack on proselytism failed, for the obvious reason that the weapon used was ineffective."[40]

(10) Justin Martyr's *Dialogue with Trypho* refers to proselyte circumcision as though it were a common practice.[41]

(11) 198–199 C.E. The *Historia Augusta* indicates that Septimius Severus sought to tighten the Roman policy by banning conversion itself.[42]

(12) Third century and later. Smallwood remarks that "Severus' explicit ban on proselytism seems to have been as ineffective as Antoninus' implicit ban."[43]

(13) The picture of successful proselytizing activity in Rome is corroborated by *Jewish sources* as well. For one, Josephus's comment at the conclusion of his *Against Apion* may not be as hyperbolic as is sometimes assumed: "The masses have long since shown a keen desire to adopt our religious observance; and there is not one city, Greek or barbarian, nor a single nation, to which our custom of abstaining from work on the seventh day has not spread, and where fasts and the lighting of lamps and many of our prohibitions in the matter of food are not observed . . . and as God permeates the universe, so the Law has found its way among all mankind."[44] At least seven epitaphs from the Jewish catacombs in Rome mention proselytes.[45]

This brief survey of reactions to Jewish proselytism has demonstrated that Judaism exercised a significant influence on Romans during the first century. It would be convenient if we could correlate these reactions— whether positive or negative—to social class or status. The case of Flavius Clemens and his wife, Flavia Domitilla, makes it impossible to speak of the senatorial aristocracy as a consistent source of antagonism. Indeed, recent studies by M. Stern[46] and S. Applebaum[47] have shown that sympathy for Judaism was common among the senatorial aristocracy throughout the first century C.E.

As for the emperors, we must speak of personal sentiments and public policy separately. As concerns policy, Gaius Caligula is the only one to depart from the precedents established early on by Julius Caesar and Augustus. What we do find, just as earlier under the reign of Antiochus VII Sidetes, are advisors surrounding the emperors who sometimes give expression to anti-Semitism: Sejanus under Tiberius during the later years of his rule;[48] Helicon under Gaius Caligula;[49] the philosopher Seneca who served as Nero's advisor from 54–66;[50] and the rhetor Quintilian whom Domitian appointed as tutor for the children of his niece, Flavia Domitilla.[51] At the personal level, we note in passing that a number of the emperors counted Jews among their friends and associates. Augustus himself knew Herod and several of his sons;[52] Berenice, the sister of Agrippa II, was Titus's mistress between 67 and 79;[53] Nero's wife Poppaea has sometimes been described, on the basis of comments made by Josephus, as a Jewish sympathizer or even a Judaizer,[54] though this inference has been called into question;[55] Julius Agrippa I was a close friend of the royal family in Rome;[56] his son Julius Agrippa II was equally a friend and protégé of Claudius.[57]

To the successful expansion of Judaism among Romans were added the Jewish revolts as a second factor that further contributed to the dislike of Judaism in conservative Roman circles. Indeed, the two factors go hand in hand in the sense that both were taken as evidence of Judaism's fundamentally anti-Roman character. Of the troubles in Alexandria between 37–41, there are no direct reminiscences in Roman authors. Indirectly, however, they left an important mark on later decades. Helicon's role in the household of Caligula has already been discussed. Apion, the spearhead of the Alexandrian anti-Semites, was an important literary figure in Rome under Tiberius and Claudius and no doubt conveyed to them his views of Jews and Judaism. It seems virtually certain that Egyptian anti-Semitic traditions began to influence Roman opinion in the context of the Alexandrian riots and the subsequent embassies.

Curiously, the Jewish war of 66–73, infinitely greater in scope than the riots in Alexandria, does not figure prominently in Roman writings at the end of the first century. The *Argonautica* of Valerius Flaccus, written to glorify the Flavians, mentions the capture of Judea (*Idume*) in the opening verses of the epic but does not mention the subject again.[58] In similar fashion, Silius Italicus's *Punica*, composed under the Flavians, includes the subjugation of Judea among the military achievements of Vespasian and comments that his son Titus, "while yet a youth, shall put an end to war with the fierce people of Palestine."[59] Once again, however, nothing further is spoken of the event or of Judaism itself. Frontinus, in his handbook on military strategy, cites the war only to illustrate how a knowledge of the enemy can be of assistance in forming military operations. He cites the example of Vespasian, who knew that the Jews could not fight on the Sabbath, and attacked Jerusalem "on the day of Saturn, a day on which it is sinful for them to do any business, and defeated them."[60] Finally, Martial's epigram in honor of Flavian military triumphs, simply lists the conquest of Judea along with other victories: "Along with his sire, thy brother (Titus) won his Idumaean [Judaean] triumph. . . ."[61]

These allusions to the Roman victory over the Jews treat the event in strictly military terms. In none of them are there further observations about Jews or Judaism. In part, no doubt, this is due to the literary exigencies of the epic form. Thus it is impossible to say whether these authors—apart from Martial—treated the war and its aftermath as an opportunity to express anti-Jewish feelings. Insofar as these authors may be taken as representing the official propaganda of the emperors themselves, it seems safe to conclude that the war simply did not generate anti-Semitism in the highest circles.

Elsewhere, however, a different picture emerges. In Book 5 of his *Histories*, Tacitus produces his famous excursus on Jewish history and customs as a preface to his account of the Jewish war. By and large, Tacitus is dependent on traditional material, including information of Egyptian origin. At the same time, however, as the length and detail of his excursus reveals, he is better informed about Judaism than most ancient authors. Modern critics have often wondered why Tacitus, who is normally critical of popular reports, should have embraced them so fully in his account of the Jews. The answer given by H. Lewy seems closest to the mark:[62] Tacitus's aim was to explain to his readers the power and rebellious character of the Jews; he did so by focusing on their religion and culture, which he characterized, in terms reminiscent of Cicero's *barbara superstitio*, as "quite opposed to those of all other religions"; Moses figures prominently in his story because it was he who "introduced new religious practices"; and as a result of Moses, "the Jews regard as profane all that we hold sacred . . .[and] permitted all that we abhor."

As far as it goes, Lewy's view of Tacitus is correct and useful. But Tacitus may have had two additional concerns in mind beyond explaining to his readers the recent Jewish uprising. First, he appears to have advanced his history as a rationale for the anti-Semitism of conservative senatorial groups in Rome.[63] In this respect it is interesting to note that in presenting the immediate causes of the Jewish war, he temporarily abandons his "cultural" interpretation of Jewish rebelliousness and refers instead to the incompetence of local Roman governors! Second, these same conservative circles were troubled at least as much by the appeal of Judaism among Romans as they were by the war. Certainly this was true of Tacitus, whose status as a *quindecimvir* made him an official guardian of traditional Roman religion. It may also be relevant to recall that Tacitus's *Histories* reach to the end of Domitian's reign in 96 C.E., and that the notorious case of Flavius Clemens and Flavia Domitilla arose during Tacitus's lifetime. So also with Quintilian, whose views influenced Juvenal and probably Tacitus. Even though it may tell us little of his personal views, Tacitus's treatment of Judaism is thoroughly in tune with the times and reflects a widespread view of Judaism in traditional literary circles of the late first century. The very fact that he can allude to Moses as "the founder of the Jewish superstition," without citing his name, is ample proof of the extent to which the issue of Judaism was alive in Rome at that time.

To complete this picture, we need to return briefly to Juvenal. Published between 100 and 127, his *Satires* cover the period from the Flavians and the Jewish revolt of 115–117. Of these, *Satire* 14 is the most interesting, not only because it attests the continued success of Jewish proselytism in Rome but also because it confirms the existence of a semi-official portrait of Judaism in Roman literary circles: the laws of Moses are antithetical to everything Roman; Jews show no kindness to non-Jews; and their customs—abstinence from pork, Sabbath-observance and circumcision—are peculiar. In short, Juvenal, like Tacitus, possessed reliable firsthand knowledge of Judaism in Rome, and, like Tacitus, he resorted to a "semi-official" anti-Semitic charter in presenting Judaism to his literary audience.

The opposition to Judaism characteristic of certain Roman authors from the latter half of the first century to the early second rests on two foundations—the Jewish revolts and the spread of Judaism among Romans. These authors saw in Judaism the expression of a fundamentally anti-Roman way of life; for them the revolts merely confirmed this anti-Romanism. In most cases, the opposition to Judaism was part of a larger movement—traditional and conservative in character—which saw in the presence of foreign peoples and cults in Rome the demise of the old Roman ways. Some have preferred to describe the views of Tacitus, Seneca, and Juvenal as "xenophobic" rather than anti-Semitic. But surely they are both; their xenophobia gives rise to their anti-Semitism.

In order to make their case, the opponents of Judaism deliberately concocted an image of Judaism, and of Moses as its founder and leader, as the quintessence of misanthropy and rebellion. Several components of this image came directly from Alexandrian sources. The unmistakable function of this image was to justify the conservative opposition to Judaism and to counter the appeal Judaism held for many Romans. Once developed, this image circulated at the highest levels of Roman literary circles. But we should not overestimate the extent or the influence of these circles. Even Domitian, whose attempts to arrest the growth of Judaizing may have inspired certain of these authors, was careful not to tamper with traditional Jewish privileges. Under Domitian and Trajan, this circle of *literati* included Juvenal, Quintilian, Pliny the Younger, Martial, and Tacitus, all familiar with one another. In some ways, these men appear as a closed circle of like-minded spirits bent on defending "the old ways."

From the time of Juvenal onward, that is, beginning in the mid-second century, traditional Roman paganism is increasingly on the defensive, with the emperors themselves providing protection for a number of non-Roman cults. Not surprisingly, this turning-point coincides with the increasing Roman preoccupation with Christianity. From this point on, we hear little more of Roman anti-Semitism.

The high-point of opposition to Judaism appears under Domitian. In part this is because the phenomenon of Judaizing among Romans reached its climax in this period. Above all else, this period reveals the extent to which Roman public opinion was divided over the question of Judaism. In the minds of many, not even the war of 66–73 proved that Judaism was incompatible with *Romanitas*. Citing the cumulative evidence from the period, S. Applebaum speaks of "the widespread influence of Judaism in contemporary Roman society"[64] and proposes the view that there was a close connection between Judaism and "the protest of the Roman upper classes against Domitian's repressive rule."[65] Indeed, the affair of Flavius Clemens, Flavia Domitilla, and "many others" suggests that the charges of Judaizing may sometimes have served purely political purposes. But the very possibility of using such accusations merely confirms the existence of the internal debate.

What becomes of this debate in later decades and centuries? This question will be answered in part in our discussion of Christian Judaizers. Already it may be suggested that the elements in Judaism that appealed to educated pagans—great antiquity, written scriptures, sense of morality, monotheism—are precisely those things that Christianity will emphasize as it presents itself as the "true Israel" to the very same audience. Can it be an accident of history that Christians begin to adopt this stance in a self-conscious manner in close chronological proximity to the final Jewish revolt of 135–37, and that Christianity offered itself, again self-consciously, as the true Israel in a very specific sense, that is, as Israel without those elements most offensive to Romans—the strong sense of identity as a nation and the attendant commitment to the autonomy of the land and its central institution, the temple?

5

Against the Stream
Sympathy for Judaism in Imperial Rome

Thus far we have seen a wide range of beliefs and feelings about Jews and Judaism in Roman society. As the complaints of poets and others make clear, Judaism exercised a powerful attraction among non-Jews in Rome. The sources of this attraction, the means by which Judaism was brought to the attention of outsiders, the degrees of attachment to Judaism, and the social standing of those attracted have all been the subject of much debate. All of this has generated a new image of Judaism's standing in the Roman world.

To complete this new image, we must examine a number of Roman authors whose views of Judaism run against the flow of those who have traditionally been seen as representative of the mainstream Roman public opinion. These authors are utterly heterogeneous; with few exceptions, they reveal no ties of kinship, social status, place of origin, or education. It is precisely this heterogeneity that gives them their value as witnesses against the traditional picture of Romans as overwhelmingly hostile toward Judaism. Unlike the *literati*, who represent the interests of a small group at a particular time and place, these others surface at random. Thus their value as indicators of Roman opinion at scattered times and places is much greater than the *literati* with whom they must inevitably be contrasted.

NICOLAUS OF DAMASCUS, DIODORUS OF SICILY, POMPEIUS TROGUS, AND STRABO

The historians and ethnographers of the early empire, in whose works Judaism appears, are Pompeius Trogus, Strabo, Nicolaus of Damascus, and Diodorus of Sicily. The earliest of these was probably Diodorus of Sicily, who produced a universal history, *Bibliotheca Historica*, toward the end of the first century B.C.E. Much of his material, including his treatment of Judaism, was drawn from earlier historians. Thus his lengthy account of Jewish origins came to him from Hectaeus of Abdera.[1] The scene in which Antiochus VII Sidetes rejects the advice of his anti-Semitic counsellors is also derived from some earlier writer, possibly Poseidonius or Nicolaus of Damascus. But these two passages do not exhaust Diodorus's treatment of Jewish matters. In 1.31.2 he describes the harbor at Jaffa; in 2.48.6–9 and again 19.98–99, he presents almost identical descriptions of the Dead Sea and its famous asphalt; and in 40.2, as part of his narrative of Pompey's campaign in Syria, he relates Pompey's diplomatic dealings in the disputes between Aristobulus and his brother Hyrcanus.

More interesting for our purposes are three additional passages in which Diodorus speaks of the Egyptian origins of the Jews. Two of them defend the claim that civilization began in Egypt and moved outward in the form of colonies. In 1.31.2 and 1.55.5, the case is based on circumcision; the fact that the Jews circumcise their male children is evidence of Egyptian origins because circumcision originated in Egypt. The third passage, 1.94.1–2, offers a list of ancient and legendary lawgivers, the founders of civilizations, whose common characteristic is that each claimed divine authority for the introduction of written laws. Mneves said that Hermes had given him the laws; Lycurgus appealed to Zeus, Zathraustes (Zoroaster) to the *Agathos Daimon*, Zalmoxis to Hestia, and Moses "to the god who is invoked as Iao." These passages are striking for the complete absence of hostility toward Judaism, especially in material which is clearly of Egyptian provenience. The two passages which argue the Egyptian origins of the Jews demonstrate that this claim was separable from and perhaps ultimately secondary to the framework of anti-Jewish polemic. They show no sign of an attempt thereby to denigrate the Jews. Even more revealing is the exalted status given Moses as a lawgiver ranking with the legendary heroes of ancient civilization. Given the time at which Diodorus was writing and the ultimate sources of his material, these texts would be invaluable witnesses for pagan opinions of Judaism even if they stood alone. But in fact they reflect a long-established tradition, shared widely by Jews and pagans alike, that regarded Judaism as a divinely revealed philosophy with Moses as its founder and spokesman. Before Diodorus, this understanding appears in Hecataeus of Abdera, Megasthenes, Clearchus of Soli, and Hermippus.[2] Later, it will persist in Numenius, Porphyry, Celsus, and Julian. In between, during the period traditionally regarded as the nadir in pagan estimations of Judaism, it will be carried forward by Strabo, Pompeius Trogus, and others.

In much the same tradition stands the work of Nicolaus of Damascus.[3] Nicolaus was a man of extraordinary talents and accomplishments. Born in Damascus of an important pagan family, he produced a *Universal History* in 144 books, various works on Aristotelian philosophy and theology, scientific treatises, dramatic compositions, a biography of the young Augustus, a *Collection of Remarkable Customs*, and an autobiography. The historical books were a major source for Josephus in the *Antiquities* and the *Jewish War* and later for the *Yosiphon*; Nicolaus's *On Plants* has been transmitted as part of the Aristotelian corpus; several of his works were later translated into Syriac and Arabic; and many of his works were still in circulation in the ninth and tenth centuries.

After serving as tutor to the children of Antony and Cleopatra in the 30s B.C.E., he spent the balance of his career as an advisor to King Herod. Nicolaus's task was a difficult one, for he had to present Herod to Greeks as a philhellene and to Romans as a loyal subject, while simultaneously defending him to the Jews as devoted to the cause of Judaism. In this capacity, he successfully defended the civic rights of Ionian Jews before Marcus Agrippa.[4] As part of the speech attributed to him by Josephus, Nicolaus defends Jewish customs generally and the Sabbath in particular:

> There is nothing hostile to mankind in our customs, but they are all pious and consecrated with saving righteousness . . . we give every seventh day over to the study of our customs and laws. . . . Now our

customs are excellent in themselves, if one examines them carefully, and
they are also ancient. . . .[5]

There can be no doubt that Nicolaus's position in the court of Herod
enabled him to acquire a knowledge of Jewish history unparalleled among
pagans in the ancient world. Clearly he possessed a thorough knowledge
of the Jewish history and of Jewish religious practices and the Jewish
Bible as well. The surviving fragments are devoid of the errors and distortions that characterize the works of his Alexandrian and Roman contemporaries. To be sure, it would be a mistake to minimize the importance of his official position as court historian in assessing his presentation
of Judaism. Certainly it accounts for the disproportionate role assigned
to Herod in the *Universal History* as well as its tendency to minimize
Herod's excesses. But by the same token, Nicolaus's position also provided him with a unique opportunity to observe Judaism at close range
over an extended period of time. Unlike other historian-ethnographers of
his time, he was not completely dependent on the idealizing traditions of
his predecessors or on apologetic accounts provided by Jews.

Pompeius Trogus's *Philippic Histories*, written toward the end of the
first century B.C.E., has survived only in the third or fourth century epitome of a certain Justinus and in an original set of prologues or summaries
for individual books. Following the customary practice of Greco-Roman
historiography, Pompeius made ample use of earlier writers, especially
in his ethnographic and geographic excursuses. His remarkable treatment
of Jewish history appears in Book 36 as a preface to the account of the
war between Antiochus VII Sidetes and the Hasmonean Jewish leader,
John Hyrcanus.

Pompeius's excursus is noteworthy in several respects. In the first place,
it combines a tradition that locates the origin of the Jews in Damascus
with the story of the expulsion of the lepers from Egypt under Moses.
Beyond Moses, who appears in the story as Joseph's son, Pompeius mentions other prominent figures in biblical history: Azelus [Hazael], Adores
[Hadad],[6] Abraham, Israhel, and Moses's son Arruas [Aaron]. Clearly
these names derive from a source that was familiar with the content
of biblical writings, but just as clearly this knowledge had been considerably muddled by the time of Justinus. Secondly, Pompeius offers vivid

portraits of Joseph, Moses, and the institution of Jewish hierocracy. Joseph, whose story follows Genesis, is envied by his brothers for his extraordinary talents (*excellens ingenium*); he wins favor with the King of Egypt by virtue of his shrewd nature (*ingenium*) and his knowledge of magic; he is eminently skilled (*sagacissimus*) in prodigies and the first to establish the science of dream interpretation; nothing of divine or human lore is unfamiliar to him; and so great are the proofs of his knowledge that "his warnings seemed to be given by god, not by a man."[7]

Moses, incorrectly identified as Joseph's son, inherits not only his father's knowledge (*scientia*), but his beauty (*formae pulchritudo*) as well. In contrast to Joseph, however, nothing further is said of Moses' person. Instead, the narrative presents a garbled mixture of the Egyptian expulsion story (Moses assumes leadership of a group afflicted with scabies and leprosy and is consequently expelled from Egypt in order to prevent the disease from spreading) and biblical history (Moses goes first to Damascus, his ancestral city and then to Sinai where he inaugurates the Sabbath as a fast day). The final panel in this triptych presents Aaron as Moses' son and a priest of the Egyptian rites. By combining the offices of priest and king, Aaron began the "custom among the Jews to have the same persons for king and priests."[8] To this Pompeius adds that "their justice combined with religion (*religio*) brought them incredible power as a nation."[9] The historical survey concludes with the remark that the Jews were "the first of all the eastern nations that regained their liberty from Rome,"[10] following a long period of subjugation to the Persians, Alexander the Great, and the Macedonians.

One aspect of Pompeius's account that deserves mention is its strongly etiological character. In part this is due to the conventions of Greco-Roman historiography, and thus to Pompeius's sources. It warrants attention here because it offers an example of the way in which traditions portraying the Jews as unsociable or even misanthropic could be handled in a manner that precluded any sense of hostility. The separateness of Jewish culture is here explained as a natural response to the expulsion from Egypt. And whereas the expulsion story itself is hardly complimentary, Pompeius's use of it places him closer to Hecataeus and Diodorus than to Apion or Tacitus.

Much energy has been expended on the question of Pompeius's

sources. The candidates have included Poseidonius, Nicolaus of Damascus, and Timagenes of Alexandria, but none of these is certain. In all likelihood Pompeius used several sources. One or two observations are significant for our present concern with pagan views of Judaism. Pompeius's excursus is not directly dependent on any extant writing on the Jews. If one chooses to regard it as derived *in toto* from a lost prototype, that prototype would add yet another testimony to the group I have described as flowing "against the stream." If, on the other hand, we decide that Pompeius himself is responsible for giving the excursus its present shape and tone, he becomes an important witness for the continued existence of an ethnographic and historiographic tradition which was not only interested in Jewish customs and history, but capable of writing about them in a dispassionate, sympathetic, and occasionally admiring manner.

The last, if not the latest of our ethnographer historians is Strabo of Amaseia. Josephus, who made extensive use of Strabo for his knowledge of Jewish history in the Hellenistic era, has preserved numerous fragments from Strabo's *History*. Whether or not Strabo followed normal practice by incorporating an excursus on Jewish origins in his historical writing is not known, but Jewish matters figured prominently in it.

Unlike the *History*, Strabo's *Geography* survived, and it includes the well-known monograph on Jewish history and religion.[11] The bulk of the monograph is given to an unprecedented recounting of the departure of the Jews from Egypt and their settlement in Jerusalem under the leadership of Moses. The story continues with the decline of the nation into superstition and tyranny in succeeding generations, with a list of ancient lawgivers whose legislation was honored because of its divine origins, with a brief summary of Pompey's capture of Jerusalem, and finally with a geographic description of Judea. Because of its extraordinary character, the story of Moses and the exodus is worth quoting at length:

> (35) For a certain Moses, who was one of the Egyptian priests, held a section of what is called the lower region (*chōra.*). But he became dissatisfied with the way of life and departed thence to Jerusalem, in the company of many who worshipped the deity. For he said and taught that the Egyptians, as well as the Libyans, were deluded in likening the deity to wild animals and cattle. Nor did the Greeks do well in fashion-

ing gods in human form. For that which encompasses us all, including earth and sea—that which we call the heavens, the world and the essence of things—this one thing only is god. And what man in his right mind would dare to fabricate an image of this god in the likeness of some mortal being? Rather we should forsake all such image-making and instead set apart a sacred precinct and a worthy sanctuary for worship without images. Some people with auspicious dreams should sleep in the temple for their own benefit and others should sleep there for the benefit of others. Those who live wisely and justly should always expect some good thing or sign or gift from god, although others should not.

(36) In so speaking, Moses persuaded not a few reasonable men and led them to the place where the settlement of Jerusalem is now located. He took it easily since the region was not desirable or such that anyone would be eager to fight for it. The area was rocky, and although the city itself was well-watered, the surrounding country was dry, arid and, within a radius of sixty stadia, rocky as well. At the same time he put forward (as a defense) the cult and the deity instead of arms, thinking it (more) worthwhile to seek a sanctuary for the deity and promising to set up a ritual and a cult which would not burden the adherents with expenses, divine ecstasies or other foolish practices. Thus Moses set up an excellent government, as a result of which the surrounding peoples were won over on account of their association with him and the advantages which were offered.

(37) His successors followed the same policies for some time thereafter, acting in a truly righteous and pious manner; but thereafter superstitious and eventually tyrannical men were appointed to the priesthood and this superstition gave rise to abstinence from meals such as is still the custom. . . .

(38) Whatever the truth of these matters, they have been believed and ordained by men. Thus the prophets (*manteis*) have been honored to the point of being treated as kings because they communicated laws and corrections to us directly from the gods. . . . Such were also Moses and his successors, who set out from good beginnings but took a turn for the worse.

This is a remarkable piece of idealizing ethnography. Its remote origins lie in Egyptian stories about early Jewish history. Yet in this version everything is turned upside down. Completely absent is the element of anti-Semitic propaganda. Together with the earlier account of Hecataeus and the roughly contemporary one of Diodorus, it demonstrates beyond any doubt that the story of Egyptian origins was not in itself anti-Semitic in character. When we find it put to such uses, we must look to local circumstances. In Strabo's case, Moses and his followers are clearly in the right. They depart because they are unhappy with Egyptian theology and ritual. Their conception of the divine—"that which encompasses us all, including sea and earth, that which we call the heavens, the world and the essence of things"—places them in opposition to all forms of image-worship; their life is one of perfect virtue; their government attracted many outsiders by virtue of its excellence. Moses and his followers are, in fact, the very models of ancient piety. Despite the eventual decline of the nation into superstition and tyranny—a favorite theme among ancient historians—Moses ranks among the legendary lawgivers of antiquity.

Much has been written on the matter of Strabo's sources. Poseidonius has been a common choice; others have pointed to Timagenes; Nicolaus of Damascus and Polybius cannot be ruled out. More recently, M. Stern has made a different suggestion. "It seems best to look for a pagan philosophical source . . . [and] that one should not, after all, exclude the possibility that Strabo is not merely derivative."[12]

No one would wish to deny that Strabo made use of sources, but neither does it seem plausible any longer to assume that his own contribution amounted to nothing more than superficial redaction. More important still is Stern's use of the term "philosophical" to characterize the passage as a whole. For Strabo portrays Moses and his followers as embodiments of popular philosophical currents current in late Hellenistic and early Roman times. As such, his portrait points back to earlier figures like Clearchus, Megasthenes, and Hecataeus, without depending on them directly. At the same time, it points ahead, in different ways, to Numenius.

A final word about relations between some of these historians. In his *Against Apion*, Josephus says the following: "Polybius of Megalopolis, Strabo the Cappodocian, Nicolaus of Damascus, Timagenes, Castor the Chronicler and Apollodorus all assert. . . ."[13] Why has Josephus cited these authors, particularly Strabo, Nicolaus, and Timagenes? The answer may lie in G. W. Bowersock's observation that "the greater Greek writers of the Augustan age were Timagenes, Dionysius, Strabo, and Nicolaus" and that "it would be surprising if these men failed to encounter one

another at Rome."[14] We may thus speak of a Roman circle of Greek
writers and their patrons under Augustus and his philhellenic successor
Tiberius. It would now appear that Judaism occupied an important place
among the concerns of this circle.

At one level, this conclusion merely strengthens the claim of those
who have argued that Judaism made a significant impact on the Roman
aristocracy in the early empire.[15] But in contrast to the passing references
of Horace and Ovid, the lengthy texts of Nicolaus, Strabo, and the
others suggest the depth and the sympathetic nature of this notice. Within
this framework, other bits of evidence regarding the extent of sympathy
for Judaism at the time take on added significance—the comment attributed to Augustus in which the emperor boasts that "not even a Jew, my
dear Tiberius, observes the Sabbath fast as faithfully as I did today";[16]
the important rhetor, Caecilius of Calacte, whom the *Suda* describes as a
convert to Judaism;[17] and the Roman noblewoman, Fulvia, whom
Josephus presents as a full proselyte.[18] In brief, it seems possible to speak
of something approaching an "official" attitude of sympathy and respect
for Judaism in the Augustan era.

LONGINUS, EPICTETUS, PLUTARCH

Though his exact name and exact date are unknown, Longinus—as we
will call the unknown author of the literary treatise *On the Sublime*—
produced a remarkable statement regarding Moses:

> In the same manner, what does the lawgiver (*thesmothetēs*) of the Jews
> say—no ordinary man, for he comprehended and brought to light in
> worthy fashion the power of the deity when he wrote at the very be-
> ginning of the laws, "God said 'Let there be light!' and there was; 'Let
> there be earth!' and there was"?[19]

These words appear at a point where Longinus is arguing that the basic
element of great writers is not literary style as such but rather a noble
and elevated mind. As examples he cites several passages from Homer, a
famous verbal exchange between Alexander the Great and his general
Parmenio, and the reference to Moses. The terms used to introduce and
describe Moses—whom Longinus assumes will be so well known to his

readers that there is no need to mention him by name—indicate that the author regarded him as at least Homer's equal in speaking of the gods. The term *thesmothetēs*, in conjunction with the phrase "no ordinary man," represents a deliberate effort to underline Moses' theological excellence. In line with his belief that great style requires great ideas, especially in matters of the gods, Longinus praises Moses' conception of a god whose word alone was sufficient for the act of creation.

What are we to make of this extraordinary text? Some have felt compelled to reject it as an obvious Jewish or Christian interpolation. Others have concluded that Longinus himself was a hellenized Jew, on the supposition that anyone who treated Homer and Moses as equals must have been Jewish. All of these proposals treat the passage in question as a "problem," that is, how to account for the presence of such laudatory sentiments regarding Moses and the Bible in a writing that is otherwise so thoroughly Greek?

By now it should be apparent that the text is problematic only within the framework of a tradition of scholarship that regards the Greco-Roman world as largely hostile toward Jews and Judaism. Once this tradition itself is called into question, the text ceases to be a problem. In light of the early Hellenistic writers like Hecataeus, Megasthenes, and Clearchus, of the ethnographic tradition represented by Diodorus, Pompeius Trogus, Nicolaus of Damascus, and Strabo, and of later writers like Numenius and Porphyry, these words of Longinus no longer stand out as exceptional. Within the overall framework of the first century, as M. Stern argues, the assumption that Longinus was a Jew is no longer either necessary or helpful. "Indeed, it would be the lack of any literary expression of such a phenomenon that would call for an explanation."[20]

Further testimony to the extent of Judaism's appeal in the late first and early second centuries is provided by Epictetus. In three of his philosophical exhortations, Epictetus speaks of Jews, Syrians, and Egyptians as the chief competitors in a struggle for religious loyalty in the Greco-Roman world:

> And is it possible at this present time that all the opinions which Jews, and Syrians, and Egyptians and Romans hold on the subject of food are rightly held?[21]

This is the conflict between Jews and Syrians and Egyptians and Romans, not over the question whether holiness (*to hosion*) should be put before everything else . . . but whether the particular act of eating swine's flesh is holy or unholy.[22]

Why, then, do you call yourself a Stoic, why do you deceive the multitude, why do you act the part of a Jew, when you are a Greek? Do you not see in what sense men are severally called Jew, Syrian, or Egyptian? For example, whenever we see a man hesitating between two faiths, we are in the habit of saying, "He is not a Jew, he is only acting the part." But when he adopts the attitude of mind of the man who has been baptized and has made his choice, then he both is a Jew in fact and is also called one.[23]

The importance of these passages can scarcely be overestimated. It is not simply that they place Judaism on a level with Egyptian (probably Isis and Serapis) and Syrian (probably Attis and the Magna Mater) cults as significant religious options in the Empire. In this they merely confirm the picture of the place of Judaism in Roman society as described by Roman writers throughout the first century. They also contribute in no small way to explaining the opposition to Judaism among conservative Romans.

Put simply, the numbers of those who protested against Judaism must now be seen as an accurate measure of Judaism's appeal in Roman society. On this point, the third of Epictetus's statements is most revealing. The context indicates clearly that he is speaking of converts to Judaism; the baptism mentioned is undoubtedly the ritual of conversion referred to in numerous Jewish texts.[24] Of greater interest, however, is the fact that the phenomena of attraction and conversion to Judaism had become common enough to have produced a proverbial saying—"He is not a Jew, he is only acting the part." Epictetus makes use of this saying in his exhortation to half-hearted adherents of his own Stoic faith! "Why then do you call yourself a Stoic, why do you deceive the multitude, why do you act the part of a Jew, when you are really a Greek?" And as the sequel makes clear, far from offering any criticism of such converts to Judaism, he presents them as models for the full acceptance of Stoicism. These comments need not be interpreted so as to make Epictetus an admirer of Judaism. Their value for our purposes lies not in what they

tell us of the author's personal views but in their testimony to the extraordinary extent to which Judaism had implanted itself on the spiritual
landscape of the Greco-Roman world by the end of the first century C.E.

The final figure in our survey of writers in the Roman period is the
Greek philosopher, biographer, and historian of religion, Plutarch. Though
he spent most of his lifetime in his native Greece, he traveled to Egypt
and Italy and taught in Rome. Plutarch's interest in Judaism, while certainly reflecting his own scholarly interests in religious matters, must also
be taken as confirming our conclusions about the extent to which knowledge of Judaism had permeated aristocratic and intellectual circles of the
late first and early second centuries.

Scattered references to Jewish history appear in a number of the
Lives[25] and the Jewish Sabbath is mentioned in *On Superstition* along
with other examples of "barbarian superstition."[26] In his treatise *On the
Contradictions of the Stoics*,[27] he cites the "opinions held on gods by
Jews and Syrians" as evidence against the Stoic argument that the view
of the gods as beneficial and humane is substantiated by universal opinion.

A rather different picture emerges from Plutarch's *Dinner Conversations*, a work of the author's maturity (c. 115 C.E.), which purports to
record the dinner conversations of himself and a number of fellow intellectuals. Two of the topics bear directly on Judaism. In 4.5, Polycrates
asks whether Jews abstain from pork because of reverence or aversion for
the pig. This topic then leads naturally to a discussion on the true
identity of the Jewish god (4.6). The topics themselves support our sense
that these two issues were among those which most interested and puzzled
outside observers of Judaism.

As for the content of the two discussions, one can only say that they
reflect Plutarch's tendency to combine sound information, misconception,
and free speculation in his treatment of Judaism. In the first category,
one must include (a) a series of brief passages, primarily in the *Parallel
Lives*, where Plutarch refers to historical events involving Jews; (b)
specific details regarding various holidays and festivals including the
Sabbath and the Day of Atonement; (c) reference to various ritual
practices including the prohibition of honey in the sacrificial cult, the
use of trumpets, tents, and palm branches during the Feast of Taber-

nacles, and the only mention of Levites in pagan literature; and (d) in the discussion of Jewish abstinence from pork, reference to the fact that the hare is also a forbidden animal.

These fragments of sound information set Plutarch apart from most pagan authors. While he reveals no knowledge of the Jewish Scriptures and is certainly no expert on Jewish ritual, such details indicate a reliable source of information rather than previous pagan authors. Perhaps he conversed with Jews in his native Boeotia or during his visits to Alexandria and Rome. It would be a mistake, however, to suppose that Plutarch was completely free from the misinformation that so frequently appears in pagan authors throughout antiquity. Like Tacitus, he reports that the Jews honor the ass because it led them to water during their sojourn in the desert. Unlike Tacitus, however, Plutarch extracts no venom from this tradition. Elsewhere he exercises his critical judgment regarding previous attempts to connect this particular tradition with the Egyptian tale of Typhon.[28]

The third and most revealing category of Plutarch's material appears in the free-wheeling speculations of the participants in the table conversations about the reasons for Jewish abstention from pork and the identity of the Jewish god. Here Plutarch's characters engage in a full-fledged *interpretatio Hellenistica* of Judaism, using details of Jewish worship to demonstrate underlying parallels between Judaism and pagan cults. The argument culminates in Moeragenes' effort to convince his colleagues that the Jewish god is none other than Dionysus.[29]

What then can be said of Plutarch's attitude toward Judaism? On the surface there appears to be a certain tension between various statements. In his early work *On Superstition*, he cites the Sabbath as an example of superstition in religion. The same tone characterizes his comments in *On the Contradictions of the Stoics* regarding the Jewish views of the divine. In his other writings, however, this censorius tone is not evident. In the *Dinner Conversations*, where he writes as a historian of religion, there is no longer any hint of criticism. Neither is there any hint of sympathy or admiration. Judaism is accepted as a fact of sufficient significance to merit the attention of a serious student of contemporary religion. Plutarch's observations not only constitute an important counter-image to the views of his exact contemporary Tacitus. They also tend to confirm the evidence of Epictetus, Longinus, Strabo, and others as to the impact of Judaism in the late first and early second centuries of the Roman Empire.

THE ESSENES

Given traditional theories of what Greeks and Romans found appealing or distasteful in Judaism, it is perhaps surprising to discover that the Essene community at the Dead Sea exercised a considerable appeal for certain pagan observers. In fact, this most separatist of all Jewish "schools" met with a strongly positive response. If we exclude Nicolaus of Damascus, who may have been a source for Josephus's accounts of Essenes, the earliest reference appears in Pliny's *Natural History* (c. 70 C.E.) in his description of the geography of Judea and the Jordan valley.[30] Although it is most unlikely that Pliny himself had visited the Essene community, it is clear that he shares with his source a sense of amazement at this "solitary tribe." Why he admires it is somewhat problematic. In the first place, it appears primarily as an ascetic community: no women, no sexual relations, no money and, though this is not stated explicitly, no involvement with urban or town life. Despite these apparent disadvantages, however, the community is constantly replenished by outsiders, "tired of life" and "driven thither by the waves of fortune." Of the beliefs and teachings of the Essenes, nothing is said—no doubt because nothing was known to Pliny or his source. Still, what he does say is enough to make it clear that Pliny saw in the Essenes an embodiment of the philosophic life as it was widely understood in popular philosophical circles of Hellenistic and Roman times. There the pursuit of wisdom lay not so much in scholastic doctrines or loyalty to particular schools as in the pursuit of a philosophical, that is, ascetic way of life.

In support of this view stands a brief comment attributed to Dio of Prusa, the second century C.E. rhetor: "he [Dio] praises the Essenes, a whole happy city beside the Dead Sea, lying at some point not far from Sodom itself."[31] Beyond these two passages, the remaining references to the Essenes are dependent on either Pliny or Josephus.[32]

Whatever their sources, Pliny the Elder, Dio, and others saw in the

Essenes an ideal community of philosophers. One reason for this perception might be found in Jewish descriptions of the Essenes, reflected in Philo and Josephus, where the Essenes were also understood and represented as a philosophical sect. In his *Every Good Man Is Free*, Philo introduces the Essenes as Jewish counterparts to those who successfully pursue virtue among Greeks and barbarians.[33] He uses the term *philosophia* several times to characterize their ethical pursuits. He also distinguishes their true philosophy from the vain study of logic and natural philosophy among the Greeks. Josephus likens the Essenes to the followers of Pythagoras: "This is a group which follows a way of life brought to the Greeks by Pythagoras."[34]

Since the discovery of the Dead Sea Scrolls, the likelihood of direct dependence of the Essenes on Pythagorean traditions has seemed less likely. But the real issue, no doubt also for Josephus himself, is not one of direct dependence but rather one of certain structural similarities and a well-established history of interpretation among ancient observers of Judaism. It is not simply, as M. Hengel put it, that "in one sense the 'Hellenized' interpretation of the Essene order by the various ancient writers was not completely mistaken."[35] More to the point is the fact that a tradition of interpreting Judaism in Pythagorean terms reaches back as far as Hermippus in the third century B.C.E. Hermippus had claimed that Pythagoras himself "copied the teaching of the Jews and Thracians . . . and introduced many points of Jewish law into his philosophy."[36] This statement, which appears in Josephus's *Against Apion*, is reinforced by Origen's comment that "Hermippus in his first book *On Legislators* related that Pythagoras brought his own philosophy from the Jews to the Greeks."[37] Finally Antonius Diogenes, author of a lost life of Pythagoras, stated that Pythagoras travelled among the Egyptians, Arabs, Chaldeans, and Hebrews and that "he learned from them the science of dream interpretation."[38]

In short, there was a continuous tradition of what one might call an *interpretatio Pythagorica* attested to and accepted by Greek, Jewish, and Christian authors, the origins of which reach back to the early Hellenistic period. Thus in regarding the Essenes as a community of philosophers, Josephus, Philo, Pliny, and others, far from being atypical, are part of a long-established tradition and must be understood within the framework of that tradition.[39]

The evidence assembled and discussed in this chapter makes it difficult to argue that the ancient world in general, and the early Roman Empire in particular, disliked Jews. Wherever such a view is propounded, this evidence is simply overlooked. The traditional interpretation is mistaken in its overall assessment of pagan attitudes in the early Empire, and it compounds the error by using this mistaken assessment as a key to understanding both earlier and later times. One counter-proposal to the traditional view has been formulated as follows by Stern—"The first century C.E. was not only the age of Apion, Chaeremon and Seneca, but was also a century marked by the unprecedented diffusion of Jewish ideas and customs among various classes of society. . . ."[40]

Stern's counter-proposal is perhaps too weak. If we exclude the situation in Alexandria and the passage from Tacitus, which is heavily dependent on Alexandrian sources, we must conclude that Roman attitudes toward Jews and Judaism were much more positive than the traditional view would allow. One might even argue that the traditional view must be stood on its head. Revisionist interpretations of the anti-Judaism in Christian authors like John Chrysostom and others see anti-Judaism as a reaction against the powerful appeal of Judaism in Christian circles. Similarly, our new view holds that the negative views expressed by Tacitus and Seneca spring from conservative and xenophobic circles opposed not so much to Judaism itself as to its successful expansion into Roman circles. We must now begin to consider an interpretation which would construe the negative views as themselves a minority expression. We need to render explicit what is merely implicit in Stern's overly modest proposal, namely, that it was precisely "the unprecedented diffusion of Jewish ideas and customs among various classes of society" which prompted the occasional words and acts of protest.

Stern has also formulated a second important revision of the traditional view. It has been customary to account for positive assessments of Judaism by referring them to Jewish sources, or in some cases by describing the authors themselves as Jews. It is interesting to note here that modern scholarship on these issues has moved consistently in a single direction. Take the case of Longinus. At one time it was assumed that the only way to explain the laudatory statement about Moses by Longinus was to dismiss the passage as a later Jewish or Christian interpolation. After this theory was thoroughly refuted, the view gained currency that Longinus himself must have been in some sense a Jew. Now, however, Stern warns us not only that such an assumption is unnecessary but that Longinus's words reflect a broad and deep penetration of Judaism in the Greco-Roman world of the first century.

The literary sources have also indicated that Judaism was a recurrent topic of conversation in pagan circles. The evidence here is overwhelming. One need only recall the fact that Longinus can refer to Moses without mentioning him by name and that Epictetus can use a proverb derived from superficial adherents to Judaism. The conversations depicted by Plutarch in his *Dinner Conversations* may serve for us as prototypes of many similar occasions throughout the period. Indeed, it is possible to say something about the specific topics of these recurrent conversations.

The *first* topic concerned the identity of the Jewish god. As Johannes Lydus puts it in his *On Months*, "There has been and still is great disagreement among theologians regarding the god worshiped by the Hebrews."[41] In light of the theological syncretism common in learned pagan circles and the various forms of religious eclecticism in Jewish circles, it is not surprising to discover attempts to identify the Jewish god with almost every significant pagan deity—Jupiter, Saturn, Zeus, Orpheus, Dionysus, Osiris, Sabazius, and Pan, not to mention various Stoic and Platonic conceptions of the divine, or the unbridled syncretism of the magical papyri.

A *second* topic of discussion was the issue of Jewish origins. Virtually every writer on the Jews espoused one theory or another, and no two are absolutely identical. Here again we are fortunate in having a catalogue of theories, preserved in the preface to Tacitus's generally hostile treatment of Judaism.[42] As we have seen, these theories served differing purposes according to the attitudes and intentions of individual writers. Generally they reflect the widespread practice of Greek and Roman historiography as well as the common Greco-Roman assumption that the key to understanding a people or nation lay in its origins. And as a rule, it follows that a particular author's attitude toward Judaism will bear a close relation to his version of Jewish origins.

The *third* and final topic of conversation was Jewish customs, notably the Sabbath, circumcision, and abstinence from pork. The reasons for the interest in these particular items are not difficult to imagine. Two of them—the Sabbath and circumcision—were central to Judaism itself, and all three seemed distinctive and peculiar when compared with Greco-Roman customs. There were also other topics that appeared somewhat less frequently. Chief among these were Jewish monotheism, the rejection of images in worship, and the figure of Moses. These in particular stand out because certain pagan authors, particularly those with a philosophical orientation, treated them with unusual respect and admiration.

The conclusions reached thus far are based on the evidence, primarily literary, that has survived. These sources demonstrate that in the first two centuries C.E., Judaism was widely discussed, examined, appreciated, and criticized. Beyond the extant sources, we must take note of an entire range of information, including brief passages as well as whole treatises, which were known at the time but have failed to survive. Among these we mention only a few: Polybius, of whom Josephus reports that he produced an account of the "Jews who live near the temple of Jerusalem, as it is called, concerning which we have more to say, especially concerning the renown of the temple, but we shall defer the account to another occasion";[43] Timagenes, the Alexandrian historian of the first century B.C.E., whose work apparently included numerous references to the Jews;[44] and Poseidonius, who is cited as a source for many later writers but whose writings have entirely disappeared.

We have seen repeatedly that ancient observers consistently represented Judaism as a philosophy. This is true both of pagans and of Jews. Thus when Josephus undertakes to describe the various sects or schools of first-century Judaism, he presents them as schools of Jewish philosophy. For Philo, Judaism is not only a competitor with other philosophies for the loyalty of Greeks and Romans, it is the true philosophy par excellence. It has been customary to dismiss such "philosophical" presentations of Judaism as either well intentioned but misleading attempts to explain

Judaism to a non-Jewish audience or apologetic efforts designed to increase Judaism's appeal to outsiders by cloaking it in the respectable garb of philosophy. Against such views, Morton Smith has argued that these easy dismissals are without any justification. They ignore the extent to which post-exilic Judaism in all of its forms was part and parcel of the Greco-Roman world. They also fail to appreciate the extended meaning of the term *philosophia* in Hellenistic and Roman times. "That world," Smith notes, "had no general term for *religion* . . . for the peculiar synthesis of all these which we call a 'religion' the one Hellenistic word which came closest was 'philosophy.' "[45] He further notes that the proper equivalent for the use of *philosophia* in the Greco-Roman world is not "philosophy" but "cult of wisdom." Thus pagan observers who represent Judaism as a philosophy need not be seen merely as providing hermeneutical aids for their readers, nor may Jewish writers be seen as seeking an apologetic advantage in describing Judaism as a whole or a particular Jewish sect as a philosophy.

Of course, not all pagans saw Judaism as a philosophy. For, as Smith comments, such a perception presupposed and expressed a positive judgment: "To those who admired Judaism it was 'the cult of wisdom' . . . and to those who disliked it it was 'atheism,' which is simply the other side of the coin, the regular term of abuse applied to philosophy by its opponents."[46] Actually, critics of Judaism often dubbed it a "superstition," a standard term of abuse applied to foreign cults, but we are nonetheless indebted to Smith for an observation of fundamental significance in assessing pagan views of Judaism—namely, that the divergence between positive and negative attitudes toward Judaism reflects tensions within Greco-Roman culture itself. The same factors that made these cults attractive applied to Judaism as well, and perhaps more. Similarly, those drawn to "philosophy" as the path to salvation were also drawn to the philosophy of Judaism. But the other side of the coin, to use Smith's phrase, was that those who were opposed to the eastern cults or to philosophy undoubtedly were opposed to Judaism, and for many of the same reasons.

> The masses have long since shown a keen desire to adopt our religious observances; and there is not one city, Greek or barbarian, nor

a single nation, to which our custom of abstinence from work on the seventh day has not spread and where the fasts and lighting of lamps and of our prohibition in the matter of food are not observed. . . . It follows, then, that our accusers must either condemn the whole world for deliberate malice in being so eager to adopt the bad laws of a foreign country in preference to the good laws of their own, or else give up their grudge against us.[47]

There is something surely still more wonderful even than this: not only Jews but almost every other people, particularly those which take more account of virtue, have so far grown in holiness as to value and honour our laws. . . . They attract and win the attention of all, of barbarians, of Greeks, of dwellers on the mainland and islands, of nations of the east and the west, of Europe and Asia, of the whole inhabited world from end to end. For who has not shown his respect for that sacred seventh day. . . . Again who does not every year show awe and reverence for the fast, as it is called, which is kept more strictly and solemnly than the holy month of the Greeks.[48]

How are we to interpret these words of Josephus and Philo as they bear on the situation of Judaism in the first 150 years of the Roman Empire? That they exaggerate is certain. The evidence surveyed above, however, forces us to consider the possibility that Josephus and Philo may stand closer, far closer, to the truth than has commonly been assumed. This does not mean that there were innumerable conversions to Judaism, and we should not look to burial inscriptions of proselytes for confirmation of our hypothesis. In many cases, the evidence points not so much to conversions as to varying degrees of sympathy or attachment. Many Gentiles adopted one or another belief or practice from Judaism, without embracing the entire system. The understanding of Judaism was not always profound. Thus the emperor Augustus himself apparently prided himself as an observer of the Sabbath, but, according to Suetonius's report, he understood the Sabbath to be a day of fast!

Two important facts have emerged about the standing of Judaism in Roman society of the early first century. First, from the comments of various Roman authors it is clear that Jews were waging a vigorous and successful campaign to disseminate their beliefs and practices. In some cases this led to conversion, in others to the adoption of certain practices, in still others to a general sympathy for Judaism. Second, the positive image of Judaism projected during Augustus's reign by various Greek writers—Nicolaus of Damascus, Diodorus of Sicily, Pompeius Trogus, and Strabo—supports the view that Judaism was seen as an attractive religious and philosophical alternative in this early period.

Toward the end of the century, during the reign of Domitian, there is again ample evidence for the appeal of Judaism among non-Jews: Dio Cassius's report that the ex-consul, Acilius Glabrio, the emperor's own cousin, Flavius Clemens, Flavius's wife Flavia, and many others had drifted into Jewish ways;[49] Epictetus's comments on the widespread appeal of Judaism throughout the empire; the evidence of Juvenal and Martial as to the successes of Jewish proselytism; and Domitian's vigorous assault on Romans who followed the Jewish way of life without formally professing Judaism.

For the period between Augustus and Domitian there is little evidence. Did the situation remain more or less unchanged during the intervening years? One might argue that Tiberius's expulsion of the Jews from Rome in 19 C.E. and the similar action supposedly taken by Claudius in 41 or 49[50] brought the Augustan era, as it applied to Jews, to an abrupt end. The various accounts of the incident under Tiberius point to a general action against foreign cults, specifically the cult of Isis and Judaism, precisely because they were enjoying considerable success in Rome.[51] Tacitus speaks of those who had been "tainted by that superstition," that is, Judaism, and adds that they could avoid expulsion "by giving up their ridiculous rites before a certain date";[52] Josephus ties the expulsion to Fulvia, a convert to Judaism and the wife of a leading Roman senator, and to proselytizing activity in Rome,[53] and Dio reports that the Jews were expelled "because they were converting many in Rome to their customs."[54]

Thus the evidence from the years between Augustus and Domitian not only fails to change the picture but strengthens it in some details. The various reports point to a situation in which some Romans fully converted to Judaism and many others adopted various beliefs and practices. Thus we find a general confirmation of Josephus's and Philo's claim that Judaism enjoyed wide popularity in this period and see that this popularity regularly took the form of Judaizing, that is, "adopting our religious observances."[55] Despite the traumatic events of the Jewish revolts of 66–73 and 115–117, both official Roman policy and unofficial expressions of sympathy for Judaism remained remarkably constant through the middle of the second century C.E. The evidence surveyed also indicates that antipathy to Judaism arose largely from political sources. This was as true for Alexandria as it was for Rome. This conclusion is supported by the fact that following the final outburst of Jewish anti-Romanism in the revolt of Bar Cochba, after which Judaism no longer posed a political threat to the Empire, signs of antipathy toward Judaism virtually disappear from the scene. There remain isolated pockets of distemper, but their sporadic occurrence substantiates the view that the earlier difficulties were largely political in origin.

6

Roman Policy Toward Judaism
and the Rise of Christianity[1]

The suppression of the Bar Cochba revolt in 132–135 C.E. marks the turning point in relations among pagans, Christians, and Jews in the empire. In the physiognomy of Judaism and in the character of relations between Jews and pagans the events leading up to 135 left perhaps their deepest impression. Jerusalem had become a pagan city (Aelia Capitolina) and was totally forbidden to Jews. Hadrian's prohibition of circumcision and other Jewish observances remained in effect, and a reorganized province (Syria Palaestina) was created with two full legions as occupying forces. Dio Cassius reports Jewish casualties at 580,000 and describes Judea as totally desolated:

> The number of those who died from hunger, sickness and fire is beyond calculation. The whole of Judea was almost like a desert, as had been predicted before the war. For the tomb of Solomon, which they revere highly, collapsed by itself and many wolves and hyenas entered their cities and howled.[2]

In religious and political activity, Galilee replaced Judea as the heart of Palestinian Judaism. The official Jewish patriarch emerged as the central figure not only in Palestine but in relations with the Diaspora and official Rome as well.[3] An indication of how significant this new office could be may be seen in the series of references in Talmudic sources to the friendship between a ruler called Antoninus and "Rabbi," the patriarch Judah I (c. 170–210).[4] M. Avi-Yonah sorts the passages into four categories: (1) historically reliable material, (2) legends, (3) anecdotes, and

(4) remains of a philosophical-theological treatise.[5] In the first category he places certain discussions between Antoninus and Judah in Palestine (Caesarea) concerning a revolt in Egypt, a statement of the emperor's desire to elevate Tiberias to the status of colony, his use of the wealthy patriarch's breeding cattle to improve his own herd, letters exchanged by the two, and finally Antoninus's gift to Judah of an inscribed golden candelabrum. The other categories contain material that is patently apocryphal, such as accounts of Antoninus's conversion.

One might be tempted to dismiss the friendship between Antoninus and "Rabbi" as the product of wishful thinking were it not for the similar relationship between the rhetor Libanius, a friend and advisor to Julian, and the Jewish patriarch Gamaliel V (c. 359–390).[6] Several of Libanius's letters to the patriarch have survived, dating from 388 to 393. Although they convey little specific information, they reveal that the two maintained regular contacts, not just about official matters but on numerous other matters of mutual concern. They also show that the patriarch corresponded with other leading figures of the time and that his son spent a period of study under Libanius. Unfortunately there is little information about relations of other patriarchs with Rome.[7] But these two instances suggest that the dialogue between paganism and Judaism depended heavily on the skill and tact of each succeeding patriarch. The Empire in turn recognized the importance of the office granting honorific titles to the incumbents. The *Codex Theodosianus* refers to the patriarchs as *viri clarissimi et illustres* and indicates that they also held the honorary office of *praefectura*.[8]

How did the wars influence Rome's view of Judaism? Granting the exaggerations of Dio's casualty figures, the impact of the wars should not be underestimated. There is ample evidence that Rome regarded them as major events—the *Judaea capta* coins issued under Vespasian and Titus, the commemorative arches of the same emperors, the drastic political measures of Hadrian, and Dio's report that after the war in 132–135 Hadrian dispensed with the customary formula, "I and the army are well," when he wrote to the senate.[9] Tacitus, in his account of the war in 66–73, accuses the Jews of harboring a bitter hatred of all men and rails against their separatism. The same themes appear in the speech of the philosopher Euphrates to Vespasian after the same war:

> For these people have for a long time rebelled not only against the Romans but against all men. By their unsocial way of life and their refusal to have anything in common with others, whether food, libations, prayers or sacrifices, they are more removed from us than Susa, Bactria or the Indians beyond.[10]

Given the precedents from earlier wars, it comes as something of a surprise to find no similar reaction among Romans to the war of 132–135. The only literary reflection of the feelings generated by the conflict is a brief remark of Fronto, the friend of Marcus Aurelius: "During Hadrian's reign, how many soldiers fell to the Jews, how many to the Britains!"[11] Of course we may simply be ignorant of sources long since disappeared. But there is some evidence to suggest that, at least in official and intellectual circles, there was no reaction like that which followed the war of 66–73. On the contrary, when we examine the policy of Hadrian's successors, beginning with Antoninus Pius but especially under the Severans (193–235) and Julian (360–363), a remarkable change of tone in the dialogue between paganism and Judaism is evident.

The new atmosphere is apparent in Dio's digression on the Jews which precedes his account of Pompey's exploits in 63 B.C.E.:

> I do not know the origin of this name [Jews], but it is applied to all men, even foreigners, who follow their customs. This race is found among Romans. It has frequently been persecuted but has prospered nonetheless and has finally succeeded in winning the right of religious freedom. They differ from other men in all things concerning daily life. Above all, they worship none of the other gods but reserve great honor for one god. Since they regard him as ineffable and invisible they have no images in Jerusalem and worship him more zealously than all men. They built a great and beautiful temple to him which had neither covering nor roof. They dedicate the day of Saturn to him. On that day they perform special duties but accomplish no serious work. Everything concerning this god, his nature, the origin of his cult and the fear he inspires in them has been discussed by many authors. . . .[12]

The tone of this passage is significant for its combination of neutrality, accuracy, and even a certain admiration for the Jewish cult. The memory of the earlier hostilities has all but disappeared.

THE NEW POLICIES ON JUDAISM

The new era began with the accession of Antoninus Pius (138–161).[13] Antoninus soon modified Hadrian's universal prohibition of circumcision and allowed the Jews alone to resume the practice: "A rescript of the divine Pius permitted the Jews to circumcise their own sons. But if anyone performs it on those not of the same religion [that is, by birth] he is punished under the code of castration."[14] Here we see both sides of the old Roman policy: on the one hand to grant freedom of religious observance and on the other hand to arrest proselytism. The effort seems to have been largely ineffectual.[15] Proselytism and even circumcision of converts continued long after Hadrian, and Septimius Severus's renewal of legislation against proselytism is but further evidence of the policy's failure.

Apart from the relaxation of laws against circumcision, we hear nothing further under Antoninus. For Marcus Aurelius (161–180) there is only one piece of second or thirdhand information of doubtful reliability. In his *History*, Ammianus Marcellinus reports that the emperor Julian applied to dissident Christian groups a saying which originated with Marcus:

> As he [Marcus] was passing through Palestine on his way to Egypt he was overcome by the malodorous and tumultuous character of the Jews and is reported to have exclaimed in sadness, 'O Marcommani, O Quadi, O Sarmati [barbarian tribes in the region of the Danube where Marcus had fought several campaigns], at last I have found a people more unruly than you.' [22.5]

From the time of Commodus (180–193) there is no direct information at all. It seems likely, however, that whatever the personal opinions of these two emperors, the *entente cordiale* established by Antoninus continued during their reigns. This assumption is supported by a comment of the Roman lawyer Modestinus to the effect that Marcus Aurelius and Commodus admitted Jews to public offices with responsibility over non-Jews and provided that they would not be required to perform duties that might offend their beliefs.[16]

For the Severans, however, there is an abundance of information. Jerome says that Septimius Severus (193–211) and Caracalla (198–217) "regarded the Jews most highly."[17] The *Digest* of Justinian reports that "the divine Severus and Antoninus [Caracalla] permitted those of the Jewish superstition to obtain public offices and imposed upon them such formalities as would not offend their superstition."[18] The *Historia Augusta* contain numerous instances of pro-Jewish sympathies among the Severans. As a young boy, Caracalla is said to have held a grudge against his own father and the father of a playmate who "had been seriously punished because of his Jewish religion."[19] The bizarre Heliogabalus ordered Jews, Samaritans, and Christians to transfer their cults to the Palatine hill as subordinate elements in a single religion dominated by the Syrian god Elagabalus.[20] Dio Cassius reports that the emperor had himself circumcised, probably in imitation of Syrian rites, and that he abstained from pork.[21] His biography in the *Historia Augusta* also includes the strange information that he occasionally displayed ostriches at banquets because "the Jews had been commanded to eat them."[22]

The biography of Alexander Severus (222–235) contains several references to his pro-Jewish sympathies. His attitude apparently earned him the unflattering title of "Syrian archisynagogus."[23] He "respected the religious freedom of Jews and tolerated Christians."[24] Remarkably, he is said to have included busts of Abraham, Apollonius of Tyana, Christ, and Orpheus in his palace shrine.[25] In politics he followed the practice of Christians and Jews in announcing the names of candidates for important public offices prior to their appointment.[26] Lastly, he used a form of the golden rule as a model in dispensing punishment:

> He often pronounced what he had heard from some Jews or Christians and had never forgotten. He also had it spoken by a herald whenever he issued a warning. "What you do not wish to be done to you do not do to others (*quod tibi fieri non vis, alteri ne feceris*)." So highly did he value this precept that he ordered it to be inscribed in the palace and in public buildings.[27]

A final piece of information from the *Historia Augusta* concerns, oddly enough, the death of Moses. In lamenting the brief reign of Claudius (268–270), the author records the following anecdote:

The most learned astrologers have asserted that one hundred and twenty years have been given to man for living and that none has been granted more. But they add that Moses alone, the friend of god (*familiarem dei*) as he is called in the books of the Jews, lived one hundred and twenty-five years. When he complained that he was dying young it is said that an answer was given him by an unknown deity (*ab incerto numine*) that no one would ever live longer.[28]

Thus far in our consideration of the Severans we have relied mainly on the *Historia Augusta*, a series of gossipy biographies of the Roman emperors from 117–284. On virtually every critical aspect of the *Historia* —date, authorship, sources, and purpose—major disagreements exist.[29] There has been a tendency to doubt its reliability in every area, not least as concerns the attitude of the Severans toward the Jews. It is not possible to substantiate the reliability of each of these passages, but it seems unlikely in the first instance that they could have been invented if there had not been some basis in fact. Thus without denying the insights of the skeptics, I would maintain that the *Historia* reflect Severan attitudes in general if not in every detail. On this point there is substantial testimony, including Jerome and the generally favorable tone of Dio's excursus on Judaism, which probably reflects Severan sentiments as well as his own.[30]

For the remainder of the third century until the first Christian rulers there is little information. As the waning pagan Empire concentrated more of its energies on Christianity, the old policies and attitudes toward the Jews seem to have persisted.

Still the last word had not been spoken. When Julian, a convert to paganism, came to power in 360 the Empire reverted immediately to its former policies.[31] In 362, following a meeting with Jewish leaders in Antioch, he announced his intention to rebuild the temple in Jerusalem and to allow the resumption of the traditional sacrifices.[32] At the same time he appointed his close associate, Alypius of Antioch, to oversee the project[33] and returned Jerusalem to Jewish control.[34] Finally, he abolished all special taxes on the Jews and urged the patriarch to abandon the annual levy (*apostolē*) which went to the support of the patriarchate.[35]

Regarding Judaism itself, his attitude appears most fully in his anti-Christian treatise, *Against the Galileans*. Here he shows a clear admiration for their sacrificial institutions.[36] In Abraham he saw a kindred spirit who "sacrificed just as we, always and continuously" and "prophesied by shooting stars, which is probably Hellenic."[37] The god of the Jews he held in high regard, though with special reservations:

> The Jews are in part god-fearing for they revere a god who is truly most powerful and most benevolent. He governs the world of sense and is worshipped by us, as I well know, under other names.[38]

> They have always worshipped a god who was always kind to me and to those who honored him as Abraham did, for he is a very great and powerful god.[39]

In other words, his attitude contains elements of both praise and criticism, though the criticism is directed not at the Jewish god himself but rather at Moses' interpretation of him. This is especially evident in the extended commentary on the Mosaic cosmogony in his *Against the Galileans*. The discussion takes the form of a comparison between Moses and Plato, with the ultimate purpose of determining the precise nature and function of the Mosaic deity.[40] Julian points out that god does not create matter itself and concludes "that according to Moses god is not the creator of incorporeal things but only the disposer of pre-existent matter."[41] The entire account he describes as "wholly mythical" and full of actions unworthy of the highest god.[42] In short, his chief criticism is that Moses "pays the highest honor to a sectional deity (*theos merikos*)" and "worships one who has been assigned the lordship over a small portion instead of the creator of all things."[43]

In the same vein, he charges that the Jews are inconsistent with their own scriptures in their refusal to honor other gods.[44] The basis of this charge is the Neo-Platonic doctrine of *theokrasia*, according to which the gods of the various nations were first shown to be identical except for name and then assigned a position in the divine hierarchy under the highest god. Thus while Julian could honor the god of the Jews as the powerful creator of the visible world, he could also deny that he was the highest god of Neo-Platonic theology.

Elsewhere, his criticisms take a less elevated tone and simply reflect the traditional themes of pagan anti-Semitic propaganda. God gave to the

Hebrews nothing of great value; they originated no scientific or philosophical discoveries; their law is "harsh and contains much that is ruthless
and barbarous"; and they have been aliens and slaves throughout their
history.[45]

What, then, are we to make of Julian's actions in view of his obviously
ambivalent feelings toward Judaism? First, there can be no doubt about
his sincerity in undertaking the temple project.[46] In a fragment of a letter
to the Jews, written after his departure from Antioch, he says that "he is
rebuilding the temple of the highest god with all haste."[47] He speaks of
the project again in his Letter to Theodorus:

> Let no one lead us astray with clever reasoning or disturb us in our
> belief in providence. Those who reproach on these matters, namely the
> prophets of the Jews, what will they say about the temple which has
> been destroyed three times and even now is not reconstructed? I say this
> not to revile them, I who had the idea after so many years to rebuild it
> to the glory of the god who is invoked there. But I use it [the project]
> to show that no human undertaking is eternal and that the prophets who
> wrote such things spoke falsely and mixed with dessicated old women.
> None of this means that this is not a great god, just that he never ac-
> quired worthy prophets or spokesmen.[48]

In other words, the letter shows a degree of disappointment, though not
despondency, at the project's collapse and also reveals that he had undertaken it in part to fulfill prophecies that the temple was eternal.

Here and there we catch glimpses of other motives. The historian
Ammianus Marcellinus, who had accompanied Julian during his campaign
against the Persians in 363, states that the emperor was motivated by a
desire "to propagate the memory of his reign by the magnitude of his
works."[49] His Christian critics saw it as a deliberate attempt to undermine
the argument that the destruction of the temple was the final sign that
God had rejected the Jews as the chosen people. No doubt there was an
anti-Christian element in his motivation, deriving in part from an understandable reaction against the religion that he had rejected. On several
occasions he goes out of his way to contrast Christians unfavorably with
Jews, as when he tells the Alexandrians that their founder was not like
any of the Hebrews "though they have shown themselves far superior

to the Galileans."[50] In addition the rebuilding of the temple was entirely consistent with his general scheme to replace Christianity with a universal pagan church. A key part of this program was his edict that temples should be restored and traditional sacrifices resumed throughout the Empire. Finally, a rapprochement with Judaism was to Julian's military advantage in his campaign against the Persians, for his actions assured him the support of Jewish communities along his route and especially in Mesopotamia.[51]

Whether this mixture of actions, attitudes, and motives justifies calling Julian a proto-Zionist, as some have suggested, is questionable.[52] Nonetheless, there can be no doubt that he was genuinely attracted to certain aspects of ancient Judaism, an attraction which he shared with other representatives of Neo-Platonism in the late empire.

With Julian's sudden death in 363 and with the official anti-Judaism of the church fully in place, we might well expect to find a dramatic reversal in imperial policy toward the Jews. Certainly the Christian emperors from that time forward, if not beginning with Constantine himself, must have succumbed to ecclesiastical pressures by translating theological anti-Judaism into imperial legislation. Just such a view has dominated the study of Judaism under Christian Rome in the fourth and fifth centuries.[53]

Recently, Jeremy Cohen has subjected this conception of relations between church and state to a searching critique. His examination of imperial decrees concerning the Jews yields several interesting results:

• A number of decrees prohibiting conversion to Judaism merely confirm earlier bans promulgated under pagan emperors, that is, Domitian and Septimius Severus.

• Valentinian I and Valens show no evidence of anti-Jewish policies.

• Theodosius I, the great champion of Nicene orthodoxy, is noted for his protection of Jewish rights against attacks on them by Christian clergy; he ordered the Christian bishop of Callinicum to rebuild a local synagogue that had been burned down by a Christian mob. Although he eventually rescinded the order under pressure from Ambrose, his motivation was not a desire to implement a set of policies based on ecclesiastical anti-Judaism. One decree in particular shows the emperor in strong opposition to ecclesiastical pressures:

It is sufficiently established that the sect of the Jews is forbidden by no law. We are gravely disturbed that their assemblies are forbidden in certain places. Your Sublime Magnitude [the Count of the Orient] will, therefore, after receiving this order, restrain with proper severity the excesses of those persons who, in the name of the Christian religion, presume to commit certain unlawful acts and to attempt to destroy and to despoil the synagogues.[54]

• Theodosius's son Honorius presents a mixed picture. On the one hand, he issued a decree that reaffirmed earlier laws requiring Jews to assume municipal offices. At a later date, however, he ordered that the tax collected by Jews for financing the office of the patriarch be paid instead to the imperial treasury. Later still, he banned Jews from all positions in the imperial bureaucracy.

• Only under Valentinian III and Theodosius II do decrees limiting Jewish privileges appear in conjunction with a clearly prejudicial tone. Still, even Theodosius continued to insist on full retribution in cases involving damage to or destruction of synagogues by Christians.

In short, Cohen finds no evidence to support either a rapid decline in the status of Jews and Judaism under the Christian emperors of the fourth century or the traditional view that such limitations as did arise can be explained on religious grounds. The emperors appear to have been motivated above all else by traditional political factors and by a desire to protect the freedom of Jews to practice their religion, a freedom first guaranteed by Julius Caesar. Rather than serving as willing instruments of ecclesiastical anti-Judaism, they appear more frequently as resisting efforts by church authorities to dissolve the status of Judaism as a protected religion. This does not make the emperors friends or sympathizers of Judaism anymore than Tiberius in the first century was a "friend of Jews." But it does suggest that church and state followed separate courses in dealing with Judaism at least until the early part of the fifth century.

A TALE OF TWO CITIES

To strengthen the picture of Judaism's status as a flourishing and appealing religion in the late Roman Empire, we turn briefly to evidence provided by two cities, Sardis in Asia Minor and Caesarea in Palestine.

Much the older of the two, Sardis had known Jewish residents since the late third century B.C.E. when Antiochus III settled a large number of Jewish families in Lydia and Phrygia.[55] Josephus, who reproduces a letter of Antiochus concerning this settlement, also records a number of documents from Sardis in the first century B.C.E. One of them, a decree from Lucius Antonius to the civic leaders of the city, reaffirms the right of Jews to live according to their native laws (*tous patrious nomous*) and to have a place (*topos*) of their own "in which they [may] decide their affairs and controversies with one another."[56] The *topos* here probably refers to a synagogue or perhaps to a special area in some public building.[57] The second is a decree issued by "the council and the people" of Sardis renewing various privileges of the Jews, including a place "set apart by the magistrates for them to build and inhabit."[58]

Beyond the evidence from Josephus, there is now a body of archeological and inscriptional material from the synagogue at Sardis, dating from the second and third centuries C.E. The synagogue itself is an extraordinary edifice, not a separate building but rather an integral part of a mammoth gymnasium complex.[59] By the second half of the third century, it had been fitted with "mosaics and revetments . . . (and) was in the possession of the Jewish community and functioning as their synagogue."[60]

What, then, may we conclude from this evidence concerning relations between paganism and Judaism at Sardis? The size and location of the synagogue appear to reflect materially the power and prestige of the Jewish community.[61] A. T. Kraabel speaks of a *"self-confident* Judaism,"[62] confident enough to appropriate symbols from the pagan environment without fear of being overwhelmed by it. Individual members of the community held titles of considerable distinction. Nine were members of the *boulē* or city council; three were part of the Roman provincial administration.[63] As for relations with Christians in the city, Kraabel has proposed that Melito of Sardis's *Paschal Homily*, a good portion of which consists of a bitter attack on Israel, was brought about by Melito's desire to uphold the legitimacy of the small and recently established Christian community against the larger, much older and powerful community of Jews in the city. In any case there can be little doubt that the cumulative evidence from Sardis enables us to speak of "intimate and excellent relations between the Jews of Asia and the Greeks in the early third century C.E."[64]

The situation in Caesarea is in many respects quite different.[65] Herod had taken over the older site of Strato's Tower in order to build the new city of Caesarea between 22–10/9 B.C.E.[66] Jews constituted about one half of the population. From the beginning, it would seem, there were difficulties between Jews and Gentiles.[67] As elsewhere in the Empire during the first century, most notably in Alexandria, the issue was citizenship. Caesarea was a Greek *polis*; the Jews were a *politeuma*, that is, a distinct body of non-citizens with guaranteed rights and privileges. At some point in the 50s, as a result of Jewish efforts to change their status, the quarrel broke out into the open. Despite Roman efforts to end the hostilities, there is evidence of continuing tension down to the first Jewish revolt (66–73).[68] By the end of the revolt, the Jewish community in Caesarea had virtually disappeared from sight, to be revived again early in the third century.[69]

When we next encounter Jews in Caesarea, the circumstances will have changed dramatically. There are no signs of the earlier difficulties. Inscriptions and literary evidence point to significant improvements in every area, particularly under the Severans. L. Levine observes that the city had become "one of the main centers of Jewish life."[70] The community included both the wealthy and the poor, the pious and the assimilated. One important new feature was the presence and influence of the rabbis. And in such a cosmopolitan environment it is not surprising that many of them were thoroughly familiar with Greek culture.

As for relations between Jews, Gentiles, and, later, Christians, there is abundant testimony. The *Vita* of St. Susanna mentions that the saint herself was a native of Caesarea, the daughter of a wealthy pagan priest and a Jewess named Martha who had raised her daughter "according to the customs and teaching of the Jews."[71] Here we have Gentile, Jew, and Christian in a single family. At an earlier date, as early as the 40s of the first century, we know of Christian missionary activity in the city. The Book of Acts (Chapter 10) mentions a certain Cornelius, a centurion in the Italian Cohort at Caesarea, and describes him as a "devout man" [*eusebes*] who feared God [*phoboumenos*]. This Cornelius "saw in a vision an angel of God" who ordered him to fetch Peter from nearby

Joppa. The story continues with a sermon by Peter and concludes with Cornelius's conversion and baptism. On the assumption that the description in Acts marks him as a Jewish sympathizer of some sort, we have in one individual a Roman soldier, a Judaizer, and a Christian. Later again, during the time of Origen's sojourn, contacts between Jews and Christians seem to have been a common occurrence. Origen refers frequently to his teacher of Hebrew.[72] His extensive familiarity with the techniques and results of Jewish exegesis shows that he learned much from Jews in the city. In turn, there is reason to believe that some rabbis may have directed comments at Origen.[73] Conversions were not uncommon. Origen speaks of Gentile converts to Judaism and of Jewish converts to Christianity. Among Christians, he also complains of Judaizing among women who keep the Jewish Sabbath, take ritual baths, and prepare unleavened bread for Passover.[74] Much of this, he says, is the result of efforts by Jews persuading Christians to Judaize.[75] As also in North Africa, public debates between Christians and Jews often attracted large audiences.

In general, and despite the inevitable tensions associated with missionary activity, the dominant mood of Caesarea was open and cosmopolitan; Jews were respected in the community. Indeed, Levine's concluding note sounds strikingly like Kraabel's assessment of the Jews of Sardis:

> . . . the Caesarean Jewish community formed one of a long line of acculturated Jewish centers which were integral parts of the Jewish world. . . . While remaining 'Palestinian,' Caesarean Jewry anticipated a uniquely Diaspora phenomenon, a striking example of the city's dual heritage.[76]

7

The Dialogue of Paganism with Judaism
in Late Antiquity
Philosophers and Magicians

Thus far we have concentrated almost exclusively on the dialogue of official Rome with Judaism, although in the case of Julian theological and philosophical matters played an important role. There was, in fact, a long history of theological interchange which prepared the way not only for Julian but for the Severans as well. As in the third century B.C.E., the cult and the deity of the Jews proved of great interest to philosophical observers.

The first figure in this stage of the dialogue is the physician-philosopher Galen (c. 131–197).[1] Like others before and after him Galen expressed dismay at the centrality of uncritical faith and authority in Judaism. He compares incompetent doctors "to Moses, who framed laws for the tribe of the Jews, since it is his method in his books to write without offering proofs, saying 'God commanded, God spoke.' "[2] Elsewhere he declares sarcastically that "one might more easily teach novelties to the followers of Moses and Christ than to the physicians and philosophers who cling fast to their schools."[3]

One notes even in these disparaging remarks that Galen appears to regard the Jews as in some sense a philosophical sect. This is confirmed by a lengthy passage in his *On the Function of Parts of the Body* in which he compares Moses with different Greek philosophers and quite explicitly engages him in a philosophical debate on the causes of creation.[4] He agrees with Moses against the Epicureans on the need for an active cause, that is, a creator god, but he rejects outright the notion of *creatio ex nihilo* and unlimited divine power. On the latter point he anticipates

Julian's interpretation that the god of Moses is only the creator of the visible world. At the same time he dismisses, at least implicitly, the view of Longinus, who praises Moses precisely because he represents god as creating merely by speaking.[5] In any case, the passage presupposes that Galen possessed a firsthand knowledge of at least the book of Genesis.[6] Beyond this it reflects the continuing fascination with Judaism among Roman intellectuals and aristocrats, dating back at least to the first century B.C.E.

Following Galen we come to a series of figures whose dominant philosophical influence was Platonism. From Celsus to Libanius, that is, from Middle Platonism to the Neo-Platonism of Plotinus and his successors, there was a persistent concern with Judaism as an ancient religion of great value. To be sure, the first of these figures, Celsus, was hardly an admirer of Judaism. His *True Teaching*,[7] the first of many anti-Christian treatises in late antiquity, contains numerous references to the Jews, in part because he devoted a large section of the work to a critique of Christianity in the form of a dialogue between a Jew and Jesus. Most of Celsus's references to Judaism are unfriendly, though there are one or two exceptions. In accordance with his fundamental belief "that it is impious to abandon the customs which have existed in each locality from the beginning," he concedes their great antiquity. The Jews themselves, however, who were Egyptians in origin, had rebelled against their native religion and committed the sin of innovation in religious matters.[8]

For Moses, Celsus has nothing but scorn. By magic and sorcery he duped his followers into worshipping one god only.[9] He refused to recognize the truth, fundamental to Neo-Platonism, that there is one god who is worshipped under many names and that "it makes no difference whether we call Zeus Hypsistos or Zēn or Adonai or Sabaoth or Amon." Moses' account of creation he characterizes as silly, containing nothing but trash.[10] His god is a weakling because he allows man to disobey him and is lacking in stamina because he needed to rest after creating the world.[11] On top of all this, Moses is guilty of having plagiarized and distorted the wisdom of ancient Greek sages. The tower of Babel (Gen. 11:1–9) is a corrupted version of the attempt by Aloeus's sons to storm Olympus, while Noah's flood is nothing but a debased account of the flood of Deucalion.[12]

While there is no mistaking Celsus's fundamentally negative attitude, we should note the historical background and setting of his work as a whole. The charge that Moses had plagiarized ancient Greek myths is a simple reversal of a Christian argument, itself borrowed from earlier Jewish apologists, that the Greeks stole their myths from biblical stories.[13] Thus Celsus's primary target is Christianity, not Judaism, and his criticisms are part of his attempt to debunk the claim of Christianity to be the new Israel. In any case, Celsus is entirely atypical of other Platonic figures among whom we hear scarcely a hint of his caustic tone.

We begin with Numenius of Apamea, who flourished in the mid-second century C.E. and exercised considerable influence on the subsequent develoment of Neo-Platonism.[14] In his effort to discover the earliest and purest sources of philosophy, Numenius prescribed a highly eclectic method:

> When the philosopher has spoken of this and confirmed it with Plato, it will be necessary to return and relate it to the teachings of Pythagoras and finally to call upon the outstanding nations, bringing the rites and doctrines and institutions which the Brahmans, the Jews, the Magi and the Egyptians established and founded in agreement with Plato.[15]

In other words, by progressively eliminating later accretions and by preserving only those elements wherein Pythagoras and certain outstanding nations were in agreement with Plato, Numenius hoped to reconstruct human wisdom in its earliest and purest form. His particular concern was to demonstrate the incorporeality of god. Origen states that Numenius included the Jews among the nations who "believe god to be without a body."[16] Elsewhere, Numenius is said to have regarded the god of the Jews as "incompatible (*akoinonētos*)," presumably with other gods, and to have called him "the father of all gods, who deemed it unfitting that any one should share his honor with him."[17]

We also know that Numenius was familiar with and used the Jewish Scriptures. Porphyry, in his allegorical treatise *On the Cave of the Nymphs*, cites Numenius in his discussion of the descent of souls, symbolized by the Naiad nymphs, into bodies:

We [Porphyry] say that the Naiads are nymphs and in particular the powers that preside over the waters. They [the theologians] use the term generally of all souls that descend into generation. For they consider, as Numenius says, that the souls rest on divinely blown water. Therefore, he says, the prophet said that the spirit of god was borne (*empheresthai*) over the water.[18]

In other words, Numenius used an allegorical interpretation of Gen. 1:2 (—"and the Spirit of God was moving over the face of the waters") to buttress his view of the coupling of soul and body. Nor is this the only occasion on which he did so, for Origen again remarks that

Numenius the Pythagorean, a man who expounded Plato with very great skill and maintained Pythagorean doctrines, quotes Moses and the prophets in many passages and gives no improbable allegorical interpretation, as in . . . his *On Numbers* and in his *On the Place*.[19]

He also knew and recorded a version of Moses' contest with the magicians of the pharaoh (Ex. 7:11–13).[20] This bit of information must have come to him from a non-biblical source, for the names he assigns to the magicians, Jannes and Jambres, appear in later traditions but not in the biblical account.

In view of these witnesses it can no longer come as a surprise that Numenius could refer to Plato as Moses speaking Attic Greek (*ti gar esti Platōn ē Mōusēs Attikizōn*).[21] E. R. Dodds has rightly pointed out that Numenius "*ought* to have described Moses as Plato talking Hebrew."[22] Indeed, this has led some to reject the saying as inauthentic, while others have supposed that Numenius must have been a Jew himself or at least a sympathizer. However, none of these solutions is necessary, given his commitment to the systematic exploitation of Oriental wisdom, a commitment neither original with him nor unusual in his time. If his views differed markedly from those of other Platonists we might suspect that he had special reasons for appealing to ancient Hebrew wisdom. In fact his views were typical and will appear in later Non-Platonists.

In Plotinus himself there is no direct mention of Judaism. On the other hand, his biographer, secretary, and disciple, Porphyry, has left numerous testimonies that must surely reflect Plotinus's views to some extent. Porphyry's early writing, *On Philosophy from Oracles*, was an attempt to create a philosophical and religious system from popular sources. In the course of the work he cites several oracles, presumably not his own creations, which mention the wisdom of the Hebrews:

> Only the Chaldeans and the Hebrews reached true wisdom, they who worship god piously, the self-born king.[23]

When asked whether speech, reason, or law was superior the oracle replied:

> God the creator and king before all things, before whom the heaven, the seas and the hidden depths of hell tremble and whom the gods them-selves hold in great awe. Their law is the father, whom the pious He-brews worship fervently.[24]

Thus in his early years, possibly under the influence of Numenius, Porphyry reckoned the Hebrews among the wise nations of the past and identified their god with the creator and king of all things.

His later writings, produced under the influence of his teacher Plotinus, continue to show signs of this fundamental sympathy. In his *Life of Pythagoras* he quotes Antonius Diogenes to the effect that Pythagoras had visited the Arabs, the Chaldeans, and the Hebrews and had "learned from the latter precise information about dreams."[25] Elsewhere, in his *On Abstinence*, he supports his argument for abstaining from meat by an extensive discussion which includes the only quotation of Josephus by a pagan author.[26] And in a passage from the later work of Johannes Lydus (b. 490), Porphyry speculates as to the place of the Jewish deity in the Neo-Platonic pantheon:

> Porphyry in his *Commentary on the Oracles* says that the god wor-shipped by the Jews is the second god, i.e., the ruler of all things, whom the Chaldean reckons to be the second god from the *hapax*, i.e., from the good. But the schools of Iamblichus, Syrianus and Proclus consider him to be the creator of the visible world [*tou aisthētou kosmou*] and call him the god of the four elements.[27]

This pasage is especially interesting because it reveals a debate among Neo-Platonists as to the status of the Jewish god within their pantheon. There was general agreement that he belonged among the cosmic or lower deities, but on his precise function within that category there were differing opinions. Porphyry shared the position of Numenius and held that he governed not only the entire created order but the other gods as well. In contrast, Julian and the schools of Iamblichus, Syrianus, and Proclus assigned the Jewish god to a somewhat lower status, as ruler of the visible world but not of the other gods.

These philosophers, most of them Platonists, have shown a persistent attraction to the religion of the ancient Hebrews. Several of them also made a systematic effort to incorporate certain aspects of this religion into their own highly eclectic systems. The *Chaldean Oracles* show traces of Jewish angelology,[28] and the first tractate (Poimandres) of the *Corpus Hermeticum* presupposes a familiarity with the creation story of Genesis.[29] This philosophical or theological aspect of paganism's dialogue with Judaism complements the official or political aspect discussed earlier, and in the figure of Julian the two become one.

THE "POPULAR" DIALOGUE: MAGIC, ALCHEMY, AND ASTROLOGY

By and large the participants in the dialogue thus far have been limited to the political and intellectual elite of the Empire. There have been few signs that other social groups were involved.[30] If we turn to ancient magic, alchemy, and astrology, what many are wont to call the "lower" manifestations of religious phenomena, we find a dialogue of a rather different kind. Here Jews were widely known as practitioners of the "divine arts." Juvenal mocked the Jewish woman who sold dream interpretations at bargain prices.[31] Pompeius Trogus described Joseph as "highly skilled in prodigies" and "the first to found the science of interpreting dreams."[32] And Hadrian is reported to have exclaimed about Egypt, "There is no Jewish archisynagogus, no Samaritan, no Christian presbyter who is not an astrologer, a soothsayer or an anointer."[33]

For the populace at large such skills were a valued possession. Satirists and critics might show scorn and intellectuals indifference, but others, including many Christians, showed great respect for Jewish magic.[34] In fact, among the enormous array of amulets, phylacteries, and recipes on papyrus, the number of items with no Jewish elements at all is quite small.[35] In popular Egyptian circles where magic flourished, the traditional lines between Jew and Gentile seem to have lost much of their meaning. Often it is easier and more accurate to speak of Jewish or Egyptian contributions to this syncretistic environment than to retain traditional labels.[36]

Among the plethora of Jewish terms in magical documents, the most common are divine names (Adonai, Iao, Sabaoth) and a host of names ending in -*ēl* and -*oth*.[37] In addition, a number of ancient Jewish heroes also appear. In *PGM* III, the suppliant appeals for help in the name of Adam (lines 145 ff.). *PGM* XXIIb contains a prayer of Jacob. *PGM* IV records a trance of Solomon that is guaranteed to work for children and adults (lines 850–929). The god of Abraham, Isaac, and Jacob is invoked several times (*PGM* XII line 287; *PGM* XIII lines 817 and 976). But the key figure was Moses, who was especially renowned for his knowledge of the divine name:

> I am Moses your prophet, to whom you committed your mysteries which are celebrated by Istrael [*sic*]. . . . Listen to me, I am the messenger of Phapro Osoronnophris. This is the authentic name which was committed to the prophets of Istrael.[38]

So powerful was Moses' fame as a magician that he became the "author" of several magical books and charms. *PGM* XIII, which contains two recensions of the same work, bears the title "Holy Book called the *Monad* or *Eighth Book of Moses on the Sacred Name*" (lines 343f. and 1077). Within the text of *PGM* XIII there are further references to books of Moses. A *Key* of Moses is cited four times (lines 22, 31, 36, and 60) and appears to reflect a rivalry between Moses and Hermes as masters of magic.[39] An *Archangelical Book* is mentioned in line 971 which may well be identical with the *Archangelical Book* of Moses which appears in Codex II of the writings from Nag Hammadi. And a *Secret Moon Book* of Moses is quoted in line 1059. Elsewhere, *PGM* VII quotes a recipe from the *Diadem* of Moses.

In the realm of alchemy, a slightly younger sister to magic, we find a similar admixture of Jewish elements.[40] In the collection of alchemical texts published by M. Berthelot and C. E. Ruelle,[41] Jewish figures play an important role. Moses appears along with Democritus, Xenocrates, and Zosimus in a list of the best known practitioners.[42] There are references to a *Diplosis* of Moses which contained a recipe for producing gold from baser metals,[43] a *Chemistry* of Moses,[44] and a *Maza* ("lump of metal") which Zosimus cites twice in his treatise on yellow-dyeing.[45] The same Zosimus, who brought together elements from various sources in compiling his handbooks, gives evidence of a considerable Jewish component in alchemical circles.[46] In addition to citing works of Moses, he notes that Solomon acquired his wisdom in these matters from the Egyptian king Membres[47] and refers to a writing entitled *True Book of Sophe the Egyptian and of the Divine Lord of the Hebrews, Sabaoth of the Powers*.[48] On several occasions he refers to a Maria who seems to have been well known among alchemists:[49]

> The entire kingdom of Egypt, dear woman, is sustained by the two arts, the art of the timely dyes and the art of stones. . . . Only to the Jews has it been given to do, record and transmit these things secretly. Therefore we find Theophilus the son of Theogenes writing about gold-mining maps, the description [of furnaces] by Maria[50] and other Jewish writers.[51]

Some of these titles may indicate the existence of Jewish schools of alchemy in Egypt though there is no evidence for them apart from the names and titles. More important is the fact that as with the magical papyri these contributions of Jewish alchemy were borrowed and preserved by non-Jews in collections designed for general use.

In the realm of astrology, the same type of Jewish influence and participation is evident. In the first tractate (Poimandres) of the *Corpus Hermeticum* details from the cosmogony of Genesis intermingle with themes from Neo-Platonism and ancient Egyptian cosmogonies.[52] An obscure astrological manuscript contains an astrological guide to the calendar.[53] For each day of the month certain deities and activities are specified as propitious. On the second day Phosphorous was born, Eve was created from Adam's side, and the day was favorable for marriage. On four of the thirty days of the first item is not a pagan deity but an event from ancient Jewish history. Thus on the first day Adam was born, on the fourth day Abel, and on the nineteenth day Moses, while on the twenty-ninth day the Jews entered the promised land. Clearly the text is an amalgamation of Jewish and Greek materials. If the original was Jewish and the editor Greek, it is an example of biblical allusions in a non-Jewish document. Otherwise, we have a "Jewish" author who juxtaposed Jewish and pagan sources without apparent concern.

Finally, as with magic and alchemy, we find writings attributed to ancient Hebrew sages. Vettius Valens, an astrological compiler of the second century c.e., reports that Hermippus (fl. c. 220 b.c.e.) had used the writings of the "most admirable Abraham" in developing travel horoscopes.[54] Somewhat later, Firmicus Maternus, before his conversion to Christianity, composed an anthology of astrological material in which he cites "that divine Abraham" as a recognized authority and places him alongside such revered figures as Hermes, Petosiris, Orpheus, and Critodemus.[55]

These Jewish contributions to magic, alchemy, and astrology are an invaluable witness to a dialogue between paganism and Judaism rather different from that of the philosophers and official Rome. Still, the fact that Moses' renown in magical circles rested on his knowledge of the all-powerful divine name cannot be unrelated to the attitude of the Neo-Platonists and others to the same god. Equally significant is the information that these sources provide for relations between pagans and Jews in Egypt. Normally when we think of Judaism in Roman Egypt we tend to focus on Apion, the riots that prompted Claudius's letter to the Alexandrians, and the so-called *Acts of the Pagan Martyrs*. But as the magical and alchemical texts have made clear, there was another side to the picture.

The explanation for this largely independent aspect of the dialogue lies partly in sociological and geographical factors. There must have been significant numbers of Jews who readily adapted themselves to the syncretistic environment of Egypt. Most of these will not have belonged to the social or economic elite. No doubt many lived in smaller communities outside Alexandria where relations were such that a good deal of Jewish lore found its way into the cauldrons that nourished magicians and alchemists. How far back we can date these relations is uncertain. The process is already evident in the Jewish military colony at Elephantine in the sixth and fifth centuries B.C.E. and it is unlikely that it burst on the scene again *ex nihilo* in the second century C.E.

Just as E. R. Dodds can speak of a dialogue of paganism with Christianity between the mid-second and the early fourth centuries,[56] we must also speak of a dialogue between paganism and Judaism in the same period. In fact, the dialogue with Judaism was generally more active, positive, and reciprocal than that with Christianity. Nonetheless there were definite limits. Our information stems almost exclusively from what might be called aristocratic circles on both sides. Even the evidence from magical and alchemical texts of the period points in this direction, for in the later Empire their appeal was no longer limited to the lower classes. As for the existence of a "popular dialogue" in the same period, perhaps based on continuing animosities from the early Empire, the pagan sources provide no information.[57] This is not to suggest that relations were perfectly harmonious, even among the aristocrats, at every moment of the period. Nonetheless, whenever we do find information it points to a positive, even if not a continuous dialogue. Conversely, I take the absence of negative voices from the pagan side to indicate that while the dialogue may have been more active at certain times, for example, under the Severans and later under Julian, it was seldom visibly hostile.

In contrast to earlier periods, the dialogue after 135 was remarkably well-informed. Before the rise of Christianity there is no clear evidence that any pagan author could claim a firsthand knowledge of the Jewish Scriptures. At best they relied on oral reports, and at worst they repeated or invented rumors, bits of misinformation, and hostile propaganda. Even Longinus, who preferred Moses to Homer in terms of his concept of god, may have known nothing beyond the single line he quotes from Genesis. With the advent of Christianity, and perhaps because of it, the situation changed. Celsus, Numenius, Porphyry, Julian, and perhaps Galen were well versed in the Jewish Scriptures and frequently used their critical insights for polemical purposes.

All of this suggests that the period from Bar Cochba to Julian represents a new and perhaps unique phase in relations between pagans and Jews in the ancient world. The explanation for the contrast lies partly in the changed situation of the Roman world itself. The age of the Antonines (138–180 C.E.) enjoyed a level of political, economic, and social stability which facilitated intercultural exchanges. Of course another element was the fact that the bases of Jewish political and military power (Jerusalem, Judea, Alexandria, and the fortress of Onias at Leontopolis) had been dismantled.

But there were other factors as well. The rise of Christianity provided Rome with a source of concern that soon became a fixation. Judaism seemed to grow in favor as Christianity grew in prominence. One of the factors in this process was Judaism's great antiquity of which all were well aware. Christianity sought to circumvent this by its claim to be the new Israel, but on this point it failed to persuade most of its critics and certainly Julian. To the Christian assertion that the Jewish scriptures themselves had prophesied the ultimate abrogation of the law, he replied angrily:

> That they say this falsely I will clearly show by quoting from the books of Moses not merely ten but ten thousand passages where he says that the law is for all time.[58]

Finally, we may now put to rest the notion that Gentile converts to Christianity brought with them, *as Gentiles*, the pervasive anti-Semitism of the Greco-Roman world. Not only was there no such pervasive anti-Semitism, but it is safe to assume that many Gentile converts were drawn from those already attracted in some fashion to Judaism. To the extent that this is so, we must reckon with the possibility that the widespread tendency toward Judaizing in early Christian communities arose not merely as the result of missionary activity within the Christian movement but also from the experience of Gentile converts whose familiarity with Judaizing predated their acceptance of Christianity.

PART III

Christianity, Israel, and the Torah

Why do you take your origin from our religion, and then, as if you are progressing in knowledge, despise these things, although you cannot name any other origin for your doctrine than our law?

A Jewish critic
cited in Origen, *Celsus* 2.4

Judaism was the dominant force in the world of early Christianity. While at one level this is simply a truism, its various implications have not always been fully appreciated. The very earliest groups of those who confessed Jesus as the Christ (Messiah) are now generally seen and studied as religious movements *within* Judaism. They observed the Mosaic commandments; they worshipped in the Jerusalem temple; and they saw in Jesus the long-anticipated prophet, teacher, and messiah who would usher in the final days of history. Of course, as is usual with reformist or revitalizing movements, these early followers of Jesus generated considerable controversy within the various circles or parties of Palestinian Judaism. This was no more true of the Jesus movement than it was of other Jewish sects of the time—the covenanters of Qumran, the Zealots, and the Pharisees, to name but the most prominent. What distinguished this movement from the others was its social constituency. Jesus himself apparently lacked the traditional credentials for religious authority or leadership and his followers were regularly accused of failing to meet even minimum standards of social and religious respectability. Thus while we must treat the early Jesus movement in Palestine as an intra-Jewish

phenomenon in every respect, we cannot ignore its peculiar social
character as a minority movement under sharp attack on a variety of
social and religious grounds.

In time, however, and for a variety of reasons, certain Christian groups
began to define themselves in opposition to Judaism, while insisting that
they had replaced historical Judaism as the true Israel. Some of these
groups emerge in Palestine, but many more appear in conjunction with
Christianity's gradual expansion into the larger Greco-Roman world.
Along with this geographical shift there appears another factor which
will have even more significance in the long run. The movement begins
to attract increasing numbers of Gentile converts. At this point in the
history of early Christianity, Judaism re-emerges as a powerful force in
shaping Christian self-understanding. We may distinguish at least three
distinct aspects of Judaism's impact on Christianity outside Palestine: (1)
once Christian groups began to differentiate themselves from Judaism, it
becomes possible for the first time to speak of Jewish influences on
Christianity; (2) once Christianity establishes itself outside the religious
sphere of Judaism proper, the phenomenon of Christian Judaizing appears
for the first time in a clear light; and (3) it is not the case that Christianity
left Judaism behind as it moved from Palestinian soil. On the contrary,
we are now able to affirm that wherever Christianity developed abroad
in the cities and towns of the Empire, it encountered a well-established,
self-confident, and widely appreciated Judaism. Furthermore this non-
Palestinian encounter between the two religions took place at precisely
the time when positive elements in pagan views of Judaism appeared with
greatest clarity. Once again Christianity had to deal with Judaism from
beneath, that is, from a position of cultural and social inferiority. And once
again the tone and substance of Christian pronouncements against Judaism
must be seen as shaped by Christianity's relative social and religious
inferiority vis-à-vis Judaism within pagan society and culture. This time,
however, the Christian attack is launched not from within Judaism but
from the outside.

Judaism remained, even outside Palestine, a primary factor in determining the process of Christian self-definition: Christian Judaizing and
Christian anti-Judaism must be seen intricately intertwined though antithetical elements in that process. In various parts of the Greco-Roman

world, Christians will encounter not only well-established and fully-integrated Jewish communities but also considerable numbers of Gentiles drawn to Judaism in various ways—as sympathizers, Judaizers, or as full converts. Some of these Gentiles undoubtedly brought such attitudes with them as they became Christians. And as we will see, there were other Christians prepared to argue that Gentile Christians, as members of the true Israel, must observe the Mosaic commandments—circumcision, Sabbath, dietary laws—in order to express and maintain their citizenship in God's chosen people. Thus we may not assume on the part of Gentile Christians a negative attitude toward the Jews of their time or toward the Mosaic commandments, whether for the "old" Israel or for the "new."

No single figure symbolizes the tortured character of these disputes better than Paul, the zealous Pharisee who became the apostle of Christ to the Gentiles. During his own lifetime and in the decades and centuries thereafter, his writings—those certainly written by him as well as numerous others penned by an incredible variety of "friends" speaking on his behalf—will serve as the foundational documents in an endless series of debates about what it meant for Christians to call themselves the true Israel. In his own lifetime he had insisted on the right of Gentiles to assume full status as Christians without observing any of the Mosaic commandments. Equally during his lifetime, other followers of Jesus had bitterly opposed him on the grounds that only those who were circumcised and who kept the law of Moses could be saved. And long after his death, the disputants agreed on one point only, namely, that Paul had proclaimed the end of the Torah as the path of righteousness. Had he not written "Christ is the end of the Law, that everyone who has faith may be justified" (Rom. 10:4)? Thus those for whom Christianity's self-designation as the true Israel meant that Christians, whether Jews or Gentiles, were fully obligated to observe the commandments of the Mosaic covenant, there was no choice but to repudiate Paul as the arch-enemy of the faith. For these and many others, Judaism continued to represent the living reality of God's ancient promises to his chosen people.

8

Judaizing and Anti-Judaism
in the
Christian Tradition

At the present time it is possible to speak of a certain unanimity regarding the settings of anti-Judaism in early Christianity. Two such settings will emerge in our discussion: first, local controversies between Jews and Christians and second, Judaizing practices among many Christians. This chapter will analyze the phenomenon of Christian Judaizing—its character, its significance, and its role as a source of anti-Judaism among Christian leaders who criticized or repudiated Judaizing practices as inimical to the true faith.

In recent discussions virtually always a distinction has been made between Judaeo-Christians—Gentiles who, for whatever reasons, observe certain Mosaic commandments as an integral part of their Christianity— and Jewish-Christians—Jews who become Christians yet do not totally abandon their observance of certain Mosaic commandments. On the emotional level perhaps we can presuppose some differences in the attitudes of the two groups toward their Judaizing practices. In all other respects the distinction is misleading. On the plane of religious or theological understanding, both groups show the same commitment to the position that observance of the Mosaic rituals is in no way incompatible with, indeed may even be required by loyalty to Jesus. Furthermore, the inability of scholars to determine whether the exponents of such views under attack in many Christian writings are Jews, Gentiles, or both should warn us that the difficulty is not lack of information but the distinction itself. Where the information available enables us to identify the audience as Jewish or Gentile we should take note. But we should understand that *in its broadest sense* Christian Judaizing is a unified phenomenon.

There can no longer be any doubt that a powerful and persistent factor in generating Christian anti-Judaism is the phenomenon of Judaizing among early Christians. Against the view which sees the development of Christianity under the banner of progressive de-Judaization, these points must be made: the evidence for Judaizing practices is even stronger in the fourth century than in the first; and the proponents of Judaizing appear to have been predominantly Gentiles rather than Jewish Christians.

Of course, it hardly needs to be stated that Judaizing itself was a complex phenomenon, ranging from the occasional use of Jewish charms for curing illness to regular observance of Jewish festivals and purity laws. No matter what form it took, however, Judaizing among Christians regularly provoked anti-Jewish polemic on the part of ecclesiastical leaders. In this respect, there is an important similarity of function between Christian and pagan polemic against Judaism. Both were bent on making Judaism seem unattractive to potential or actual converts and sympathizers. Long after the intense ideological conflicts of the early decades, the tradition of anti-Jewish polemic was kept alive by the presence of Judaizing Christians.

John Chrysostom[1]

In 386, while still a presbyter at Antioch, in western Syria, Chrysostom interrupted his addresses against the Arians and began a series of eight sermons directed against Judaizing Christians in the city. The timing of these sermons is of interest in that they are addressed not to the Christian calendar but rather to the Jewish festivals (Rosh Hashanah, Yom Kippur, and Sukkoth) of the autumn season. The reason for this unusual proceeding, as Chrysostom himself plainly reveals, is that numerous Christians in the city were accustomed to celebrate these festivals with the Jews. John hoped to dissuade them from doing so.

The immediate audience of the homilies, it should be noted, is neither the Christian Judaizers nor the Jews themselves but members of Chrysostom's own congregation. His announced aim is to combat their complacency regarding the Judaizers. With dire threats of perdition, he urges his listeners to seek them out in their homes and to dissuade them from their foolish ways. But if loyal Christians are the audience of the sermons, the Judaizers are the targets of his wrath and the Jews its victims. His method is to turn the tables on these Judaizers, by likening the synagogue to a theater or a brothel rather than a place of power (I. 2–3). Better to die of illness, which he calls a martyr's death, than to make use of Jewish charms and spells (VIII. 5–8).

Throughout the homilies, but especially in the first and last, his language is intemperate. At one or two points in the first homily he appears to pause, as if members of the audience had expressed dismay at his words, in order to justify his choice of words. "I know that some will condemn me for daring to say that the synagogue is no different from the theater. . . ." (I. 2). But he will not be deterred. The Jews have degenerated to the level of dogs. They are drunkards and gluttons. They beat their servants. They are ignorant of God. Their festivals are worthless and were proclaimed as such by the biblical prophets. Their synagogues are the dwelling places of demons. "If our way is true, as it is, theirs is fraudulent. I am not speaking of the Scriptures. Far from it. For they lead me to Christ. I am speaking of their present impurity and madness" (I. 6). And by way of summing up: "What more can I say? Rapacity, greed, betrayal of the poor, thefts, keeping of taverns. The whole day would not suffice to tell of these things" (I. 7).

What were the activities of these Judaizers that so outraged the eloquent presbyter? They attend the Jewish festivals and join in their fasts. They undergo circumcision. They observe the Sabbath. They honor the synagogue as a holy site. They make use of Jewish charms and spells as cures for diseases. They sleep in the synagogue at Daphne, a suburb of the city, for the purpose of receiving dream-revelations. In Chrysostom's own words, they "have high regard for the Jews and think that their present way of life is holy" (I. 3). Furthermore, the "sickness" was not limited to a few. On numerous occasions Chrysostom speaks of them as many (*polloi*) and at one point warns his listeners not to announce the full number lest the reputation of the church suffer damage.

What are we to make of this extraordinary tirade from one of the leading Christian figures in the fourth century? Several of his techniques are worth underlining. The very violence of Chrysostom's language demonstrates the potential for a linkage between anti-Jewish beliefs and anti-Semitic feelings that has been explored in more recent work. In this regard, we may compare Chrysostom with the much earlier Cicero in that much of their language reflects the standard implements of rhetorical invective.[2] John is particularly fond of biting metaphors. But his techniques are no less harmful for being artful or traditional. They convey ominous overtones. While he does not advocate the use of force against the Jews, he is not opposed to it as a means of recovering a fellow Christian from the fellowship of "the Christ killers" (I. 4). At another point he admits that he has come to lust for combat agaist the Jews (VI. 1).

Clearly this is an extreme case. And yet, how far removed are we from Cyril, bishop of Alexandria in 412, or Ambrose, bishop of Milan from 374? Cyril, shortly after having ascended his episcopal throne, expelled the large Jewish community from the city of Alexandria.[3] As for Ambrose, in 388 he countermanded an edict of the emperor Theodosius concerning the destruction of a synagogue in Callinicum (Asia Minor).[4] According to Ambrose's own letters, the synagogue had been burned by a Christian mob under the leadership of the local bishop. In justifying his opposition to the emperor's edict, the bishop denies that the incident amounted to a crime and adds that it was only his own laziness that had prevented him from burning down the synagogue of Milan! Thus even while choosing to regard Chrysostom as an extreme example of Christian anti-Judaism, Simon is forced to deny in virtually the same breath that he is an exception: "Both the spirit and the method of his polemic reappear, with more or less clarity, wherever the question of the Jews emerges in Christian writings of the period."[5]

The "question of the Jews" mentioned by Simon is the final item worth underscoring. For what disturbed Chrysostom so profoundly was that members of his own congregation not only failed to share the official view of Judaism as contemptible and inimical to true faith but had even gone so far as to involve themselves in Judaizing practices. Here the connection between popular Christian Judaizing on the one side and official Christian anti-Judaism on the other side could not be more apparent. To this we need only add that it is all but certain that all of the Judaizers in Antioch were Christians of Gentile origins.

Syriac Christianity in the East

Before leaving Syria in the fourth century, it will be instructive to look briefly at two major figures representing the Syriac-speaking Christianity of the East rather than the Greek-speaking churches of the West.

Aphraat stands as the first articulate literary spokesman of eastern Syriac Christianity. His native land was Persia. A monk, he appears to have served as abbot superior of a monastery near Mosul (Iraq) north of ancient Nineveh. In him we encounter a distinctive Christianity, strongly ascetic and deeply influenced by its Jewish environment and its biblical roots. At the same time, in his views of Judaism—preserved in a number of his *Demonstrations*—Aphraat shares numerous common themes and concerns with earlier, non-Eastern writers.[6] Whether these similarities reflect literary dependencies, or rather the inevitable results of common sources and antagonists, or both, cannot always be determined.

As his repeated references to the Jewish "debater of the people" make clear, Aphraat was keenly aware of contemporary Jewish criticisms directed against Christianity—criticisms based on the view that the Jewish Scriptures failed to sustain the Christian case.[7] For this reason, Aphraat's own response regularly took the form of counter-exegesis. At least some of these arguments and criticisms were almost certainly voiced in public debates.

The Jewish argument seems to have emphasized four issues: that Christians worshipped a man rather than God; that Christian celibacy was contrary to the Torah; that Christians were persecuted and thus not protected by God; and that the Christians, as Gentiles, cannot be the true people of God. In each case, Aphraat replies with counter-examples from the Hebrew Bible: the Christian designation of Jesus as son of God is in tune with the heroes of Israel who were called both God and sons of God; Moses himself remained celibate after his descent from the mountain and many of the prophets did not marry; persecutions, far from indicating rejection or disgrace, have been signs of true faith from the very beginning; and, finally, the call of Gentiles was prefigured long ago in the figure of Abraham and is echoed in prophetic utterances on the uselessness of the Israelite cult. In brief, Aphraat's response rested on two basic assertions: first, that the Jews have been rejected by God and no longer have any claim to be his people; and second, that the cultic practices of Judaism "do not now and never did lead to salvation."[8]

While there can be no doubt that Aphraat's attitude toward Judaism is determined to a degree by criticisms of Christianity from Jews of his own time and place, we must ask whether his writings also point to Judaizing tendencies among the faithful of his time. His writings contain no explicit references to such tendencies, and thus we will have to look in other directions. The first of these is what we may refer to as Simon's model: wherever we find anti-Jewish literature aimed at specific Jewish rites we may suspect the presence of Christians who are observing these rites.[9] Among Aphraat's *Demonstrations*, four deal with practices fully attested in connection with Judaizers elsewhere: On Circumcision (XI), On the Passover Sacrifice (XII), On the Sabbath (XIII) and on Making Distinctions among Foods (XV).

A second direction takes us back to the very origins and character of Christianity in eastern Syria itself. While the evidence is scanty, recent work has moved toward a consensus that "Syriac Christianity long retained some features which can only be accounted for in a thoroughly Jewish form of Christianity."[10] Even the asceticism which permeated the Christian ethos in Syria from its earliest manifestations may well have derived from a sectarian form of Judaism, not unlike what we find at Qumran, where ascetic ideals lay at the very heart of the community's self-understanding. Speaking of later relations between Christians and Jews in Syria, Robert Murray has observed that "the two communities must have remained socially connected . . . but by the fourth century they had quarrelled irrevocably."[11] Or better, perhaps only the leaders quarreled, for a direct corollary of Simon's model is that polemic directed against specific Jewish practices points to a split *within* Christian circles.

Before considering earlier stages of Syriac Christianity, we may look briefly at Aphraat's contemporary Ephrem (d. 373). Ephrem mentions the Jews in several of his writings. In general his arguments reflect a continuous tradition which reaches from the fourth century to Dionysius bar Salibbi in the twelfth century.[12] Ephrem shares with Aphraat a common tradition of biblical testimonies and religious symbols.[13] Both defend the view that Christianity has replaced Israel as the vehicle for God's plan of salvation.[14] And both argue that Sabbath observance, circumcision, and purity laws which earlier served to prevent Israel from lapsing completely into paganism are no longer necessary for Christians. Their faith, unlike that of the Jews, is perfect. Ephrem, however, unlike Aphraat, "hated the Jews."[15] He regularly used the term "crucifier" as synonymous with the Jews.[16]

In seeking to account for the differences in tone and spirit between Aphraat and Ephrem, Murray singles out the political factor. Aphraat lived in the Persian Empire, where Christians were less favored than Jews and where both were minorities. He lived among Jews and knew them well, while not unconscious of Jewish inroads among his flock. Ephrem, by contrast, lived in the Roman Empire under a Christian ruler—with only a brief respite during the reign of Julian—and at a time when pagan anti-Semitism had combined forces with Christian anti-Judaism and Christian political ascendancy to create the inevitable turn of events in Jewish fortunes which will become evident in the early fifth century. Clearly, political conditions alone will not account for all of the differences, but in the case of Aphraat we see an interesting set of circumstances under which Christian anti-Judaism did *not* spill over into anti-Semitism.

To these conclusions we need to add Stanley Kazan's important observation about the setting of Ephrem's anti-Judaism. In several of his writings, Ephrem argues vehemently that Jewish customs including the unleavened bread of Passover, circumcision, and prayer in synagogues no longer possess religious legitimacy of any kind. Kazan sees in these warnings a reaction against Jewish proselytism among Christians. At the very least he takes them as evidence for Judaizing tendencies by Christians in Nisibis.[17] Speaking generally of Syriac Christianity in the fourth and fifth centuries, Kazan sees its pervasive anti-Judaism as a response of ecclesiastical leaders to the fact that "Christians were practicing circumcision, were celebrating Jewish festivals and holidays, and were frequenting the home of the Jewish magician for amulets they believed to possess magical powers."[18]

Before leaving eastern Syria, we must say a word or two about the time before the literary tradition established by Ephrem and Aphraat.[19] From the very beginning there are strong indications that Christianity from Antioch in the West to Mesopotamia in the East was strongly influenced by Judaism. On this issue there is virtual unanimity. In some cases we may speak of Jewish influences, as in Aphraat's emphasis on the elements of the Jewish Passover in the celebration of the Eucharist and of Easter. In other cases, as we have seen, this influence expressed itself as a tendency among Christians to observe elements of Jewish ritual. In still others, the influence went much deeper. Furthermore, these forms of Christian piety almost certainly did not represent a minority or sectarian view in an area otherwise dominated by "orthodox" beliefs and practices but were in fact the "normative" tradition.

The Pseudo-Clementine writings in particular contain literary materials ("The Homilies of Peter" and "The Epistle of Peter") which reach back to the early second century in Greek-speaking areas of western Syria. These materials go well beyond what we normally mean by Judaizing.[20] Jesus here is seen as the manifestation of the "true prophet" who had revealed himself earlier in Adam and Moses. The revelation he brings is identical with the Mosaic commandments; baptismal instruction takes the form of enjoining full observance of these commandments.

The attitude toward Judaism reflected in these materials is of a different kind from that found elsewhere in early Christian literature. Not only is there no trace of anti-Jewish polemic, but the validity of Jewish tradition is extended down to the author's own time: ". . . the fruit of his precaution [that is, Moses was careful not to reveal his tradition to an outsider] is apparent until the present. For his fellow nationals everywhere hold to the same rule of monotheism and the same moral constitution . . ."[21] At one point Peter cites what must have been the favorite testimony of Judaizers everywhere (Matt. 5:18—"one jot or tittle shall not pass from the law") against those who falsely represent Peter himself as having advocated a break with the Mosaic commandments: "For to take such a position is to act against the Law of God which was spoken through Moses and whose eternal endurance was attested by our Lord."[22]

In pronouncing these words of censure against those who have misrepresented his views, Peter identifies his (Christian) enemies as Gentiles who have accepted "a lawless and silly teaching of the enemy."[23] Else-where the text gives the name of this arch-enemy as Simon Magus, the mysterious figure who appears briefly in the Acts of the Apostles and is later attacked by Christian heresiologists as the father of gnosticism. But there is now general agreement among students of the Pseudo-Clementines, based on clear indications in the texts themselves, that Peter's true opponent is none other than Paul![24] Peter's polemic against Paul is lengthy and passionate: Paul has deliberately falsified Peter's teachings on the continued validity of the Mosaic commandments;[25] Paul is a spiritual descendant of the false, female prophet who has resisted true prophecy from the beginning of time;[26] and Paul's claim to apostolic authority is vitiated because it derives not from direct contact with Jesus but from an ephemeral and deceptive vision.[27]

What troubles Peter more than anything else is that Paul has taught his "lawless and absurd doctrine" to Gentiles.[28] Whether the author(s) of these writings was Jewish we do not know. What is certain is that the community behind them, as well as their intended audience, is predomi-nantly Gentile.[29] In other words, it is Gentiles, not Jews, who are the intended audience for Peter's Torah-based Christianity. We can only conclude that the literary materials embedded in the Pseudo-Clementines reveal a stream of Christianity in close contact with contemporaneous Judaism, committed to the observance of the Mosaic commandments for all of its members, and constituted to a significant degree by Gentiles. This Christianity looks back to the preaching of Peter, purified of distortions introduced by anti-Judaizers, and sees in Paul the arch-enemy of the true faith. This Christianity also looks very much like the combination of beliefs and practices so strenuously resisted by Chrysostom, Ephrem, and Aphraat.

In turning to the *Didascalia*, a compendium of ecclesiastical teachings on a variety of subjects (for example, the laity, the role of bishops, the sacraments), we find much the same picture. Written initially in Greek, probably between 200 and 250, the book enjoyed wide circulation throughout Syria and was translated into Syriac before the time of Aphraat and Ephrem. Like other Syrian literature, the *Didascalia* presents us with a Christianity much influenced by contacts with Judaism.[30] Thus the orthodox view which the document repeatedly claims to represent must be seen as orthodox in a quite particular sense, that is, this Syrian orthodoxy presupposes both an open dialogue between Jews and Christians and a significant degree of Jewish influence on Christian belief and practice.[31]

In the final chapter (23) of the *Didascalia*, the author addresses a number of heresies and schisms. Following a general condemnation of all heresies, the author turns to a specific group. This one argued "that one should abstain [only] from the flesh of pigs, and should eat what the law declares to be clean, and ought to be circumcised according to the law." In later passages it becomes clear that this group also observed the Sabbath and prescribed ritual baths following sexual contaminations. Whether the group consisted of (Christian) Jews, Gentiles, or both is not certain. What is certain is that the presence of Gentiles cannot be ruled out given our general knowledge of Judaizing tendencies throughout Syria.

The relationships between Christianity and Judaism in the *Didascalia* are thus rather complex. First, we have a typical case from Syria in which the beliefs and practices of the "orthodox" community are already shaped by Jewish traditions. Next, we find a second group, possibly representing the majority position, in which Judaizing is the norm. Against this group the *Didascalia* advances its theory of the "secondary legislation" (*deuterosis*), according to which the ritual and ceremonial rules, that is, the secondary law, were imposed on Israel as a punishment for its worship of the golden calf, whereas the true law is expressed in the Ten Commandments. Thus the old Israel is not now and never was meant to serve as an expression of the divine will. Those who observe the ritual laws do so in vain. Finally, some have argued that specific aspects of the *Didascalia*'s own prescriptions regarding the celebration of Easter[32] can only be accounted for if we assume that the author, under pressure from large numbers of Judaizers, has deliberately modified certain liturgical customs in an attempt to neutralize the appeal of Judaism among the faithful.[33]

Can we speak of anti-Judaism in the *Didascalia*? In the sense that it declares the ritual commandments to be absolutely without validity, inasmuch as they were imposed on Israel as a form of punishment, the answer must be affirmative. At the same time, Simon reminds us that the writing as a whole betrays a genuine sense of sympathy for "the people" and that it refers to Jews as brothers, albeit disobedient ones. Far more significant is the observation that the author's sole preoccupation in the writing is not with Jews but with Judaizing Christians. Thus we find ourselves confronted once again by a set of circumstances in which anti-Judaism arises in direct response to a form of Judaizing Christianity. This should cause no surprise. By now we have encountered similar circumstances repeatedly, in different times and places. In response to Murray's expression of dismay that anti-Judaism should arise in circles permeated by Jewish influence,[34] we might say that anything else would be cause for dismay.

IGNATIUS OF ANTIOCH

Turning from the *Didascalia*, dated between 200 and 250, and the sources of the *Pseudo-Clementines*, reaching perhaps as early as 200, to Ignatius, we arrive at Antioch in the first decade of the second century. In our discussion of John Chrysostom we have already discovered disputes at Antioch regarding Christians and the observance of the Mosaic commandments. With Ignatius we encounter once again a protest by an ecclesiastical leader against the observance of Jewish practices in that city by persons who regarded themselves as Christians.

To be sure, the letters of Ignatius bear only indirectly on the city of Antioch. They were written during Ignatius's forced journey toward martyrdom in Rome, and they address issues which he encountered in Christian communities along the way. The tone of several passages suggests that Ignatius was genuinely surprised by the Judaizers whom he encountered on his journey.[35] In view of what we know about the previous and subsequent history of Christianity in Antioch, however, it seems unlikely that Ignatius was completely unfamiliar with the phenomenon of Christian Judaizers. Perhaps what surprised him was the discovery that they were not limited to Antioch!

Two of Ignatius's letters contain clear references to Judaizers. In *Magnesians* his warning "not to be led astray by strange doctrines or old tales which are without benefit (8.1)" is directed at those who had been living according to some form of Judaism. The contrast between the

Sabbath and the Lord's Day in 9.1 may point to Sabbath observances. Finally in 10.3 he completes the picture, though adding no new information, by expostulating that "it is foolish to talk of Jesus Christ and to Judaize."

In his letter to the *Philadelphians*, he says the following:

> If anyone should undertake to interpret Judaism to you, do not listen to him. For it is better to hear of Christianity from a man who has been circumcised than to hear of Judaism from someone who is uncircumcised. [6.1]

Ignatius's words are not altogether unambiguous, but the situation appears to involve an effort on the part of Gentile converts to Judaism, or perhaps Gentile Judaizers, to suggest that the two faiths be regarded as complements rather than opposites.[36] Unfortunately, nothing further is said about those who were "interpreting Judaism" except that they were not born Jews. Perhaps they were like the Judaizers in Magnesia. Or again, perhaps we should interpret the words of 6.1 in the light of the later passage in 8.2:

> For I have heard some men saying. "If I do not find it in the archives (*archeiois*), I will not believe it in the gospel." And when I said that it was written there, they answered, "That's just the issue." For me Jesus Christ is the archives. The unshakeable archives are his cross and death, resurrection and faith through him. . . .

If this dialogue took place between Ignatius and the interpreters of Judaism mentioned in 6.1, we would then have a bit more information about them. Their position appears to be that any Christian belief or practice ("the gospel") which does not find direct corroboration in the Hebrew Scriptures ("the archives") is simply not acceptable. While such a position does not necessarily lead to Judaizing, neither is it inconsistent with such a possibility.

Ignatius's response to what he had learned is characteristically direct. Those who continue to live according to Judaism are said to confess that they have not received grace (*Magn.* 8.1). The ancient prophets already lived according to Jesus Christ and for that reason they were persecuted

(*Magn.* 8.2). Those who fail to speak of Jesus Christ are "to me tombstones and graves of the dead" (*Philad.* 6.1). Clearly for Ignatius, Christianity has superseded Judaism and allows no room whatsoever for Jewish ritual observances.

Apart from his tendency to assert rather than argue, the absence of exegetical arguments from his polemic is curious.[37] To the Judaizers in Philadelphia, who seem to have refused beliefs or practices unless they could be documented in the Hebrew Scriptures, Ignatius responds, "the *archeia are* Jesus Christ" (*Philad.* 8.2). If we may see in the Philadelphian position something of the later Antiochian skepticism regarding the unbridled Christological exegesis of the Old Testament, then perhaps we may also see in Ignatius's retort a foreshadowing of the logic that will later be used by Marcion.

PAUL AND THE CONTROVERSY OVER GENTILE BELIEVERS

Antioch was not only the city where, according to the Book of Acts, the followers of Jesus were first called Christians (Acts 11:26). According to the Jewish historian Josephus, it was a city with a large Jewish population of long standing. On relations between Jews and Gentiles in the city he reports the following:

> Moreover, they were constantly attracting to their religious ceremonies multitudes of Greeks, and these they had in some measure incorporated with themselves.[38]

In short, there was already a tradition of Gentile Judaizing—Josephus does not speak of converts—in Antioch before Christianity arrived. Thus, we should not be surprised to learn that Antioch was also the site of the first reported controversy concerning the status of Gentiles in the new movement.

The reasons for the controversy are not hard to find. A number of texts preserved exclusively in the gospel of Matthew reflect a point of view that may well have been predominant in the earliest stages of Christianity in Palestine and Syria. Since these texts clearly do not represent Matthew's own views, we must assume that they stem from an earlier source which he has incorporated into his own gospel:

(a) The community continued to worship in the Jerusalem temple. The command in 5:23–24 to settle disputes before offering a gift at the altar makes sense only for a community that regularly made such offerings at the only available altar, namely, in the Jerusalem temple. That this was the common practice is, of course, confirmed by Acts 2:46—"And day by day, attending the temple together. . . ."

(b) The Mosaic covenant remained fully binding; indeed its commandments were radically intensified. Strong warnings were issued for any who sought to abolish or even relax any of them. In 5:17–20, Jesus says that he has come not to abolish the law and the prophets but to fulfill them: "For truly, I say to you, till heaven and earth pass away, not an iota, not a dot, will pass from the law until all is accomplished" (5:18). And the passage concludes with the warning that his followers cannot enter the Kingdom unless their righteousness *exceeds* that of the scribes and Pharisees (5:20). Again there is confirming evidence in Acts, where certain followers of Jesus from Judea proclaim, regarding Gentiles, "Unless you are circumcised according to the custom of Moses, you cannot be saved" (15:1) and "It is necessary to circumcise them, and to charge them to keep the law of Moses" (15:5).

(c) Their missionary activity was limited to Israel. In reporting Jesus' charge to the disciples, Matthew alone records these words: "Go nowhere among the Gentiles, and enter no town of the Samaritans, but go rather to the last sheep of the house of Israel" (10:5f.; 15:24). To this we may add that this movement was presumably open to Gentiles, but only if they were prepared to accept full responsibility for the Mosaic covenant.

Such sayings constituted a powerful force among numerous early followers of Jesus. At the same time, however, we hear of other believers —Jews also—whose attitude toward Gentiles took a different turn. Most of them are just names: Titus, Barnabas, Timothy, Silas, and Stephen. Two things in particular differentiated them from their fellow believers: they saw the Gentiles as their primary audience and, more importantly, they did not require Gentile adherents to observe the Mosaic commandments. Inevitably these differences led to conflict, and it was to resolve this conflict that a meeting was held in Jerusalem.

Two reports of this meeting have been preserved—one in Acts 15, one in Paul's letter to the Galatians. We need not concern ourselves here with the enormous literature surrounding what has been anachronistically called the Jerusalem Council. For our purposes, what matters is the aftermath. On one matter only do we know that the two parties reached an agreement: Paul and his co-workers were granted full authority to broadcast their gospel to the uncircumcised, while James, Peter, and others would focus their attention on the circumcised. Despite the significant concessions made by the Jerusalem leaders, a close look at events immediately following the meeting suggests that the agreement soon broke down. Peter (Cephas) came under pressure from "certain men from James"—whether they had participated in the meeting is not made clear—and again refused to eat with those Gentile converts who were not observant. According to Paul, Peter acted out of fear of "the circumcision party," by which he presumably means "the men from James" referred to in the same verse. Even Paul's trusted co-worker Barnabas, together with "the rest of the Jews," was persuaded by these dissidents. Acts 15:39 refers to this dispute between Paul and Barnabas as a "paroxysm" and adds that the two subsequently parted company; in Gal. 2:13 Paul reports that he accused Barnabas of acting out of hypocrisy. Beyond this, we know from Paul's own letters that his later missionary efforts among Gentiles were constantly disrupted by those who insisted that Gentile converts were required to assume at least some of the Mosaic commandments. As for Paul himself, he appears to have had little to do with Antioch from that point on. Can it be that he regarded his efforts at establishing his Torah-free gospel to Gentiles as a lost cause in that area?[39] Certainly the subsequent history of Gentile Judaizing in Antioch and Syria generally would appear to point in this direction.

One final observation is necessary. Our earlier analysis of Judaizing among Gentiles in the Greco-Roman world should warn us not to suppose that Gentile Christians in Antioch who followed certain Jewish rituals were acting under any external constraint, say, from spokesmen for the Palestinian believers. And if we add the specific comments of Josephus regarding Gentile sympathizers and Judaizers in Antioch, we need not look beyond the prevailing cultural climate for an explanation of Christian Judaizing in that city and beyond. Thus I would conclude that we may have the very opposite of what some have presented as the result of Christianity's arrival in areas where Jews were already well-established. It is wrong, or at the very least misleading, to view Christianity as having accelerated the process whereby Jews assimilated to their pagan environment, by offering them an "exceptionally attractive" form of Hellenism.[40] In many areas we know that the reverse was true, for Christianity was far less attractive to many Hellenes than was Judaism. Thus many Gentile Christians adopted a variety of Jewish customs precisely because they accorded well with elements of their own pagan and Hellenistic culture.

Our survey of a wide range of Christian writings has revealed that Judaizing Christians were a common feature of the Christian landscape from the very beginning. This phenomenon seems to have been particularly prevalent and persistent in Syria, but it was by no means limited to one region of the Empire.[41] In Asia Minor, it appears not just in the letters of Ignatius but in the pseudo-Pauline letter to the Colossians. The Gentile recipients of this letter are rebuked by the author for undertaking certain Jewish observances—"Let no one pass judgment on you in questions of food and drink or with regard to a festival or a new moon or a Sabbath" (Col. 2:16). And in the Book of Revelation, the author writes two of his introductory letters to the same Christian communities at Smyrna and Philadelphia later addressed by Ignatius. In both places (2:9 and 3:9) he vents his anger at "those who say they are Jews and are not, but are a synagogue of Satan." Here is a case of Gentile Christians calling themselves Jews—presumably because they behaved like Jews—being repudiated by another Christian, himself probably of Jewish birth, as a synagogue of Satan!

Also from Asia Minor come the canons of the Council of Laodicea (held in 360), several of which address the issue of Judaizing among Christians: Canon 29 forbids resting on the Sabbath rather than on the Lord's Day; Canon 16 requires that if Christians worship on the Sabbath they must read the gospels along with the other Scriptures, that is, the Hebrew Scriptures; Canons 27 and 38 forbid Christians to participate in Jewish feasts and ceremonies. Similar prohibitions appear in canons from the Council of Antioch (341), forbidding Christians to eat Passover with Jews (Canon 1) and as far away as Spain, where the Council of Elvira (c. 300) expressly prohibits the blessing of fields by Jews (Canon 49) and the sharing of feast with Jews (Canon 50).[42] Origen mentions Jews who "want to accept Jesus as the one prophesied and to observe the law of Moses just as much as before"[43] and elsewhere criticizes others who observed both the Jewish Sabbath and Passover.[44] From Latin-speaking regions, individual Christian writers—Jerome, Augustine, Novatian, Commodian, and others—reveal a similar pattern of recurrent, if not pervasive, Judaizing among Gentile believers.[45]

What accounts for this continued attraction to Judaism? Once we clear away the debris of earlier misconceptions about the status of Judaism in the Greco-Roman world, the question begins to answer itself. In the first place, we need to recall that the New Testament itself preserves a vivid account of Judaizing among the earliest followers of Jesus. "Think not that I have come to abolish the law and the prophets. . . . Whoever then relaxes one of the least of these commandments and teaches men so, shall be called least in the kingdom of heaven" (Matt. 5:17–19). "But some men came down from Judea and were teaching the brethren, 'Unless you are circumcised according to the custom of Moses, you cannot be saved'" (Acts 15:1). These and other passages convey a sense of the logic which seemed so apparent to the earliest Christian Judaizers, and they may also have communicated it to others at a later time. In this case, we are fortunate in being able to hear both sides of the internal debate during its early stages. Later on, we hear only the official voices of the church.

It would appear, then, that popular Christianity was not nearly as convinced as were its leaders that the beliefs and practices of Judaism had been rendered powerless by the appearance of Christianity. John Chrysostom's homilies against the Jews are revealing on this point. At the least they prompt Meeks and Wilken to question whether it was "Chrysostom himself and other leaders of the church who are exceptional."[46] Beyond this they provide specific examples, at points where Chrysostom appears to be quoting the Judaizers themselves, of what motivated their behavior. For significant numbers of Christians in late antiquity, Judaism continued to represent a powerful and vigorous religious tradition. Unlike their ecclesiastical and theological superiors, they saw no need to define themselves in opposition to Judaism or to cut themselves off from this obvious source of power.

9

Controversies and Debates
Between Jews and Christians

We turn now to the second major setting of Christian anti-Judaism—debates and controversies between Jews and Christians in the early centuries. As with the phenomenon of Christian Judaizing, these debates are at once simple and complex: simple in the sense that they involve one basic issue, namely, the legitimacy of each side's religious self-understanding; complex in the sense that the debates themselves varied according to time, place, and participants. As with the question of Judaizing, the debates about the legitimacy of Christianity and Judaism were complex in the additional sense that the spokesmen for "official" Christianity had as their opponents not just Jews as such but many of their own fold. Just as arguments against the validity of the Mosaic ritual commandments were at least as often directed against Christians as against Jews, so the debates were carried on not simply with Jews who stood outside Christianity but with those who stood within.

This chapter deals with those expressions of Christian anti-Judaism that must be seen as products of a prolonged debate, whose origins go back to the very beginning of Christianity, between Christian and Jew at various times and places. The issues, themes, and biblical prooftexts in this debate remain fairly constant for two basic reasons: first, the fundamental problem is that both parties laid exclusive claim to the legitimate heritage of the divine convenant with Israel, and second, both parties built their case around the same documents, that is, the Hebrew Bible.

Jewish criticism of Christianity was wide-ranging and persistent.[1] It is a mistake to judge its extent by the scattered references to Christianity in rabbinic literature. The Jewish critique held that Jesus was not the Messiah, that beliefs about him amounted to a repudiation of monotheism, that Christians had misunderstood and distorted the Scriptures, and that they had forfeited any right to the promises of Israel by their abandonment of ritual observance. Furthermore, until the advent of Constantine and the Christian empire, Jews had pleaded successfully before official Rome that Christianity was a new religion, distinct from Judaism, and thus not deserving of respect or recognition. Wherever these criticisms were voiced and in whatever form, they prompted a Christian reply.

A second major reason the Jewish critique could not be left unanswered concerns—one hesitates to use the term—the essence of Christianity or at the very least its historical origins. This factor is at once more profound and more elusive than the need to defend oneself against outsiders. The point has been made repeatedly, from Isaac and Simon to Ruether, that the origins of Christianity within first century Judaism and its painful separation from Judaism meant that its sense of identity and legitimacy took shape within the framework of opposition to Judaism. Or as Ruether has put it, "for Christianity, anti-Judaism was not merely a defense against attack, but an intrinsic need of self-affirmation."[2] This was certainly the case during the earliest decades, when Christian communities sought, in settings of competition and conflict with local synagogues, to create and maintain a symbolic universe of their own. The early gospels and the letters of Paul bear direct testimony to the intensity of the struggle as seen from the Christian side. Beyond this, the very formation of the Christian canon, beginning as early as the second century with a collection of gospels and Pauline letters, preserved a permanent record of this struggle at the very heart of the Christian theological charter, that is, the New Testament.

THE EARLY DEBATE—THE CANONICAL GOSPELS AND THEIR SOURCES

Apart from Paul, our earliest sources for controversies between Jews and Christians are the New Testament gospels. In them Jesus and his followers appear frequently in situations of tension and debate with various Jewish opponents. These opponents are variously identified as Pharisees,

Sadducees, scribes, elders, priests, high priests, and sometimes simply as
Jews. It is fair to say, however, that many of these disputes, or at least
the specific identification of these opponents, represent occasions not so
much from Jesus' lifetime as from later times, the times of the gospels
themselves, which have been read back into Jesus' career.[3] In any case,
we may be certain that these controversy-passages helped to shape the
self-understanding of those early Christians who later produced the
written gospels.

If it is in fact the case that these controversy-stories reveal a particular
line of development in Christian views of Jews and Judaism—a line
moving from internal disputes between different Jewish groups, including
groups of Jesus' followers, toward a situation in which the Jews, as a
people, stand against the Christians—we may be able to use them to
locate points at which the Christian critique ceases to be intra-Jewish
polemic and becomes Jewish-Christian or even gentilizing anti-Judaism
instead.

Oral and Written Traditions Before the Gospels

A fundamental axiom of modern biblical scholarship is that collections
of sayings and stories of Jesus circulated in oral and written form before
being incorporated into our written gospels. There is even evidence to
suggest that such traditions continued to circulate in oral form after the
composition of the earliest gospels, whether Mark, Matthew, or John.

Inasmuch as the sole, or rather primary source for these pre-gospel
traditions are the gospels themselves, any attempt to detect and disengage
them from this present setting in the written gospels must depend finally
on our ability to discriminate early material from later, the gospel writers'
sources from their own contributions. If, as has been traditional, we regard
Mark as a written source used by both Matthew and Luke, we are in a
position to make just such discriminations for these two gospels. Further
comparisons between the two reveal that they made use of other sources
as well; some of these sources they used in common, for example, the
famous Q, which consists of common sayings found in Matthew and
Luke but not in Mark, whereas other sources appear to have been available only to Matthew or Luke. But how are we to make such distinctions

within Mark (or Matthew for those who prefer to regard this gospel as prior to the others) when we have no direct evidence of its sources other than the gospel itself? By the painstaking, highly technical, and seemingly endless task of literary analysis—analysis here in the literal sense of breaking down the text into smaller units of material—students of the gospels have sought to re-create the origins and development of the gospel traditions before they were written down in their present form. Among these students, some have even ventured to push behind the traditions to the figure of Jesus, arguing that it is possible to identify certain sayings and stories that originated with him rather than in the communities which preserved and transmitted the traditions or, in the final stages, in the creative work of the gospel writers themselves. As indicated earlier there are good reasons for skepticism about the feasibility of this final step.[4]

For the present it will be enough to pursue these traditions themselves, to discover what they reveal about very early followers of Jesus and their relationship to Judaism, and to leave to others the determination of whether these traditions reflect the views of Jesus himself. In analyzing these traditions and the individual sayings or stories within them our goal will be to determine whether they reveal a different attitude toward Judaism from the attitude of the gospels in their final form. Or put differently, has the editorial process of creating the gospels resulted, whether or not deliberately, in modification or transformation of the very meaning of the pre-gospel materials?[5] If the answer is yes, can one then use these materials, along with Paul, to reconstruct a more complete picture of interaction between Christians and Jews in the earliest decades of the Christian movement? For purposes of limiting this discussion we will concentrate on three forms of the pre-gospel traditions: first, the materials common to Matthew and Luke but not found in Mark, that is, the so-called Q tradition; second, traditions found only in Matthew; and third, material unique to Luke.

Q

Q designates material common to Matthew and Luke but not found in Mark. As such it is a purely hypothetical, though not improbable reconstruction of a source available only to Matthew and Luke.[6] Its great value is that it takes us behind not only Matthew and Luke but simultaneously to sources independent of Mark as well.[7]

The Q tradition is dominated by a small number of basic themes:

• the role of Jesus as eschatological prophet and bringer of divine wisdom (Luke 7:26)[8]

• the intense expectation of the final judgment and the end of the present age in the near future, together with warnings of doom and a call to repentance (Luke 12:57; 13:20)

• predictions concerning the role of a/the Son of Man as the one who will carry out God's act of judgment (Luke 12:40)

• statements about how to prepare for the imminent judgment and about the fate of those who will be condemned (Luke 11:31)

Running through these themes are a number of threats and warnings directed against those who fail to heed Jesus' proclamation of the coming judgment. Most of these fall within the rubric of prophetic anti-Judaism. The saying of Jesus (Luke 10:21) in which he thanks God "that thou hast hidden these things from the wise and understanding and revealed them to babes. . . ." is a typical example of sayings that make a sharp distinction between insiders and outsiders. But both groups clearly stand within Israel; there is no trace of the view that Israel as a whole is to be rejected, that the followers of Jesus represent a new Israel or that Gentiles will replace Jews as the true Israel. To this same category belongs the lengthy tirade against the Pharisees and their brand of piety in Luke 11:39–52. The language here is tough and uncompromising, but as I have argued elsewhere, this tirade in its original form and setting must be seen as a classic expression of resentment by outsiders, in this case the early followers of Jesus, against a highly self-conscious religious establishment which defined itself in such a way as to exclude certain sectors of Palestinian Jewish society.[9] In this particular case, the anti-Pharisaic polemic is strictly an intra-Jewish affair. Quite similar in tone and structure is the parable of the Great Supper in Luke 15:15–24. Here the contrast is between the initial invitees who refuse to attend the banquet and the second group ("the poor and maimed and blind and lame" in Luke 14:21; "as many as you can find" in Matthew 22:9), with no further evidence of a general anti-Jewish or pro-Gentile thrust. Only Matthew turns the parable in this direction by introducing the line that the host, the king, "was angry, and he sent his troops and destroyed these murderers and burned their city" (Matt. 22:7).[10]

Somewhat different in tone and content are passages where Jesus appears to speak in a more general way of those who stand against him. Luke 11:29–32 relates Jesus' saying against the current generation ("This generation is an evil generation; it seeks a sign. . . .") which it contrasts unfavorably with the queen of the South (". . . will arise at the judgment with the men of this generation and condemn them") and with the men of Nineveh (". . . will arise at the judgment with this generation and condemn it."). Although a contrast between Jews and non-Jews (the men of Nineveh = Jon. 3:5; the queen of the South = 1 Kings 10:1ff. [Sheba]) is implicit in the saying, the language is otherwise typical of prophetic condemnations in the eschatological literature of this period.[11] Other contrast-prophesies make a more explicit distinction between Jews and non-Jews. In Luke 10:13–16 Jesus pronounces woes against two Galilean towns, Chorazin and Bethsaida, for failing to respond positively to his works: "if the mighty works done in you had been done in Tyre and Sidon [that is, Gentile cities to the North], they would have repented long ago. . . ." Even more pointed are two laments over Jerusalem. In Luke 13:34–35, Jesus speaks of the city "killing the prophets and stoning those who are sent to you! . . . Behold, your house is forsaken." In 19:39–44, again in a saying artificially directed against the Pharisees (19:39—"And some of the Pharisees in the multitude said to him. . . ."), Jesus "predicts" the imminent destruction of the city (19:43—"your enemies will cast up a bank about you. . . . ") "because you did not know the time of your visitation."

In the overall context of Luke and Matthew, it is apparent that these contrast-prophecies belong to a general structure of insiders-outsiders in which the two sides are understood as Gentiles and Jews. But whether the isolated stories, in their pre-gospel versions, conveyed the same message is less clear. The most likely interpretation is that these earlier, pre-gospel versions reflect a controversy *within* Judaism between competing communities or regions.[12]

One final group of sayings in Q may take us yet another step in the direction of Jewish Christian or even Gentilizing anti-Judaism. Luke 7:1–10 records Jesus' healing of a (Gentile) centurion's slave. At the conclusion of the healing proper (Luke 7:2–8), there appears what may well originally have been an independent saying, "I tell you, not even in Israel have I found such faith" (7:9). Here again, Matthew sharpens the Gentile, anti-Jewish focus by attaching still another Q saying (8:12— ". . . the sons of the kingdom [Israel?] will be thrown into outer darkness. . . . "). Even here, however, the point of Luke's version is not that Israel has been rejected but that a Gentile has done what Israel should have been doing all along. Much the same pattern apears in Jesus' warning to his disciples that they will be brought before "the synagogues and the rulers and the authorities" (Luke 12:11). Matthew's version has the disciples also being "dragged before governors and kings for my sake, to bear testimony before them and the Gentiles," thus expanding the scope of the saying. But even in Matthew the passage as a whole deals with Jesus' instructions to his disciples for their mission to Israel alone. Finally, Luke 16:16 presents the difficult saying about John the Baptist and the prophets: "The law and the prophets were until John; since then the good news of the Kingdom of God is preached and every one enters it violently." While the precise meaning of this saying may be unclear, the general sense is not. It is intended to clarify the relationship between the law and the prophets of old and John the Baptist and the intense eschatological expectations of the speaker's own times, and to assert that the coming End is in fact the culmination of the line that leads from the law and the prophets through John to Jesus. Far from cancelling either the law or the prophets, the saying in its pre-gospel version presupposes the very opposite, namely, that they lead to and find their culmination in present events.

The final picture which emerges from the Q tradition fits easily into the framework of prophetic anti-Judaism. The picture includes typical elements of Jewish eschatological expectations from the first century: (a) the coming Kingdom will cause a division within Israel, as does already its proclamation; (b) harsh language is used to describe those who reject the proclamation; and (c) the Kingdom concerns Israel primarily, although pious Gentiles are sometimes included. Only in the later literary setting of the gospels, where they are incorporated within an increasingly Gentile Christian setting, are these elements regularly reinterpreted in such a way as to turn prophetic into Gentilizing anti-Judaism.

Matthew's Special Traditions

To confirm the results obtained from the preceding analysis of Q, we may look briefly at a series of sayings from a source or tradition that must have been known only to Matthew. The material preserved in this tradition enables us to reconstruct an image of some early Christian community—whether or not it represented the view of Jesus' earliest followers in Jerusalem, or even those of Jesus himself, is not of importance here—in which the Q tradition might well have been generated and transmitted to later times. The following picture emerges from this pre-Matthean tradition:

· The community continued to worship in the Jerusalem temple.

· The Mosaic covenant remained fully binding; indeed its commandments were radically intensified.

· Their missionary activity was limited exclusively to Israel.

Apart from the picture of an early Christian tradition, earlier certainly than Matthew and probably than Mark, which these sayings convey, their special value lies in the fact that they so obviously fail to reflect Matthew's own point of view. For whatever reasons, he has seen fit to incorporate a body of material that unmistakably derives from a movement within Judaism. What, then, of the relationship between this tradition or community and the prophetic anti-Judaism of the Q materials? Of course there may be no connection whatever, in which case the two traditions would simply reflect two early, but separate communities with different points of view. If, on the other hand, the tradition stems ultimately from the same source or community, we would be able to assert beyond any doubt that the prophetic anti-Judaism of Q is strictly and fully an intra-Jewish matter.

Here would be a clear case in which discipleship of Jesus would not involve any form of anti-Judaism in the strong sense. For here we encounter a religious movement whose self-understanding placed it firmly within the circle (and in this case a reasonably tight one at that) of Judaism. This movement was open to Gentiles but only if they were prepared to accept full responsibility for the Mosaic covenant which the movement itself declared to have found its fulfillment in the figure of Jesus.

Luke's Special Sources

In its present form, the gospel of Luke appears to have been written for Gentile Christians and to reflect their special concerns. In contrast, a number of passages appear to be addressed exclusively to Israel and to reflect concerns not at all characteristic of Gentiles. As reconstructed by Lloyd Gaston, these special pre-Lucan traditions offer us yet another insight into encounters between Jews and Christians in the period before the written gospels:[13]

(a) The birth stories focus on Israel "as the people of the promises . . . [and] rejoice confidently and positively that redemption, also in its political sense, has come to Israel in the fullest meaning of the Old Testament expectation."[14]

(b) In the birth stories Jesus is described in classically biblical terms: "Son of the Most High" (1:32), anointed (Messiah) of God (2:11, 26), ruler over the house of Jacob (1:33), and so on. Elsewhere, these traditions reveal a two-stage view of Jesus: in the first, he is a prophet like Moses; in the second, following his death-resurrection-ascension, he becomes Messiah and a prophet like Joshua. The second stage in particular places so much emphasis on Jesus' role as savior of Israel that Gaston is inclined to call it nationalistic.[15]

(c) On relations between Israel and the Gentiles in Luke's special sources, Gaston comments that while missionary efforts were directed exclusively to Israel, these optimistic efforts show signs of disappointment at Israel's failure to respond. This disappointment is the setting for the polemical statements regarding Israel. In particular, the high priests and temple authorities are seen as enemies of Jesus (19:47; 22:52, 66; 23:10, and so on), where the people or the crowds are quite specifically contrasted with their leaders as sympathetic to Jesus. As for the Pharisees, whom the other gospels portray as uncompromisingly hostile to Jesus, they are sometimes presented in a quite positive light here (7:36; 11:37; 14:1; Acts 5:34-39; 15:5).

(d) The overall ambivalence toward Israel reflects the basic pre-occupation of these materials with preaching the good news to Israel, coupled with a warning of judgment for those who refuse to obey. These warnings point forward to an apocalyptic crisis about to overtake Israel and her cities and towns (Luke 12:54–13:4; 13:22–30; 17:20–18:8; 23:27–31). Nowhere are these warnings coupled with the prospect of a mission to Gentiles.

At this point there is no need to speculate about possible relationships between the material of Q, the special traditions of Matthew and the special sources of Luke. Whatever their ultimate source(s), they share certain fundamental features. The judgmental statements found in them, whether as imprecations against Israel's leaders or as eschatological warnings to Israel as a whole, clearly fall into the category of intra-Jewish polemics. The issues separating the followers of Jesus from Israel's disobedient leaders take us back to our earlier discussion concerning the religious sources of Christian anti-Judaism. According to Gaston's analysis of Luke's sources, the polemical attitude arose from disappointment at Israel's failure to follow Jesus. This result appears to contradict Ruether's assertion that messianic claims about Jesus were the sole source of Christian anti-Judaism. But inasmuch as the claims about Jesus were undoubtedly the basic issue of dispute between followers of Jesus and other Jews, Ruether's assertion is actually supported. Finally, all of these materials confront us once again with a fundamental law of religious dynamics: the closer the parties, the greater is the potential for conflict. There is no paradox in the repeated juxtaposition of strong Jewish influences and strong anti-Judaism.

Mark

Our discussion of the pre-gospel traditions has introduced a note of caution with regard to our reading of the written gospels. Not only must we distinguish between early and late material in them, but we also need to reckon with the probability that a story or saying that had one meaning in an early setting may have acquired a quite different meaning later on in a new setting. This is not to say, however, that we should now reinterpret the gospels in the light of the pre-gospel traditions. The procedure is rather the other way around. For by our ability to distinguish between the evangelists' sources and their own contributions, we are in a better position to isolate their own distinctive attitudes as well as to examine the techniques by which they reinterpreted earlier material in accordance with these attitudes.

D. R. A. Hare concludes his analysis of the gospel of Mark with the assertion that it "contains only the barest traces of prophetic and Jewish-Christian anti-Judaism, and not the slightest evidence of that gentilizing anti-Judaism that was later to dominate Christian theology."[16] He argues that certain passages, traditionally interpreted as expressing an anti-Jewish ideology (4:11f.; 11:12–25), will not bear such a reading. Others, which are anti-Jewish in the prophetic vein, are directed not at Israel as such but at her religious leaders (11:12–25; 12:1–12). The same contrast appears elsewhere in the passion narrative (15:10) and in general throughout the gospel (7:1–23). In response to his own question—"Why does Mark not take the next logical step and dissolve the distinction between wicked leaders and the people as a whole?"—Hare answers that the explanation lies in the fact that Mark wrote before the failure of the mission to Israel and before the theological explanations generated by that failure.[17]

This is certainly the strongest possible attempt to minimize the level of anti-Jewish material in Mark's gospel. And yet, the analysis of anti-Judaism in the written gospels requires something more than a narrow concentration on isolated words and phrases. The context of these passages in the larger text and the broader context of the gospel itself must be taken into account. Thus Hare has not succeeded in demonstrating that Mark is devoid of Jewish-Christian or even gentilizing anti-Judaism, but rather that these themes are less explicit in Mark than in Matthew or John. In his analysis of the same passages, S. G. F. Brandon concludes that "the reader of the Markan gospel is led to see Jesus as both rejected by, and in turn rejecting his fellow-Jews."[18] In its negative aspect, this theme runs through a series of encounters between Jesus and various groups of Jewish leaders. Its other side, that is, the acceptance of Jesus by Gentiles, expresses itself in the confession of faith in the crucified Jesus attested by the Roman soldier at the moment of Jesus' death. By contrast, in the account of Jesus' appearance before Pilate, it is the leaders *and* the crowd who insist on Jesus' crucifixion. As Brandon notes, the passage "greatly magnifies the culpability of the Jews, both leaders and people, for the death of Jesus."[19] Similarly, Peter Richardson detects clear signs of Mark's preoccupation with the Gentile mission. The transition from secrecy to openness in chapters 6–8 is "an indication of the Jews' rejection and of the turn to the Gentiles."[20]

In the early part of the gospel, before the transition, Mark presents a number of scenes in which the Pharisees and others reveal their inability to comprehend Jesus and his actions (chapters 2–3). These are followed in chapter 4 by the parable of the sower, to which Mark has attached his theory of the parables in general (4:10–12). The peculiar theory of the parables is that Jesus used them as a kind of code whose purpose was to convey the truth to insiders while purposely concealing it from "those outside" so that they may not understand or be forgiven. This is a harsh passage, presupposing an unbridgeable gap between insiders who understand and outsiders who do not. Yet there are two important observations to be made before we read this harshness as a form of gentilizing anti-Judaism.

First, the passage itself makes no reference at all to Jews, only to outsiders. One might wish to argue that the location of the passage in its Markan context makes it clear that the outsiders are Jews. Thus Richardson concludes that Mark has transformed a pre-Markan tradition about the meaning of the parables "into a theory to explain Jewish obtuseness."[21] But even this is not certain, for while chapter 3 speaks of opposition by Pharisees (3:6) and scribes (3:22), the immediately preceding material in 3:28–35 addresses insiders rather than outsiders. Furthermore, in chapter 5 the opposition comes not from the Jews but from an unclean demon (5:1–20) and the second half of the chapter relates the story of Jairus, "one of the rulers of the synagogue," whose request that Jesus heal his dying daughter is granted (5:21–24, 35–43).

Second, and more importantly, the theme of incomprehension is a *leitmotif* throughout Mark. The most uncomprehending figures in the gospel, and thus the targets of Jesus' most severe rebukes, are not outsiders at all but rather the disciples themselves. Peter above all the others receives a rebuke much harsher than that directed against any "outsider" (8:33 "Get behind me, Satan! For you are not on the side of God, but of men."). In other words, outsiders in Mark include all the participants in the gospel narrative, especially those closest to Jesus. Only those outside the narrative, namely, Christian readers who understand the full story of Jesus' death and resurrection, are able to know the whole truth.[22]

There are also clear signs in Mark that the author is aware of a Jewish polemic and opposition to Christianity. In 2:6f. the "scribes" accuse Jesus of speaking blasphemy for pronouncing forgiveness of sins; in 3:22 the "scribes from Jerusalem" declare that he is possessed by Beelzebul and casts out demons by the prince of demons; in 2:24 the Pharisees ask why Jesus' disciples were doing unlawful labor by plucking grain on the Sabbath; and in 3:6, after Jesus performs a healing on the Sabbath, the Pharisees consult with the Herodians about how to destroy him. Finally, in 6:2, during his unsuccessful visit to Nazareth, the natives, not the leaders, question his teaching and "take offense" at him.

As for the customary contention that Mark distinguishes between the leaders of the Jews (Pharisees, scribes, elders, priests) and the people as a whole, two points must be made: first, that the distinction is not maintained consistently (cf. 15:6–15; 6:3) or developed systematically in the gospel, and second, that it is precisely the leaders and institutions of Judaism, not the simple faithful of Israel, who constitute the main target of Christian anti-Judaism. At a later time, when the notion of Christianity as the new Israel or the new people of God comes to full expression, this very distinction will serve to justify the Christian claim that it stands, in opposition to apostate Judaism, in an unbroken line of descent from ancient Israel.

Finally, several interpreters of Mark have noted that the internal structure of the gospel points us in the direction of Gentile Christianity. According to Richardson, "the movement from secrecy to revelation occurs during the chapters (6–8) which bring Gentiles into special prominence."[23] The Gentile soldier at the foot of the cross is the first to confess Jesus' true identity. Richardson notes at the conclusion of the gospel "a very close relationship between Jesus' death, the rending of the veil, and the centurion's confession that is consistent with the idea that a transition has occurred."[24] Nor is there any sign of an eventual restoration for the Jews. What is not yet present in Mark is a fully articulated vision of a "new Gentile church, or . . . a new people of God."[25] Such a vision, prompted by increased hostility between Jewish and Christian communities, will emerge in Matthew. But its basic elements are already present in Matthew's sources, among them Mark.

Matthew

To the elements of prophetic anti-Judaism present in Mark, Matthew adds the theme that "the Jewish people, . . . because it has rejected Jesus and his missionaries, has now been rejected by God."[26] Thus for Hare, "Matthew's pessimism is unrelieved."[27] There is no remnant and no restoration. Here the traditions of prophetic, Jewish-Christian and gentilizing Judaism come together within a perspective that may itself be described as Jewish-Christian. But the fact that Matthew himself may have been a Jew and that his gospel is permeated with Jewish learning in no way alters the fact that he claims for Jewish and Gentile followers of Jesus the full prerogatives of the "old" Israel.

In contrast to Mark, Matthew places the blame for Jesus' death on the whole people (*pas ho laos*):[28] "His blood be upon us and on our children" (27:25). In the parable of the vineyard, Matthew has expanded Mark's version: "Therefore I tell you, the kingdom of God will be taken away from you and given to a nation producing the fruits of it" (21:43). To the parable of the great supper, he adds the conclusion, "The king was angry and he sent his troops and destroyed those murderers and their city" (22:7).[29] And in line with this theme of Israel's rejection, there is a tendency throughout the gospel to appropriate for Christians the attributes of Israel.[30]

Matthew has also taken over Mark's scattered references to Jewish anti-Christian polemic. No doubt on the basis of encounters between Matthew's own community and Jews in the area, this theme of Jewish opposition to Christianity is significantly more prominent here. Jesus and his disciples violate the Sabbath (12:2); Jesus is called a friend of Beelzebul (12:24), a blasphemer (9:1ff.), a glutton, drunkard, and friend of tax-collectors and sinners (11:19). The chief priests and elders question the legitimacy of his authority (21:23).

Of course these passages sit side by side with others of a rather different sort. Whereas Jesus' final words to the disciples point to an exclusively Gentile mission (28:19),[31] earlier in the gospel Jesus instructs the disciples "to go nowhere among the Gentiles . . . but go rather to the lost sheep of the house of Israel" (10:6; cf. 15:24). And alongside his imprecations against the Pharisees, we find Jesus saying that he has come not to abolish the law but to fulfill it:

> I say to you, till heaven and earth pass away, not an iota, not a dot, will pass from the law until all is accomplished. Whoever then relaxes one of the least of these commandments and teaches men so, shall be called least in the kingdom of heaven. . . . For I tell you, unless your righteousness exceeds that of the scribes and Pharisees, you will never enter the kingdom of heaven (5:17–20).

How, then, to account for the juxtaposition in Matthew of unmistakably prophetic (for example, 5:17–20) and gentilizing (for example, 21:43; 27:25; 28:19) forms of anti-Judaism? Hare's view is that the position of the gospel is clearly that of the latter. If so, we must then see the prophetic variety as reflecting either the voice of a body of material that Matthew has appropriated but not fully integrated into his own framework or a developmental scheme according to which the rejection of Jesus by the Jews leads to their rejection as the people of God and to the Gentile mission.[32] As Hare concludes, Matthew represents an "attempt on the part of Jewish Christians" to give a theological accounting for the separation between church and synagogue.[33]

In his discussion of Matthew, Hare also articulates his divergence from Ruether on the relationship of christology and anti-Judaism. He notes that Jewish opposition to Christianity plays an important role in Matthew's polemic against Judaism and that the figure of Jesus is not always at issue. There is, however, a measure of inconsistency in Hare's position. For while denying any "essential relationship" between christology and gentilizing anti-Judaism in Matthew,[34] he concedes "that there will always be tension between Jews and Christians as long as Christians insist that hopes and expectations articulated in the Hebrew Scriptures find some kind of fulfillment in Jesus of Nazareth. . . ."[35] Quite apart from the fact that Hare's phrase "some kind of fulfillment" rather understates the stand of historical Christianity, Ruether's point is precisely that all forms of anti-Judaism derive ultimately from claims and counter-claims about the figure of Jesus.

Luke–Acts

There are widely differing views regarding the status of the Torah and Israel in the two books known as Luke–Acts. On the one side, Hare has discovered each of the three kinds of anti-Judaism characteristic of early Christian literature. Prophetic anti-Judaism expresses itself as "invective directed against the people as a whole" (for example, Luke 3:7f.; 11:29; Acts 7:51) and in the "popular theme that Israel has always resisted and persecuted God's prophets" (Luke 6:23; 11:47–51; Acts 7:52).[36] Jewish Christian anti-Judaism appears in the passion narrative where Luke clearly places the blame for Jesus' death on the entire people (Luke 23:13; Acts 2:22; 3:14f.; 4:10; 5:30; 10:39; 13:28). Finally, Gentilizing anti-Judaism is reflected in the use of the term "the Jews" to designate the enemies of the Christian mission throughout the book of Acts (9:22f.; 20:3, 19; 23:12).[37] While noting the presence of anti-Judaism in its various forms, Hare also argues that Luke has sought to moderate its impact by a variety of means.[38] He softens his accusation that the people as a whole have rejected Jesus by introducing the theme of remorse in the crucifixion account (Luke 23:27, 48), by asserting that the Jews acted in ignorance (Acts 3:17) in demanding Jesus' death, and by stressing divine pre-ordination as the primary force behind the events of Jesus' life and death (Luke 24:25f., 44–46; Acts 4:27f.).

A rather different view of Luke–Acts emerges from J. Jervell's *Luke and the People of God*.[39] In contrast to earlier interpreters, he resists the notion that Luke presents the Jews either as rejecting the Christian message or as supplanted by Gentiles as the new Israel. On both accounts he is able to cite impressive evidence that Luke, while fully cognizant of a mission to the Gentiles, nonetheless introduces that mission only *after* the mission to the Jews has been *successfully* undertaken and completed. Given the large number of Jews who are shown as embracing the faith and the strict observance of the Torah among the early followers of Jesus, including Paul, Luke offers a vision in which the Jewish charges against Christianity are fully refuted, that is, Christians have not rejected the Mosaic convenant. Christianity is not so much the new Israel, as the true Israel, whose continuity with the past is preserved in those loyal and observant Jews who follow Jesus. From this it follows for Luke that

Jews who reject Jesus thereby show themselves to be unworthy of the promises to Israel. And far from seeing the Gentiles as replacing an old Israel, Luke views their acceptance of the Christian gospel as the complete fulfillment of the promises to Israel.

Jervell's interpretation of Luke–Acts is in line with others to the extent that it places both the success of the Gentile mission and Jewish criticisms of Christianity at the center of Luke's theological concern. All emphasize the schism within Israel provoked by Jesus and the inclusion of the Gentiles in the divine plan of salvation.[40] In contrast to Jervell, however, Richardson sees a pronounced movement toward seeing the Gentiles, in place of the Jews, as the inheritors of Israel's promises. Despite their differences on specific issues, interpreters agree that Luke–Acts requires special consideration within the context of early Christian literature. Ruether notes that Luke alone stresses the positive response of the Pharisees to Christianity.[41] At the same time, however, she has pointed to other passages, mostly in Acts, that portray the Jews as a whole as enemies of the Christian faith. Stephen's speech in chapter 7 explicitly denies that the temple in Jerusalem is God's dwelling (7:48–50) and has as its principal theme Israel's persistent disobedience and rejection of the divine will. As for the claim of Jervell that Luke–Acts is utterly devoid of gentilizing anti-Judaism, it must be noted that the book of Acts as a whole is structured around the movement from Jewish Jerusalem to Gentile Rome and that Stephen's speech is a crucial turning point in that movement. In other words, the period of Christianity's contact and continuity with Judaism belongs entirely to the past.

Finally, it is impossible simply to dismiss the concluding episode in Acts and its place in the book as a whole. Paul's arrival in Rome provokes a division among the Jews of the city. But in his speech, which clearly echoes the earlier words of Stephen in chapter 7, no account is taken of this division. Instead, Paul cites Isa. 9:10 and Ps. 67:2f. to demonstrate that the rejection of his message by "this people" is not merely a fact of history but part of the divine plan. And he concludes with the announcement that "this salvation of God has been sent to the Gentiles; they will listen" (28:28). As Paul's final word in Acts, we can hardly see this as anything less than an expression of gentilizing anti-Judaism. Even if one chooses to smooth over these difficulties by accepting Jervell's proposal that the speech is directed, despite the phrase "this people," not at the Jewish people as a whole but only at those who have rejected the gospel, it still remains true that obedient Jews are defined by Luke as those who have accepted Jesus as the fulfillment of Israel's promises. It is less certain, however, whether this means that such obedient, that is, Christian Jews had relativized the Mosaic covenant to a mere predictive status and emptied ritual observances of their salvific values.[42] What is certain is that for Luke, Jews who view the covenant in terms of observance alone, to the exclusion of Jesus, have forfeited their claim to be the true Israel (Acts 7:51–53; 13:46; 18:6). Nor does Luke envisage a moment in the future when they will repent and return. As Gaston has put it, speaking of the contrast between Luke's own views and those of his sources,

> what in Proto-Luke still was an alternative, either salvation to Israel or destruction of Jerusalem, becomes in Luke temporal succession: first salvation to part of Israel, then the fulfillment of the threat, then the fulfillment of the salvation for the Gentiles, and finally the end.[43]

John

For Ruether and many others, early Christian anti-Judaism reaches its peak in the gospel of John.[44] Throughout, the author uses "the Jews" universally and without internal distinction as a synonym for the opponents of Jesus. He holds to a replacement theory in which Israel no longer has any but a negative status before God. As John Townsend puts it, "Jesus is a challenge to all the essential elements of the Jewish religion."[45]

Nowhere is this theological anti-Judaism more apparent than in the dialogue between Jesus and the Pharisees in chapter 8. In response to the Pharisees' assertion that *they* are the children of Abraham, Jesus replies as follows:

> You are of your father the devil; and your will is to do your father's desires. He was a murderer from the beginning, and has nothing to do with the truth because there is no truth in him. When he lies, he speaks according to his own nature, for he is a liar and the father of lies. But, because I tell you the truth, you do not believe me. [John 8:44–45]

These are breath-taking statements. According to this version of anti-Judaism, the Jews have never worshipped God. Their rejection of Jesus does nothing but manifest their condition from the beginning. Their father, that is, their god, is the devil. This is how Jesus answers their assertion, "We have one Father, even God."

Quite apart from the intensity of the language, there are indications in the text that the gospel grew out of local tensions between John's community and a local synagogue. A number of scholars have argued convincingly that the Johannine community came into being as a distinct entity only after being expelled, as a group, from a Jewish community.[46] The trauma of this expulsion was such that a myth was evolved to express the total rupture between "those from above," namely, Jesus and those who love him, and "those from below," namely, Moses and his descendants. This myth, together with a detailed refutation of a polemic directed against the Johannine community by the synagogue, make up virtually the entirety of the gospel.

As with the synoptics, this polemic includes certain standard charges: Jesus violates the Sabbath (5:16); he utters blasphemy by equating himself with God (10:33); he is possessed by a demon (8:48). Above all else, Jesus' opponents question his authority at every opportunity; as a result, much of the gospel is devoted to a defense of Jesus' legitimacy as a spokesman for God (5:36ff.; 6:41ff.; 7:16ff.; 8:13ff.; 10:22ff.; 12:44ff.; 16:25ff.; 17:1ff.). More specifically, J. Louis Martyn has shown that three quite specific challenges lie behind the distinctive cast of John's response:

(a) Christological claims about Jesus needed to be supported by detailed proofs and texts. John replies that searching the scriptures will not reveal Jesus' identity (5:39) and that only the Paraclete can show who Jesus is;

(b) Moses, who had himself ascended into heaven and returned with a knowledge of its secrets, made the Christians man from heaven, namely, Jesus, unnecessary. To this John replies that no one except Jesus has ever seen God (1:18; 3:13);

(c) Christians worshipped two gods. To this John replies with the repeated assurance that Jesus and God are one (17:11,22).[47]

To this we may add:

> (d) Christians fail to observe the commandments. Jesus replies in a counter-thrust that the Jews, who perform the act of circumcision on the sabbath, thereby violate their own law (7:19–24).

Some have sought to deny the fundamental anti-Judaism of the fourth gospel.[48] Part of the case depends on a demonstration that John does not always use "the Jews" in a derogatory manner and that Jesus' words sometimes cause divisions among the Jews (10:19). In a somewhat different fashion, J. Townsend undertakes to show that the anti-Judaism of the gospel is not as pronounced as many suppose.[49] His evidence for this assertion is rather curious: John does not hide the Jewish setting of the narrative or the Jewish origins of Jesus; John is not alone in arguing that in Christ the "old Israel" has been replaced (he cites Paul as the prime example!);[50] John's attitude toward the Jerusalem temple must be read in view of the fact that the temple and its cult had already been destroyed.

As for what Townsend calls the relatively pro-Jewish elements in the gospel, it is difficult to imagine what he has in mind. It is true that not all Jews in the gospel reject Jesus (7:43; 9:16; 10:19) and 11:45 reports that "many of the Jews therefore, who had come with Mary and had seen what he did, believed in him." But within the total framework of the gospel this surely means that such individuals cease thereby to be Jews. It is also true that the gospel presupposes a significant level of familiarity with beliefs and practices of first century Judaism. But this should cause no surprise. There is no paradox in the statement that John's gospel "is most anti-Jewish just at the points it is more Jewish."[51]

LATER DEBATES BETWEEN JEWS AND CHRISTIANS

We have seen that from its inception, the Christian movement provoked criticism and polemic from Jewish opponents. We have also seen that Christian responses constitute one of the principal spawning grounds of anti-Jewish arguments. Sometimes this response took the form of writings known generally as *Adversus Ioudaeos*, lengthy treatises against the beliefs and practices of Judaism.[52] At other times it took the form of written

accounts of dialogues between Christian and Jewish spokesmen. Whatever the form, we can always detect in the background clear echoes of
public debate and persistent Jewish criticism. From the confrontations
between Jesus and various Jewish figures in the gospels of the first century
to Aphraat's debater of the Jews in the fourth century, there is an unbroken string of debate, criticism, and response.

Not infrequently these debates took place in public settings, before a
gathered audience. Tertullian witnessed such a debate in North Africa;
the dialogue between Justin Martyr and Trypho unfolds in a public
square; the dialogue of Timothy (the Christian) and Aquila (a Jew) makes
explicit reference to bystanders;[53] and Origen, who mentions several such
occasions, cites one in particular when many people were present to
judge what was said.[54] At other times, the discussions took the form of
private conversations. In either case, we can conclude that public debates
between Christians and Jews were a familiar feature of the Greco-Roman
landscape for at least the first three hundred years of Christianity's
existence.

The purposes of the debates were several. In the first place, it is now
clear that Judaism and Christianity were regular competitors for the
religious loyalties of Gentiles. Literally as well as figuratively, they faced
each other in the marketplace. In the second place, both sides stood to
lose some of their own adherents if they appeared to lose badly in public debate, whereas a resounding success could only have the opposite
effect. In the third place, we may refer to our earlier comments on the
intrinsic need of a religious community to justify its symbolic universe,
that is, its system of beliefs and practices, whenever they come under
attack. And finally, we must also assume that these public debates presuppose the presence of a silent audience, namely, Christian Judaizers.
For whenever we hear criticisms of specific observances in the Mosaic
covenant we must suppose that they are being directed at least as much
at Christians as at Jews. In this sense, these debates have an unmistakable
intramural significance for Christians despite their formal character as
encounters between Christians and Jews.

On the Jewish side, these debates also appear to have been an important matter. Origen warns Christians not to arrive ill-prepared in
biblical knowledge.[55] As often as not, it would appear that Jews took

the initiative and came well-prepared. Jerome comments that they frequently showed familiarity with the New Testament.[56] The Jewish document used by Celsus as part of his attack on Christianity similiarly indicates a thorough knowledge of the gospels.

Inasmuch as these debates dealt almost exclusively with the interpretation of passages from the Jewish Bible/Old Testament, a sound knowledge of the relevant texts was essential. Memory alone would not do. Early on, perhaps as early as the first century, it appears that Christians prepared lists of biblical prooftexts (*testimonia*), organizing them by topics.[57] The regularity with which specific biblical passages, both individually and in combination with others, recur in widely separated places suggests that written collections of *testimonia* were regularly deployed in written treatises and oral debates. One such collection, written around 250 c.e. by bishop Cyprian of Carthage, is the earliest surviving example.[58] It consists of twenty-four headings, each followed by several biblical citations. These headings offer us a detailed outline of the debates from the Christian point of view:

1. That the Jews have fallen seriously under the wrath of God because they forsook the lord and followed idols.

2. Also because they did not believe the prophets and murdered them.

3. That it was foretold that they would neither know the lord, nor understand him, nor receive him.

4. That the Jews would not understand the holy scriptures and that they would become intelligible only in the last times, after Christ had come.

5. That the Jews would be able to understand nothing in the scriptures unless they first believed in Christ.

6. That the Jews would lose Jerusalem and leave the land they had inherited.

7. That they would lose the light of the lord.

8. That the first circumcision of the flesh is abrogated and a second circumcision of the spirit is promised.

9. That the former law given through Moses would cease.

10. That a new law was to be given.

11. That another dispensation and a new covenant was to be given.

12. That the old baptism would cease and a new one begin.

13. That the old yoke would be abrogated and a new one begin.

14. That the old pastors would cease and new ones begin.

15. That Christ would be the house and temple of God and that the old temple would cease and a new one be established.

16. That the old sacrifice be abrogated and a new one be celebrated.

17. That the old priesthood would cease and that a new priest would come who would be forever.

18. That another prophet like Moses was promised, one who would give a new covenant and who should be listened to instead.

19. That two people were foretold, a greater and a lesser, the old people of the Jews and the new one which would consist of us.

20. That the church which had been sterile would have more children from the Gentiles than the synagogue had previously had.

21. That the Gentiles would instead believe in Christ.

22. That the Jews would lose the bread and cup of Christ and all his grace, while we would accept them, and that the name of Christians would be blessed on earth.

23. That the Gentiles rather than the Jews would reach the kingdom of heaven.

24. That Jews are able to receive pardon for their sins only if they wash away the blood of the slain Christ through his baptism and if they come over into the church and obey his teachings.

The reason for the Jewish interest in these debates is not difficult to imagine, though there is little concrete evidence. As early as the book of Acts, it is possible to see a double concern on the part of Jewish synogogue authorities. Its religious aspect appears as the fear that Christian missionaries might, as they sometimes did, make converts; the political aspect is reflected in passages like 17:6 ("These men who have turned the world upside down have come here also. . . .") and 18:13 ("This man [Paul] is persuading men to worship God contrary to the law."). These charges are made not to the synogogue community or to a general public but to local Roman officials. Jews throughout the Empire must have been deeply concerned that Christianity would upset the delicate balance which governed relations between Jewish communities and local authorities.

Worse yet, as Christians in the second and third centuries began to advance the claim that they were the true Israel, Jews must have seen them as a direct threat to their social and political standing. If the violent language of Melito of Sardis is any measure of the intensity with which Christians pressed the line that Rome's interests were best served by protecting the new Israel, we may well imagine that for the powerful Jewish community of Sardis the issue was not just religious but social and political as well.

In stressing the social and political aspects of these debates, however, we should not neglect their religious and theological significance. A. Marmorstein has shown that specific Christian arguments in these debates must have hit their targets with some regularity.[59] The rabbis simply "could not ignore the taunt" that God had abandoned his people, a charge increasingly prominent in Christian anti-Jewish literature of the late second and third centuries.[60] And while the rabbinical texts attribute such taunts to "the nations," that is, pagans, everything points to Gentile Christians as the true antagonists. Other passages deal with further charges: Israel's exile is proof of divine rejection; the destruction of the temple is an act of divine judgment; God hates Israel; Israel's worship of the golden calf was the cause of their rejection and led to the imposition of the ritual commandments as a form of divine retribution; circumcision and the Sabbath were never intended to be interpreted or observed literally as expressions of true faith; and so on. Here, then, we must conclude that the Jewish participation in these debates, like that of the Christians, stems from an intrinsic need to defend and justify one's symbolic universe whenever it is the target of serious attack. In this sense, for Jews as well as Christians, it was a matter of life and death.

In line with the view that these debates were of great importance for all parties, internally as well as externally, we must consider one final motivating factor on the Jewish side. No doubt Jews in general were puzzled by the Christian claim that they were the true Israel, despite having renounced all of the practices that had defined Israel for centuries. But they must have been appalled to find their own scriptures cited against them, not just on specific issues but on the fundamental question of Israel's status as the chosen people. Beyond the need to refute these anti-Jewish interpretations drawn from the Jewish Scriptures, some Jews must have noticed the occasionally striking parallels between specific Christian charges and traditions reflected in post-biblical Judaism. The common argument that the ritual commandments were never meant to be taken literally in the first place, but to be understood in their moral and spiritual sense appears for the first time not Barnabas or Justin Martyr but among the allegorizing Jews whom Philo criticizes for having abandoned literal observance of the laws once they "discovered" their inner, spiritual message.[61]

To be attacked in this way, with one's own weapons, added insult to injury. Perhaps this helps to explain why, according to Jerome, Jews seemed so anxious to engage Christians in debate or why, according to Cyril of Jerusalem, Jews were always ready for controversy.[62]

There is no need here to review in detail the subject matter and themes of the debates or to trace their development over time. While there were significant variations according to time and place, there was also a remarkable thematic consistency. On the Christian side, the basic themes appear already in the first century and vary little thereafter: christological assertions about Jesus, supported by biblical texts designed to show that everything of importance was foreseen by God and predicted in the scriptures; a critique of the Mosaic covenant and in particular of its ritual commandments; proofs concerning the abrogation of that covenant, except for its moral elements, in particular the ten commandments; assertions regarding God's rejection of the Jews and their replacement by the Gentiles as the new Israel; and, following the defeat of the Bar Cochba revolt in 135, the destruction of Jerusalem and the Roman decree forbidding Jews to inhabit the city begins to be used as final proof of Judaism's abandonment by God.

On the Jewish side, the arguments were as follows: Jesus and his followers were unworthy outlaws; given the manner of his death Jesus cannot be the messiah; Christians give impossible interpretations to biblical texts and sometimes even corrupt the wording of the texts to suit their purposes; by virtue of refusing to honor the ritual commandments, Christians have forfeited any right to the prerogatives of Israel; and finally, God never intended his commandments as punishment for Israel's sins or as a temporary revelation.

Obviously, these are serious charges; and they were taken seriously on both sides. Christians in particular were stung by the accusation that they used faulty versions or bad translations of the Hebrew originals. Origen's enormous undertaking to create a reliable Greek version of the Hebrew canon must be seen as growing directly out of these controversies. Others, however, simply reversed the accusation, charging that Jews had manipulated biblical texts to their own ends.

Finally, when neither textual criticism nor exegetical discussion proved capable of settling any of the major issues, Christians resorted to the simple assertion that the Jews, as God's rejected people, were blind to the meaning of their own scriptures. At this point debate ended and diatribe began.

10

Anti-Judaism in the Theological Response to Marcion and the Christian Gnostics

At this point, one might ask why Christianity, faced with the serious and theoretically endless task of legitimizing itself in the face of a vigorous and critical Judaism, failed to resolve the dilemma once and for all by severing its ideological connection with Israel and seeking its legitimacy elsewhere, for example, in classical philosophy or mystical revelation. The answer, of course, is that all of these possibilities were explored and that some of them, like the appropriation of Middle- and Neo-Platonic philosophy by such theologians as Justin, Clement of Alexandria, Origen, Ambrose, and Augustine, eventually came to play an important role in the formulation of Christian doctrine. The other option, including a radical break with Israel, was elected by Marcion and many Christian Gnostics.

By excluding the Jewish Bible from his canon of scriptures, Marcion eliminated the issue of whether Christianity or Judaism stood as rightful heir to the promises of Israel. But as Marcion soon realized, relinquishing the Jewish Bible was not enough. The synoptic gospels and Pauline letters (especially Galatians and Romans) were riddled with quotations from and allusions to the Old Testament. Without these references, the gospels and letters would be literally and theologically incomprehensible. Yet for Marcion to have kept them as they stood would have left him with a blatant self-contradiction. True to his intellectual rigor, he systematically removed those passages which posited a continuity with Israel and justified this action with the claim that the gospels and letters had been corrupted by numerous interpolations from the hands of Judaizing Christians.

Marcion's solution was roundly rejected. Instead, what emerges in the development of the Christian Bible is a distinction between the Old and the New Testaments, and within that distinction a subordination of the Old to the New.[1] For our present concerns, the New Testament canon itself becomes an important witness of the extent to which Jewish polemic and Christian response shaped the self-understanding of what eventually became mainstream, orthodox Christianity. Indeed, the very existence of the New Testament reflects a sense that Christian exegesis of the Jewish Bible was not sufficient to establish and defend the Christian claim. Thus a new and separate body of writings was created to reflect Christianity's view of itself as the new Israel, separate from the old.

We must also remember that the writings in the New Testament were not chosen at random or for the purpose of representing all points of view. By its structure and contents it expresses and conveys a particular image of what early Christianity should have been like. It is, if you will, a polemical statement. Given the great importance generally assigned to Marcion as a force in giving shape, by way of reaction, to the final collection of New Testament writings, we must now consider whether it is possible, perhaps even necessary, to correlate Marcion's influence in the development of the canon with a more general influence, again by way of reaction and refutation, on Christian religious self-understanding vis-à-vis Judaism.

One element in the reaction against Marcion was to insist on retaining the "Old" Testament as part of a twofold canon. But the retention of the Jewish Bible had its price. Part of that price may be seen in the resurgence of anti-Jewish motifs that accompanied the refutation of Marcion's position, as demonstrated by David Efroymsen with respect to the anti-Marcionite writings of Justin Martyr, Origen and, above all, Tertullian.[2] "The God of the Hebrew Bible," he concludes, "was 'salvaged' for Christians precisely by means of the anti-Judaic myth."[3] We must also confront the likelihood that one principle used for including a particular writing in the New Testament was its expression of the same anti-Judaic myth.

MARCION AND HIS THEOLOGICAL OPPONENTS: TERTULLIAN, JUSTIN MARTYR, AND ORIGEN

All of Marcion's writings have disappeared, but they have left their mark. There can be no doubt that Marcion had a decisive influence on the development of Christianity in the second century, even if by way of the violent reaction against him. In all of the discussion of his influence, however, very little has been said about his anti-Judaism and its impact on his critics.[4] This is all the more peculiar inasmuch as anti-Judaism must be seen as the very foundation of Marcion's Christianity. Only recently, in an essay by Efroymsen, has this aspect of his gospel been taken seriously.[5]

Efroymsen summarizes the relevant aspects of Marcion's position as follows:[6]

1. The law is to be ignored as being beneath the dignity of humans and beneath the dignity of any God who could be called wise and kind.

2. The God who enacted the law must be relinquished as completely unwise, overly concerned with justice (as opposed to mercy or kindness), and (perhaps) as humankind's enemy, the Creator of this evil world.

3. The "Old" Testament is to be abandoned as scripture but "kept" as an account of that god, that world, and that history from which Christians are liberated by the God revealed in Jesus.

This is, of course, a radical point of view, one to be refuted and rejected by a long line of Marcion's theological opponents. It is an extreme form of Christian anti-Judaism, though with clear roots in earlier literature. The rejection of the "Old" Testament is perhaps anticipated, though certainly not in any systematic fashion, by Ignatius's angry reply to his Judaizing opponents in Philadelphia—"Jesus Christ is the archives!" Even the introduction of a god both distinct and superior to the god of the Jews is foreshadowed in the Gospel of John, in the assertion that the father of the Jews is the devil. Still, Marcion's critics find nothing in him worthy of the Christian tradition.

The most thorough of these critics was Tertullian. What enraged Tertullian was not so much Marcion's view of the Mosaic covenant—after all it had been abrogated by Jesus—but rather his theology of the two gods. Most relevant to us is his defense of the God of the "Old" Testament, especially in the lengthy *Against Marcion*. In Book II, Tertullian counters Marcion's claim that the Mosaic covenant is unduly harsh with the assertion that its harshness was due not to any harshness of God but to the disobedience of his people (II. 15.1–2). The law was given in order to hold in check "that stiff-necked people, devoid of faith in God" (II. 18.1). Against Marcion's insistence that the refusal of the Jews to follow Jesus must mean that they worship some God other than his, Tertullian answers that the disobedience of the Jews was predicted long in advance of Christ's appearance (III. 6.4). The cancellation of the previous dispensation is no proof of a new God, for the prophets had predicted that God would wipe out the old observances (V. 4). And against Marcion's attempt to draw Paul to his side, Tertullian replies that Paul's criticisms are directed against the Jews, not against their God (V. 8, 11, 13, 14). Thus Paul becomes for Tertullian the primary mouthpiece of the radical newness of Christianity and the total demise of Israel.

Efroymsen's analysis of Tertullian's anti-Judaism begins with a seeming paradox. Why is it, he asks, that "the largest block of anti-Jewish material . . . is to be found not in his early treatise, *Against the Jews*, but in the later *Against Marcion?*"[7] His answer is that Tertullian has taken traditional anti-Jewish motifs and used them to create an anti-Judaic myth whose function it is to recover the God, the scriptures, and the ancient pedigree of Israel from Marcion's damaging attack. In earlier times the question was whether or not the Mosaic covenant was still valid for Christians, but Marcion forced Tertullian and others to pose a new question: "If, as 'everyone' agrees, the law is to be abandoned . . . how can one take seriously the *God* who enacted this inferior law in the first place?"[8] And Tertullian's answer is the anti-Jewish myth which enables him to rescue for Christianity the God of Israel: the " 'inferiority' of God's 'old' law and/or cult cannot be due to any inferiority on God's part, but must be accounted for by the 'inferiority' of the people with whom God was working at the time."[9] Or, as Efroymsen restates the results of the myth: "God and Christ must be anti-Jewish too."[10]

Tertullian's anti-Judaism is not limited to *Against Marcion* and *Against the Jews*. Elsewhere Efroymsen has shown that it permeates every aspect of his thought.[11] For him the Jews are the very anti-type of true virtue: they resisted the prophets and Jesus; they insult and persecute Christians; they rebel against God. Their crimes are manifold. They embody the principle of *vetustas*, or obsolescence.[12] In short, what emerges in Tertullian is a rekindling of traditional Christian anti-Judaism in which the full burden of Marcion's assault of the God of the Jews is deflected onto the Jews themselves. And in his case, the intensity of language clearly crosses the boundary between anti-Judaism and anti-Semitism.

Before leaving Tertullian, we may pause to ask whether there were other factors, apart from Marcion and Tertullian's own personality, which might have prompted his anti-Judaism. While he gives no indication of Judaizing among the Christians of North Africa, there are signs of competition between Christianity and Judaism for pagan adherents.[13] A good deal of this competition must have taken place in formal, public debates. Tertullian's *Against the Jews* is in fact the result of such a debate in North Africa between a Christian and, significantly, a Jewish proselyte (I. 1). The debate lasted until nightfall and was attended by large numbers of partisans for both sides. Whether Tertullian was the Christian participant in the debate is uncertain. In any case, he informs his readers that he intends in his treatise to clarify certain issues raised in the debate. From his tone in the opening sentences of the treatise, it can be surmised that Tertullian was particularly troubled by the fact that the spokesman for the Jewish side was a Gentile and that the debate appeared to have gone against the Christians. There is thus reason to suppose that competition for pagan adherents was among the factors which helped to shape Tertullian's anti-Judaism.[14]

More briefly, we turn to Justin Martyr. With Justin we find a striking contrast between the tone and the substance of his encounter with Judaism. L. W. Barnard speaks of the "amicable spirit"[15] and good knowledge of post-Biblical Judaism[16] in Justin's works. His *Dialogue with Trypho* points to "a closer intercourse between Christians and Jews in the first half of the second century than has usually been supposed."[17] Barnard's assessment is seconded by Theodore Stylianopoulos in his study of Justin's view of the Mosaic law. He speaks of an "irenic spirit" which pervades the *Dialogue*,[18] a spirit which reflects the conviction that "a

remnant of the Jews remains to be saved in Justin's own time."[19] As for
the context of the debate, Stylianopoulos comments that it presupposes
a successful missionary activity between Jews and Christians and that
on the Jewish side the primary aim was to restore observance of the
Mosaic commandments.[20]

But Justin's polite tone and gentle manner are only part of the story.
The other part is a sustained theological anti-Judaism nourished by the
need to refute Marcion. The Mosaic law is no longer valid (*Dial.* 11);
the prophets spoke openly of Israel's lack of faith (*Dial.* 12); Jews read
their scripture at a literal level and thus fail to comprehend its true
meaning (*Dial.* 14); and the suffering of the Jews in Justin's time is to be
taken as divine punishment for their murder of Christ and persecution
of Christians (*Dial.* 16f.). In line with Tertullian, Justin asserts that the
ritual law of Moses was given only because of the Jews' hardness of
heart (*Dial.* 18). The entire law is simply God's effort to keep Jewish
sinfulness in check (*Dial.* 19–23). Thus while his tone is utterly different
from Tertullian's, the underlying position is essentially the same.[21]

Much the same picture emerges with respect to Origen, writing at
the end of the second and the beginning of the third century. At one
level, he merely confirms the existence of an important facet in Jewish-
Christian relations throughout this period: the existence of "a lively
debate" between Christians and Jews.[22] We have already noted that
Origen complains in several places of Judaizing practices among Christians.[23] Thus despite his scholarly discussions with Jews in Caesarea and
his very considerable knowledge of Judaism, he will "explicitly forbid
any mutual give-and-take between the Church and the Synagogue."[24]

As with Tertullian and Justin, Origen's anti-Judaism often expresses
itself in passages where the target is Marcion. Thus in *On First Principles*
he argues that the failure of the Jews to read their scriptures at their
true, spiritual level explains their refusal to believe in Jesus (Book 4. 2.2).
When read properly, that is, spiritually, the Jewish Bible itself prophesies
its ultimate fulfillment in Jesus and Christianity, and that fulfillment puts
an end to the ritual law and to Jewish control over their native land (4.
1.3–4). They have now been replaced as God's people by the Gentiles
(ibid.). He criticizes their ingratitude in rejecting God's chosen son

(*Cels.* 2.38), their slanders against Jesus and his followers (*Cels.* 2.29), their adherence to doctrines that he describes as "myths and trash," and their role in the death of Jesus:[25]

> On account of their disbelief in Jesus and all their other insults to him the Jews not only will suffer at the judgment. . . . Some already suffered more than others. What nation but the Jews alone has been banished from its own capital city and the native place of its ancestral worship? They suffered this because they were very ignoble people; and although they committed many sins they did not suffer for them any comparable calamities to those caused by what they had dared to do against our Jesus.[26]

Elsewhere, to be sure, Origen is capable of adopting a different stance. In the *Against Celsus*, in refuting Celsus's anti-Jewish polemic, Origen comes to the defense of the Jews. Here we find a Christian author quite explicitly and self-consciously turning aside familiar elements of pagan anti-Semitism.[27] But we must not mistake the purpose of these passages or their bearing on Origen's own anti-Judaism. Celsus had introduced his criticisms of Judaism in the first place in order to attack not Jews but Christians who were calling themselves the true Israel. Thus Origen's concern is not to champion the Jews as such but rather to rescue for Christianity those attributes of Israel that were fundamental to Christian self-understanding at the time.

Chief among these attributes was the claim to antiquity. An important strand of Christian apologetic in the second and third centuries consisted of claiming Israel's great antiquity for the church and denying it to the synagogue. Given the significance of this motif, it was essential for Origen to undermine Celsus's argument at two points: first, by showing that Christianity was not a "newcomer" with no pedigree but rather the true fulfillment of ancient Israel; and second, by refuting Celsus's charge that Israel was a barbarous nation, ignorant and unphilosophical, which had failed to contribute anything of value to human civilization (*Cels.* 4. 31). To this set of charges Origen replies that the Jews were a nation of the greatest antiquity (*Cels.* 1. 16), and that Moses was a distinguished philosopher (*Cels.* 1. 18) far superior to Plato (*Cels.* 1. 14–20) who, he claims, plagiarized his philosophical ideas from Moses (*Cels.* 4. 39).

If Origen's "defense" must be understood as benefiting Christianity rather than Judaism, so also we must not misread his mild tone. Here again Efroymsen has drawn attention to the need to distinguish between tone and substance. What separates Justin and Origen from Tertullian and Ignatius is not their fundamental religious and theological attitude toward the religious legitimacy of Judaism but rather the feelings and actions that result from these common beliefs. The issue is not whether certain writers "liked" Jews or Judaism, but rather "the development of an attitude toward Judaism (or a theology of Judaism) that led to what Jules Isaac called the 'teaching of contempt.' "[28] In this regard, Origen is absolutely typical. For while he is by and large devoid of the personal bitterness so evident in Tertullian, he is uncompromising on the underlying theological issues: Christianity has triumphed over Judaism; God has rejected the Jewish people and made manifest his decree in their defeat and expulsion from Jerusalem; Jewish beliefs and practices are of no religious value for Christians or Jews. In principle, there was nothing to prevent Jews from abandoning the literal interpretation of the scriptures. But for Origen, to perceive that meaning is simultaneously to abandon Judaism.

CHRISTIAN GNOSTICISM IN THE NAG HAMMADI DOCUMENTS[29]

The discovery of the Nag Hammadi writings in 1945 added a new chapter to the story of religious movements in late antiquity.[30] Christian Gnosticism in particular, once known primarily through the reports and refutations of its "orthodox" opponents, is now directly accessible through a number of writings written by Gnostics themselves. Although the study of these documents is still in its infancy—perhaps we should say because it is still in its infancy—there are significant disagreements on every issue of importance. One of the most hotly disputed has been the question of the relationship between Gnosticism and Judaism. No one doubts that certain of the Nag Hammadi writings show Jewish influence. Even Hans Jonas, who represents the skeptical extreme in the debate, is willing to concede that Gnosticism seems to be "derived from a Jewish milieu" and that it owes "not a little to Judaism."[31] Many are willing to go much further than Jonas and to point not just to Jewish influence but to Jewish

origins for Gnosticism as such.[32] Some have located these origins in circles
of Jewish apocalypticism;[33] others have pointed in the direction of Jewish
wisdom piety and especially its use of the heavenly Sophia;[34] still others
find the roots of Gnosticism in the radically skeptical wing of the Jewish
wisdom movement (Koheleth);[35] and some even speak of its development
from "the esoteric traditions of Palestinian Pharisees."[36]

Of course, it must be added that none of these theories posits a
straight-line theory of development from Judaism, of whatever sort, to
Gnosticism. The specifically Gnostic principle of revolt against the
cosmos and of value-inversion must be added to the equation in order for
it to yield a Gnostic result. Thus G. Marcrae surmises that the Jewish figure
of Sophia must have been combined with a mythical version of Eve in
order to arrive at the fallen Sophia of Gnosticism. Even Gilles Quispel,
among the earliest and most vigorous defenders of the theory of Jewish
origins, admits that the "Gnostics have removed themselves [far] from
these origins."[37] And Birger Pearson, who is inclined to locate the gnostic
revolt within Judaism, nonetheless adds that "it is axiomatic that once
Gnosticism is present 'Judaism' has been abandoned."[38]

Despite an emerging consensus in this area we cannot speak of
unanimity. Even if he stood alone, Hans Jonas would carry great authority, for he more than any other has shaped the modern study of
Gnosticism. Jonas describes the typical Gnostic use of biblical material as
follows: vilification, parody, caricature, conscious perversion of meaning,
wholesale reversal of value-signs, savage degrading of the sacred, and
gleefully shocking blasphemy.[39] This leads him not only to reject the
likelihood of Jewish origins but to characterize the Gnostic view of
Judaism as saturated with an "anti-Jewish animus."[40] Reporting a conversation with Gershom Scholem, Jonas reports that this great student of
Jewish mysticism saw Gnosticism as "the greatest case of metaphysical
anti-Semitism."[41] In sum, while admitting that Gnosticism reacted against
Judaism wherever the two met, and while admitting that Gnosticism may
have originated as a revolt against Judaism—"in a zone of proximity and
exposure to Judaism"[42]—Jonas remains unconvinced that the revolutionaries were themselves Jewish.

Perhaps the distance between Jonas and the advocates of Jewish
origins is not as great as either side imagines. Jonas rejects Quispel's state-

ment that esoteric Jewish mysticism "led to the origin of Gnosticism."[43] But Pearson and others lay great stress on the element of revolt and departure from Judaism which accompanies the birth of Gnosticism. It must also be said, against Jonas, that not all references to Judaism in the Nag Hammadi writings are hostile. The *Exegesis of the Soul* (CGII. 6) cites several biblical texts, alongside Homer and the New Testament, in a straightforward manner.[44] Jonas himself writes that the "elevation of Sabaoth" in the *Hypostasis of the Archons* (CGII. 4) and *On the Origin of the World* (CGII. 5) betrays "a streak of sympathy for Judaism."[45] The *Tripartite Tracate* (CGI.5), after speaking of "what has come from the race of the Hebrews and what is written by the hylics," that is, lower non-Gnostic persons, as though the two categories were identical, goes on to cite "other men of the Hebrew race . . . namely, the righteous ones and the prophets" who spoke properly, "in faith," of the things above.[46] And in one of the few writings where we find any consistent concern with Jews, as opposed to the Jewish deity or the Jewish Scriptures, the Hebrews are said to be, not Jews, but "the apostles and the apostolic men," namely, non-Gnostic Christians![47]

As for the anti-Jewish material, it may be divided roughly into two categories: first, disparaging comments about Jews or Jewish practices, and second, interpretations of biblical passages based on the principle of value-inversion. The first category comprises very few passages. In this respect gnostic anti-Judaism is utterly dissimilar to what we find more generally in Christian literature of the same period. Furthermore, virtually all of these passages appear in two writings, the *Gospel of Philip* (CGII. 3) and the *Gospel of Thomas* (CGII. 2) and derive directly from New Testament sources, for example, *Gospel of Thomas* 40.7 = Matt. 23:13; 40:24 = John 8:19, 25; Matt. 7:16–20; *Testimony of Truth* (CGIX. 3) 29.12–15 = Matt. 16:1ff. Only in the *Gospel of Philip* is there a conscious effort to separate the community of the gospel from the Jews: 52.21f.—"When we were Hebrews we were orphans . . ."; and 75.30–34—"And, [as a] Christian [people] we [ourselves do not descend] from the Jews."

The second category of anti-Jewish material is considerably larger. It includes numerous passages in which the god of the cosmos utters the words of Isa. 45:21; cf. 46:9 ("I am God and there is no other!") as proof that he cannot be the true god (for example, *Gospel of the Egyptians* [CGIII. 2] 58.24); passages in which the words of Moses are refuted (for example, *Apocryphon of John* [CGII. 1] 22f.); texts that mock the biblical god as envious, ignorant, malicious, blind and jealous (*Testimony of Truth* 47.14–48.15); a writing that dismisses as a laughingstock every hero (Adam, Abraham, Isaac, Jacob, David, Solomon, the twelve prophets, and Moses) of the Jewish Bible (*Second Treatise of the Great Seth* [VII. 2] 62.27–35); and many others.

Where, then, does this leave us with respect to anti-Judaism in the Nag Hammadi documents? In one sense, it makes little difference whether Gnosticism itself originated inside or outside Judaism. We are no longer surprised to discover Jewish elements and anti-Jewish polemic side by side. But it is important properly to characterize this particular version of anti-Judaism. We have already noted differences between the Gnostic version and that which appears in mainstream Christian literature of the second and third centuries. In general scope and specific detail there is little comparison. Beyond this, it seems impossible to place the anti-Judaism of Gnosticism in any of the categories outlined earlier. It is certainly not intra-Jewish or Jewish Christian and it goes well beyond gentilizing anti-Judaism. In contrast to each of these categories, which share the common theme of an effort to rescue the name and attributes of Israel for a particular group of believers, Gnostic anti-Judaism stands outside and against Israel altogether. The polemic here is directed not against Jews, or only rarely, but against the heroes, the scriptures, and the god of the Jewish Bible according to the principle of value-inversion. It is thus to be distinguished from anti-Semitism in that its animus is not against Jews as persons, and from Christian anti-Judaism in that it has little interest in claiming itself to be the true Israel. Here the revolt proceeds well beyond the abrogation of the law or the rejection of Israel— indeed these themes hardly appear at all. Here the revolt is against everything about the cosmos, including and especially its creator.

Could such a revolt have originated within Judaism? The answer depends on the fertility of one's imagination. Here we may simply note that the possibility of a revolt against Judaism, in the manner characteristic of gnosticizing anti-Judaism, is by no means limited to Jews. Jonas, searching for concrete instances of proximity to and resentment against

Judaism, mentions the Samaritans and reminds us that Simon the Magician from Samaria was the candidate of many Christian writers as the fountainhead of all subsequent Gnosticism.[48] Finally, it must be remembered that it was precisely in the second and third centuries that pagan intellectuals first developed a thorough knowledge of the Jewish Bible and, among Platonists, began a lively debate over the nature and status of the Jewish god, ultimately denying that he was the highest god and locating him somewhere within the realm of the visible cosmos.

By way of testing the plausibility of Jonas's doubts concerning possible connections between Judaism and Christian Gnosticism, it may be useful to look briefly at the Gospel of John and Marcion. Alan Segal's hints regarding the genesis of Christian Gnosticism are very much like the current views concerning the circumstances surrounding the original Gospel of John: first, "proto-Gnostic interpretations of angelic mediation originated in a thoroughly Hellenized kind of Judaism or among gentiles attracted to synagogue services";[49] then, "gnosticism arose in Judaism out of a polarization of the Jewish community over the issue of the status of God's primary angel."[50] In both cases, the expulsion of one group from a synagogue leads to the formulation of a dualistic myth in which the deity of the "mother" community is devalued and demoted. How different are the results! In John's version of anti-Judaism the full brunt is borne by "the Jews," whereas in Gnosticizing anti-Judaism the target is divine.

Consider the contrasting case of Marcion, a Gentile, whose name is absent from much of the recent debate about the Jewish origins of Gnosticism. The issue is not whether Marcion is himself a Gnostic but whether similarities between his views and those of the Nag Hammadi writings can shed any light on their respective forms of anti-Judaism. Like the Gnostics, Marcion's theology posits two gods, with the lower god clearly identifiable as the creator god of the Jewish Bible. Like the Gnostics, Marcion uses a number of biblical texts to establish the inferiority of that god. More to the point, he cites the oath of Isaiah 45:5 ("I am the Lord, and there is no other, besides me there is no God. . . ."), a favorite text of the Gnostics, to establish his case.[51] Elsewhere, he cites additional passages that reappear in Nag Hammadi documents: Gen. 1:26; 2:7; 3:22.[52] And in interpreting these texts, Marcion uses the same hermeneutical principle—a fundamental and systematic inversion of values: biblical heroes become villains, while the reprobates are saved.[53] In general terms, the sole value accorded to the Jewish Bible is that it preserves a vivid record of divine and human existence in this fallen world. As a result, Marcion's anti-Judaism, like that of the Nag Hammadi documents but unlike that in the Gospel of John, focuses almost exclusively on the god and the scriptures of Judaism and says little of Jews as such. Indeed, as we have seen earlier, it was rather among the Christian *opponents* of Marcion that the focus shifted from the god of the Jews to the Jews themselves.

Before leaving Marcion and the Christian Gnostics, we must say a word or two about a further connecting link between them—Paul. For Marcion, Paul was simply "the apostle." The letters of Paul, purged of their "Judaizing" accretions, were the heart of Marcion's New Testament. Paul had proclaimed Christ to be the end of the law (Rom. 10:4), and Marcion therefore saw no need for the Old Testament or for its god or its people. Taking this together with his view of Paul as the apostle to the Gentiles, Marcion simply cut loose all connections between Christianity and Judaism—no Old Testament, no Israel, no God of the law and creation. Christianity was radically new. All of this was proclaimed by Marcion in the name of Paul and on the basis of Pauline texts. In his own mind, this radical gospel was nothing more than an effort to restore Christianity to its pure, that is, Pauline beginnings.

Much the same picture emerges from the Nag Hammadi materials. These documents now make it possible to confirm the reports of various heresiologists (Irenaeus, Hippolytus, Clement of Alexandria, and so on) concerning Paul's influence among various Christian Gnostics.[54] Valentinus claimed to have derived all of his teachings from Theodas, a follower of Paul.[55] The *Gospel of Truth*, found among the Nag Hammadi writings and frequently taken as a work of Valentinus, contains numerous allusions to Pauline texts. Basileides cites Paul in support of his views on the transmigration of souls. For Theodotus, Paul himself appeared as the Paraclete (Holy Spirit), preaching the gospel.[56] Some of these interpretations are based on secret oral traditions alleged to go back to Paul himself, whereas others are achieved by applying special rules of exegesis to his written letters. In either case, Paul emerges as the apostolic witness not simply for radical types of Christianity in the second and third centuries, but types whose distinguishing mark is an effort to sever all ties between Christianity and Judaism. In the apostle to the Gentiles these radical exponents of Gentile Christianity discovered their founder and hero. Just how persuasive their image of Paul has been, centuries after Marcion and the Gnostics, we will see in the following chapters.

Paul's Friends and Enemies

Throughout the preceding chapters, the figure of Paul has loomed large in every phase of the controversy regarding Christianity and Israel. Of course his influence was felt on other issues also but nowhere more than here. His persuasive presence led earlier historians of Christianity to define Paul as the second founder of Christianity. But which Christianity? Marcion's? The Christian Gnostic's? The radically ascetic faith depicted in the later *Acts of Paul and Thecla*? What are we to make of Tertullian, himself a vigorous defender of emergent orthodoxy in the Latin-speaking West, who does not hesitate to dub Paul "the apostle of the heretics." Or, to put the same question in a slightly different form, which Paul? The author of Galatians and Romans? Of Ephesians? Of the Pastoral Epistles? The figure depicted in Acts of whom certain Jews reported that he fought against the Jews, their law and their temple (21:21)? Or the figure whom the author of Acts describes as having circumcised his co-worker Timothy, the son of a Jewish mother and a Gentile father (16:3)? It is not surprising, then, that certain Christian leaders in the second century seemed reluctant to make use of him.[1]

Given this confusing picture, it seems wise to track Paul's influence in the centuries following his death before turning to Paul himself. We will do so by limiting ourselves to the issues of Christianity and Israel, and by looking first at Paul's "friends," then at his "enemies," and finally at the conditions under which his writings were ultimately included in the New Testament canon.

PAUL'S "FRIENDS"

Paul's friends—those who invoked his name and cited his letters in support of their theological position—fall into two distinct categories: those who will eventually come to be regarded as heretics by mainstream Christianity and those whose views will eventually flow into and merge with the mainstream itself.

As many observers have noted, the most striking thing about Paul's influence in the second century is not those figures who rely on his authority but those who ignore him—Ignatius, Polycarp, Hegesippus, Justin, and Athenagoras.[2] Only with Irenaeus, toward the end of the century, does the effort begin to reclaim Paul for "orthodox" Christianity. Among those who had early claimed him as their spokesman, Marcion and the Christian Gnostics were prominent. As we have already seen, Paul was everything for Marcion—his apostle, his scripture and his theological guide in such matters as the radical newness of Christianity, the opposition between law and gospel, asceticism as a mark of the Christian life, and strenuous resistance to any form of Judaizing among believers. Put simply, the most thoroughgoing and systematic repudiation of Judaism in early Christianity was articulated under the banner of Pauline authority.

Paul assumes the same role among the Christian Gnostics. For Valentinus, Basileides, the Naassenes, and numerous writings from the Nag Hammadi codices, Paul was scripture. Himself a true gnostic, it was he who received the esoteric teachings directly from the risen Christ, transmitted them in oral form to an inner circle of chosen followers, and instructed them to discern the inner meaning of scripture through spiritual exegesis. Indeed it is probably among the Valentinians that systematic exegesis of Paul's letters had its beginning.

Beyond the use of spiritual or allegorical techniques of interpretation, for which Paul himself was cited in evidence (2. Cor. 3), his "heretical friends" made use of two further techniques. Marcion argued that the copies of Paul's letters in circulation toward the middle of the second century no longer represented the original texts. They had been tampered with by Judaizing Christians who had inserted positive references to the

Old Testament and its God. In accordance with this assertion, Marcion "restored" the letters to their original purity by removing all positive references to the Old Testament.[3]

Irenaeus, to be sure, calls this an act of mutilation. But we need to remind ourselves that additions to and excisions from ancient texts were not a rare occurrence. We have already seen that mutual accusations of textual tampering plagued attempts by Christians and Jews to discuss the meaning of biblical texts. And the author of the book of Revelations, anticipating just such a fate for himself, concludes with a somber warning:

> if anyone adds to them [the words of the book] God will add to him the plagues described in this book, and if anyone takes away from the words of the book of this prophecy, God will take away his share in the tree of life and in the holy city, which are described in this book. [2.18]

A far more common procedure was simply to produce a new writing, reflecting one's own point of view, and to attribute it to Paul. Of this there are numerous examples. Both sets of Paul's friends resorted frequently to such inventions. The so-called Muratorian canon, a discussion of canonical and non-canonical writings dating from around 200, complains of letters forged by Marcionites in Paul's name.[4] The *Acts of Paul* were similarly penned in Paul's name, probably with the purpose of claiming Paul's authority for the ascetic orientation which they advocate. Tertullian, protesting the use made of these *Acts* as a basis for allowing women to teach and to administer baptism, writes the following:

> in Asia, the presbyter who composed that writing, as if he were augmenting Paul's fame from his own store, after being convicted and confessing that he had done it from love of Paul, was removed from his office.[5]

The second group of Paul's friends can only be understood with reference to the first. More specifically, Paul's orthodox supporters, making use of the very same techniques as his heretical interpreters, undertook a systematic campaign to reclaim him for their own cause. The campaign insisted that Paul had been repeatedly and deliberately distorted by heretics who simply misunderstood his letters. And when counter-exegesis failed to convince, "orthodox" documents were written in his name so as to deter any future misunderstandings. Among the New Testament writings, 2 Peter contends that "the ignorant and unstable" twist Paul's letters to their own destruction. Ephesians and the Pastoral epistles (1–2 Timothy and Titus) are later productions whose obvious purpose is to present Paul as the implacable foe of heresy. And the letter of James aims a polemical thrust at unnamed antinomian believers who must have cited Paul on their own behalf (2:14–26).

In examining some of those orthodox inventions, we will distinguish between two groups; the earlier, in which it is not always possible to detect an anti-heretical purpose (Ephesians, Hebrews), and later ones in which Paul's "heretical friends" are clearly in the background.

Ephesians

Although it presents itself as written by Paul (1:1), the letter to the Ephesians is one of several New Testament writings whose Pauline authorship is still debated today. In itself, the question of authorship is of no interest to us here. What must concern us is the extent to which a decision for or against Pauline authorship yields consequences for the interpretation of particular passages. What difference does it make for our reading of Ephesians 2:14–15 ("For he is our peace, who has made us both one, and has broken down the dividing wall of hostility, by abolishing in his flesh the law of commandments and ordinances, that he might create in himself one new man in place of two. . . .") if we assume Pauline or non-Pauline authorship? Or does it matter? The question is not a simple one. In the first place, we need to know which Paul we are speaking of—the Paul of traditional exegesis for whom Christ is "the end of the law" (Rom. 10:4) or the Paul of those exegetes who begin with passages like Rom. 11:1 ("I ask, then, has God rejected his people? By no means!"). If our Paul is the latter rather than the former *and* if we take Ephesians to be genuinely Pauline, we will have no choice but to interpret 2.14f. in a manner which flies in the face of virtually all previous interpreters. Conversely, if ours is the former Paul, we will give a traditional reading of the passage and resolve the issue of authorship on altogether independent grounds.

The key passage in the letter reads as follows: "For he is our peace,

who has made us both one, and has broken down the dividing wall of
hostility, by abolishing in his flesh the law of commandments and ordinances, that he might create in himself one new man in place of the two,
so making peace. . . ." Of the many questions arising from the text, only
two are of interest to us here:

(1) Does the passage deal with the relationship between Jews and
Gentiles generally in the light of what has been accomplished by the
Christ or more narrowly with the relationship between Jews and Gentiles
in the church?

(2) Do these verses point to a total abolishment of the "law of commandments and ordinances," such that it is no longer valid for any Jew
or Gentile, or rather to its removal as a barrier between Jews and Gentiles
in the church?

Unlike Colossians, the recipients of which are reprimanded explicitly
for Judaizing tendencies ("Let no one pass judgment on you in questions
of food and drink or with regard to a festival or a new moon or a
sabbath. . . ." (2:16), the specific situation addressed in Ephesians is not
clear.[6] Instead the discussion turns in a general way on the new status
of "you Gentiles" (2:11) in relation to the commonwealth of Israel and
the covenants of promise (2:12) and of both, that is, Israel and the
Gentiles, to each other following the reconciling action of Christ.
Throughout the passage the author speaks of and to his Gentile addressees
in the second person plural, while also using the first person plural to
indicate Gentiles and Jewish Christians.[7] Whereas verses 11–12 focus on
the alienated, hopeless, and godless condition of Gentiles ("you") prior
to the Christ, and thus clearly presuppose the primacy of Israel in God's
action, verses 13–22 stress the new situation in which the former enmity
between Jew and Gentile has been overcome. Gentiles no longer stand
outside the household of God (2:19) as strangers, separated by the
dividing wall of hostility. Jews and Gentiles, formerly two, are now
made one.

The question now arises whether Israel retains its primacy in the
era after Christ and if so, in what sense. There can be no doubt that the
basic thrust of the passage is that the Gentiles who once stood outside
Israel and the covenants have been brought near and made full citizens.

In other words, Gentiles have now been incorporated into Israel *on their own terms*. The dividing wall of hostility formerly represented by the law of commandments and ordinances, that is, the Mosaic covenant as expressed in the Hebrew Scriptures, has been broken down. Thus the answer to our question concerning Israel's continuing primacy must be affirmative, but with two important modifications. First, in contrast to previous Jewish expectations, the incorporation of the Gentiles has not taken place through conversion. Gentiles have been drawn near *as Gentiles*. The dividing wall has been broken down in the sense that Gentiles are no longer required to observe the commandments and ordinances as a condition of covenantal citizenship.[8] And second, even in positing the continued primacy of Israel, the author obviously conceived of Israel in a new way, by incorporating Gentiles as Gentiles. In this sense there is no real tension, as some have supposed, between 2:11–13 which speak of bringing the Gentiles into the covenant, and 2:14–16 which describe Christ as creating in himself one new man in place of the two. For the new man, here understood as a corporate entity, is none other than this "new Israel."

Of course this interpretation stands in sharp contrast to virtually all previous exegesis of Ephesians. Traditional as well as many modern exegetes have argued that the abrogated law refers to the so-called ceremonial regulations, for example, food regulations and circumcision, whereas the so-called moral law, the ten commandments, remains in effect. According to this analysis, the entire ritual law has been cancelled. Other difficulties apart, however, this traditional interpretation violates a fundamental principle of all exegesis, namely, close attention to the literary context of a passage and to the situation of its addressees. The universalizing exegesis of 2:14–15, that is, that the full law has been terminated for all time, totally ignores the specific circumstances of this passage and of the letter as a whole.[9]

From this important insight two others follow: first, that the author nowhere speaks openly of Israel apart from Christ; and second, that there is no hint of rejecting either Israel or the Torah. Here it is essential to stress the "empirical" nature of the assertion that the wall of hostility has been broken down, for the early churches consisted of Jews and

Gentiles. Jews and Gentiles now existed side-by-side on an equal footing; the Mosaic commandments no longer stood between them as a barrier, whether religious or social.[10]

The view of Ephesians developed here clearly sets this writing apart from a number of positions attested elsewhere in early Christianity. It is fundamentally incompatible with the position of those who insisted that Gentile converts were required to observe some or all of the Mosaic commandments. Nor is there any sign of a replacement theory. In Ephesians, Gentiles have been incorporated into Israel. Finally, there is no evidence to suggest that the author's conception of the "new man" (2:15), understood as a reference to Israel in its new form, involves an understanding of Christianity as an altogether new entity, a *genus tertium*, consisting of Jews and Gentiles, but identical with neither. One thing is thus clear: if the author was Paul, he simply did not address the general issue of Israel and the Jews as in Romans and Galatians.

How, then, may we understand the relationship between Ephesians and the other Pauline letters if we assume a non-Pauline authorship? Was it an effort to clarify ambiguities in Paul's statements about the status of Jewish and Gentile believers? Is it intended as a correction to specific misunderstandings? Independent of this letter, we know that Paul was the center of two controversies during his lifetime: one concerned relations between Jews and Gentiles in the church, while the other involved the refusal by some of the early followers of Jesus to associate with Gentile converts unless they observed the Mosaic commandments. Not coincidentally, these two issues lie at the heart of Ephesians. Thus we may perhaps see in this letter an effort to clarify certain continuing difficulties in post-Pauline circles concerning the understanding of the church in relation to Israel.

Hebrews

The letter to the Hebrews is an enigma in all respects, very much like the fatherless and motherless figure of Melchizedek who dominates its central chapter. Though it made its way into the collection of New Testament writings as a letter of Paul, it is clearly neither Pauline nor epistolary.[11] Nothing in it enables us to identify its author, its date, its place of origin, or its intended audience. Furthermore, its heavy concentration on cultic language and imagery—the temple, sacrifices, and the nature of priesthood—make it unlike any other piece of early Christian literature, canonical or otherwise. Yet in one essential respect this document is utterly typical, for it reflects the general preoccupation of Christian-writers in the late first century with demonstrating the absolute superiority of Christianity over Judaism.

The nature of the situation to which Hebrews is addressed has been the subject of much discussion. That the community had experienced external pressure or persecution of some sort is clear. Several passages suggest that by the time of writing these difficulties lay in the past, "But recall the former days when, after you were enlightened, you endured a hard struggle with sufferings. . . ." (10:32) and also that they had not led to the death of any of its members, "In your struggle against sin you have not yet resisted to the point of shedding blood. . . ." (12:4). Whether the source of these persecutions is to be located in a nearby Jewish community is less certain. While we know that various punishments were administered by synagogue authorities to renegade Jews, that is, Christians (for example, Paul in 2 Cor. 11:24; John 7:22; 12:42; 16:2), we also know that pressures of various kinds were applied by Gentiles as well (2 Cor. 11:26—"danger from my own people, danger from Gentiles").

Of more immediate concern to the author is a fear that the community is slipping away from what he defines as the true faith, "Therefore we must pay closer attention to what we have heard, lest we drift away from it!" (2:1). The argument of the document as a whole, the superiority of Christianity over Judaism, leaves no doubt that this slippage involves Judaism. Apart from this, the text provides almost no further information. It is not clear whether this is a sliding back into Judaism by Jewish converts, or a divergence into Judaizing by Gentile converts. At most we may say, on the basis of what we have learned of Judaizing tendencies among Christian and non-Christian Gentiles, that the addressees are not necessarily Jews slipping back into Judaism. In any case, we should not imagine that these were Christians about to abandon Christianity altogether. Instead, like those addressed in Paul's letters to the Galatians and to the Philippians, they were inclined to view their Christianity as not incompatible with a certain level of involvement in Jewish beliefs and practices.

Against this Judaizing inclination, which we must now regard as widespread in early Christianity, the author mounts an extended polemic, complete with threats of eschatological judgment (2:2f.).

The heart of the argument appears in chapters 7–10, where it is stated that the old covenant, imperfect and flawed from the beginning, has been superseded by a new and better covenant, inaugurated by Jesus as the perfect high priest. Of the inadequacies and provisional character of the old covenant, the old temple, and the old sacrifices, the author leaves no doubt:

• "Now if perfection had been attainable through the Levitical priesthood (for under it the people received the law), what further need would there have been for another priest to arise after the order of Melchizedek . . ." (7:11);

• "They serve a copy and shadow of the heavenly sanctuary" (8:5);

• "For if that first covenant had been faultless, there would have been no occasion for a second" (8:7);

• For since the law has but a shadow of the good things to come instead of the true form of these realities . . ." (10:1);

The complement to these negative statements is the claim that Jesus, the perfect high priest, has inaugurated a new and better covenant, which renders the old one obsolete:

• "Jesus has been counted worthy of as much more glory than Moses as the builder of the house has more honor than the house" (3:3);

• "This makes Jesus the surety of a better covenant" (7:22);

• "In speaking of a new covenant he treats the old one as obsolete. And what is becoming obsolete and growing old is ready to vanish away" (8:13);

• "Therefore he is the mediator of a new covenant . . . since a death has occurred which redeems them from the transgressions under the old covenant" (9:15);

• "For Christ has entered, not into a sanctuary made with hands, a copy of the true one, but into heaven itself . . ." (9:24);

•". . . Jesus the mediator of a new covenant" (12:24).

Although the process of replacing the old covenant with the new is not yet complete, the fundamental imperfection of the old, not only now but from its very beginning, is clearly established. Israel failed to see beyond the shadow. Christians participate in the true, heavenly reality. Thus, the author concludes, any return to the old covenant would represent a senseless and dangerous exchange of good coin for bad, of reality for shadow.

The overall argument of Hebrews presents us with the most sustained case of early Christian writings against the continued validity of the old covenant. And yet there is no trace anywhere of either Jewish Christian or Gentile anti-Judaism. Unlike most other Christian writings of the same period, Hebrews says nothing at all about the Jews as such and shows no inclination to identify the recipients of the new covenant as Gentiles. Certainly there is no sign that Jews are rejected by God or stand under a curse.[12] In fact, chapter 11 contains a long list of biblical figures who exemplify the very attitude of faith that the author is urging upon his readers. This, I would argue, is entirely consistent with the observation that the target of the polemic is Judaism per se rather than the Jews as a people. One might be tempted to conclude that Hebrews represents a critique of Judaism from within, not unlike that of those first century Jews known to Philo who held that observance of the old, "physical" commandments was no longer necessary once their true spiritual meaning was brought to light.[13]

Nevertheless, we must not fail to appreciate the radical character of the position taken by the author with regard to the old covenant as such. His familiarity with the Jewish Scriptures and techniques of interpretation are put to use in the service of the doctrine that a new covenant has rendered the old one obsolete (8:13a): "What is becoming obsolete and growing old is ready to vanish away" (8:13b). Nothing else remains of the old covenant, which was never more than "a shadow of the good things to come" (10:1).

The author of Hebrews was undoubtedly a Jew. But in the final analysis his Jewishness reduces itself to his background and culture. Take away that background and culture, and we are well on the way toward Marcion. As we have just seen, the Gospel of John already points in that direction, while Barnabas and Ignatius will begin to make

explicit what is merely implicit in Hebrews. In any case, it is not difficult to understand why the letter to the Hebrews should have been
accepted as Pauline, despite the obvious difficulties of which even the
defenders of Pauline authorship were aware. For it offers the most
sustained and systematic case against Judaizing to be found anywhere in
Christian literature of the first century. What is merely alluded to in
Colossians, "These [ritual observances] are only a shadow of what is to
come; but the substance belongs to Christ" (2:17), is here stated with
unmistakable clarity.

Acts

In Luke's book of Acts, we find ourselves in rather different circumstances. Whereas Ephesians was written in Paul's name and Hebrews was
honored as though from Paul, Luke writes *about* him. Here, for the first
time, it is possible to see a conscious desire to correct misunderstandings.

What picture does Acts give concerning Paul, the Jews, and the
status of the Mosaic commandments?[14] We may begin with the following
list of important themes:

• Paul's missionary activity always begins in synagogues; he turns to
Gentiles only after being turned out by the Jews (17:17);

• He recognizes and submits to the authority of the Jerusalem leaders
(chapter 15);

• He circumcises his co-worker Timothy (16:3);

• He agrees to the so-called apostolic decree concerning limited ritual
observances for Gentile converts (15:22-16:4);

• He cuts his hair in accordance with an ancient Nazirite vow (18:18;
21:18–28);

• He travels to Jerusalem in order to participate in religious festivals
(20:16);

• When on trial, he stresses that he is a Pharisee (23:6; 26:5).

This is not the place to rehearse the lengthy debates concerning the
historical accuracy of Luke's picture. My own view is that there are
sound reasons for doubting every element in this picture. At the very

least we may agree with the contention that Luke's version of the Jerusalem meeting—just one item from the list—was precisely what Paul was trying to counter in Galatians 2.[15]

More interesting is yet another suggestion, first made by John Knox. Finding a coherent structure in Luke's presentation of Paul, he asked whether this structure might have been designed as an antidote to some earlier, unacceptable version of Paul's understanding of Israel and the Torah. The answer, of course, is yes, and the author of that version is Marcion. Marcion, Knox notes, had insisted that Paul was utterly independent of the original disciples (Gal. 1:16f.; 2:1f.) and was equally adamant about his freedom from constraints of any sort. Thus Knox argues that Acts—or at least its treatment of Paul—was produced quite specifically to counteract Marcion's treatment of Paul, to reclaim him from the camp of the heretics. In its final form, Acts "reflects an awareness of the attitude of Marcion (and perhaps others) to the Old Testament, toward Paul . . . and a knowledge of the use such men were making of a particular gospel [Luke] and of Paul's letters."[16]

To Knox's proposal we may add one footnote: one important factor shaping Luke's picture of Paul is a desire to exonerate him from accusations that he fought against the Jews, their law, and their temple (21:20f.; 18:13). These accusations may have originated at first in Jewish counterattacks against the renegade Pharisee; Luke's purpose would have been to show that such charges were groundless. But Acts is a Christian document, written for a Christian audience, and thus we ought to look within Christian circles for those who proclaim Paul as the apostle who fought against the law. Once again, the needle points to Marcion or, as Knox allows, to others who held similar views at about the same time.

What can we say about the consequence of Luke's efforts to reclaim Paul from his heretical friends? The fundamental issue was the legitimacy of Gentile Christianity itself. Radically repudiated by Jews for having abandoned the Mosaic covenant, some Gentile believers responded with the equally radical affirmation that true Pauline Christianity had no connection or continuity whatsoever with Israel, Judaism, or the Mosaic commandments. In turn, Luke's challenge to Marcion, as well as his case for the legitimacy of Gentile Christianity, takes the form of emphasizing "both an exaggerated sense of continuity of the church with Israel and a radical discontinuity with contemporary Jews, the election of the church as the people of God and the rejection of the Jews as those cut off from that people (Acts 3:23)."[17]

Central to Luke's challenge is the figure of Paul—the Pharisee called by God to preach Jesus as the fulfillment of Israel's hopes and expectations; the apostle who turns to the Gentiles only after being turned out by the Jews; and the spokesman for Gentile Christianity whose mission is confirmed in Acts by Luke's careful transformation of the Jews from sympathizers of the followers of Jesus in Jerusalem at the beginning to enemies of Paul at the end. Gaston observes that, ironically, "of the three charges made against Paul in Acts 21–28, of preaching against the people and the law and the temple, *Luke is guilty of all three*, and particularly of 'teaching men everywhere against the people'."[18]

Paul's "Enemies"

Paul's enemies were by no means limited to the Jews. To judge from his own letters, he was far more concerned with his opponents among the faithful than with those outside. It is for these Christian foes that he reserves his harshest language. In Philippians he calls them "dogs" and "evil-workers . . . who mutilate the flesh" (3:2). In 2 Corinthians, those who have challenged his authority are called, with deep sarcasm, "super-apostles" (11.5).

Nor did these enemies disappear at his death. Centuries later Judaizing Christians of various sorts would continue to anathematize Paul for teaching against the people, the law, and the temple. As late as the early fifth century, these Christians and their treatment of Paul would be the cause of a painful exchange of letters between no lesser figures than Augustine and Jerome.

If Paul's place in the Pseudo-Clementine writings, we may simply refer to what has been said earlier.[19] In *The Letter of Peter to James*, Peter violently attacks those, namely, Paul, who have spread false reports about Peter's abandonment of the Mosaic covenant. In the *Homilies*, Peter assails Paul's credentials as an apostle and describes him as a spokesman for the lying female prophet.

Elsewhere, the following groups join in repudiating Paul:

(a) The followers of *Cerinthus*, according to Epiphanius, use the gospel of Matthew, assert that Jesus was circumcised and insist that Christians must also be circumcised. "They break with Paul because he does not accept circumcision, but they also reject him because he said, "You who would be justified by the law have fallen away from grace" [Gal. 5:4] and 'If you receive circumcision, Christ will be of no advantage to you' [Gal. 5:2]."[20]

(b) The *Ebionites*, representing a broad movement of Judaizing Christians, also denounced Paul as an apostate from the law. Some of them even developed a legend to explain Paul's opposition to the law:

> They declare that he was a Greek. . . . He went up to Jerusalem, they say, and when he had spent some time there, he was seized with a passion to marry the daughter of the priest. For this reason he became a proselyte and was circumcised. Then, when he failed to get the girl, he flew into a rage and wrote against circumcision and against the Sabbath and the Law.[21]

(c) Certain *Encratites*, according to Hippolytus, rejected his epistles.[22]

(d) The *Elchasaites*, another Judaizing group described by several heresiologists, uttered blasphemies against Paul.[23]

(e) Irenaeus speaks in general of "those who do not recognize Paul as an apostle."[24]

Thus from the 30s of the first century until the late fifth century, there existed groups of Judaizing Christians among whom Paul's name was anathema. Surprisingly, a number of "orthodox" writers did not regard these groups as heretical. In reply to Trypho's question whether Judaizing Christians will be saved, Justin Martyr replies in the affirmative.[25] His only reservation was that they should not force Gentile believers to behave likewise. While expressing disapproval of Gentile Christian Judaizers, Justin does not deny them salvation. Similarly, Origen disparages but does not entirely reject those who observe the ritual laws even after recognizing their spiritual meaning.[26] But for Ignatius in the early second century, and Epiphanius in the fourth, there is manifestly no room for such Judaizers. They are, says Epiphanius, "Jews and nothing more."[27]

For some, then, the very existence of Judaizing Christians was tantamount to a denial of Christianity, or rather of Gentile Christianity. Thus
they were led of necessity to declare such believers as heretics. Still,
the fact that the New Testament writings spoke of some early followers
of Jesus as continuing to observe Jewish customs—as the Judaizers themselves were certainly quick to point out—served to call such judgments
into question. Thus Origen is forced to take the position that Jesus and
the disciples continued in their former ways merely as a concession to
their Jewish audience.[28] As a missionary strategy it was appropriate that
those sent to the circumcision should not abandon Jewish customs.

Much the same issue animates the series of letters exchanged by
Augustine and Jerome on the issue of Jewish observances among the
early apostles, including Paul himself.[29] Jerome had written in his commentary on Galatians 2:1 that the two apostles, knowing full well that
the law had been terminated by Christ, "staged" the entire dispute so as
to convince the Jerusalem believers that their practices were mistaken
without having to confront them face-to-face.[30] Against Jerome's interpretation, Augustine replied that both Peter and Paul continued in their
loyal observances after becoming apostles. Peter's only error was in
requiring observance of Gentile believers. As for Paul, he remained loyal
to the observances so as to show

> that they were not dangerous to the conscience of those who wished
> to keep them, as they had received them from their parents under the
> law, even after they had come to believe in Christ.[31]

The final phrase, "even after they had come to believe in Christ," triggered Jerome's lengthy and passionate response:

> So this is your view of the matter: After the coming of Christ's gospel,
> believing Jews are justified in keeping the commandments of the law,
> that is, if they offer sacrifices as did Paul, if they circumcise their sons,
> if they keep the sabbath. . . . If this is true, we lapse into the heresy
> of Cerinthus and Ebion. . . . If necessity requires us to admit Jews
> together with their legal prescriptions, if they are allowed to observe in
> the churches of Christ what they have initiated in the synagogues of
> Satan, I will tell you my view—they will not become Christians, they
> will make us Jews![32]

Finally, in reply to Jerome's blast, Augustine protests that he had been misunderstood, that Jewish converts were allowed to keep the ancient customs only in the time of the apostles, and that he fully endorses Jerome's opinion that "the ceremonies of the Jews are both baneful and deadly to Christians and that whoever keeps them, whether Jew or Gentile, is doomed to the abyss of the devil. . . ."[33] Elsewhere, in a letter to bishop Ascellicus, he speaks bluntly about a certain Aptus who was teaching Christians to observe certain Mosaic commandments. To this Augustine responds that the former observances have been nullified by the New Testament; only the ten commandments "are obligatory at this time."[34]

This exchange of letters, and particularly Jerome's contribution, perfectly summarizes the ongoing problem: by their very existence, observant Jewish believers undermined the official teaching that the new covenant had completely abrogated the Mosaic dispensation. Even worse was the attempt to impose these abrogated practices on Gentiles. Once again, Judaizing Christianity proves to be the catalyst for Christian anti-Judaism. Jerome, writing from Bethlehem, must have come to know this Christianity at first hand. And in his remarkable theory of the "rigged" confrontation between Peter and Paul, we seem to hear a continuing echo of those who insisted that Paul was an apostate from the Torah.

Just as Paul in his letter to the Galatians recited the events of Jerusalem and Antioch, some twenty years after the initial dispute, in order to attack Judaizing tendencies among Gentile believers, so Jerome rehearses the same events more than three hundred and fifty years later for the same purposes. In both periods, and in between, the issue was the same— the legitimacy of orthodox Christianity. For whenever believers argued, in the name of the founding apostles, that Christianity could not claim to be the true Israel without also honoring Israel's covenant, the self-understanding of those who represented mainstream, orthodox Gentile Christianity must have seemed threatened. And whenever such arguments required refutation, the greatest authority was Paul.

PAUL'S PLACE IN THE CANON

". . . if it was inevitable, given Marcion's practice, that the letters of Paul be canonized, it was likewise inevitable that they should not be canonized alone."[35] Paul's friends had seen to that. As we have seen, the assault against him came from both extremes, from those who wished to dissolve all ties between the new faith and the old covenant and from those who insisted on an unbroken continuity. On one, and only one issue was there agreement between the two extremes—Paul had declared the old covenant null and void.

For a variety of reasons, Paul's orthodox friends made the decision to rescue him from his heretical champions.[36] They did so by a variety of techniques: they wrote letters in his name (Ephesians, 1–2 Timothy, Titus) and they wrote about him (Acts). Beyond this, they placed his writings at the heart of the emerging New Testament canon. Paul the apostle to the Gentiles was made to serve as the scriptural centerpiece of orthodox Gentile Christianity. To the accompaniment of the repeated assertion that the heretics had simply misinterpreted the Pauline letters, these techniques presented a thoroughly orthodox Paul—enemy of useless speculation, moderate on the issue of asceticism, spokesman for the authority of bishops, and herald of the end of the law.[37]

Much energy has been expended on discussion of the first two of these techniques; relatively little attention, however, has been given to the order of writings in the New Testament and to Paul's place in that order. If, as is generally agreed, the process of creating a New Testament canon was profoundly influenced by the various internal controversies of the second and third centuries, we should not fail to inquire how the anti-heretical thrust of the canon determines not simply its individual components but their order as well. This may be so obvious that it has been taken for granted.

We first encounter Paul in the New Testament not in his own letters but in the book of Acts. As E. J. Goodspeed observed long ago, even the position of Acts in the canon cannot be merely fortuitous.[38] With its depiction of Paul's friendly relations with the Jerusalem community and of his missionary activity—as always beginning with the synagogue— Acts is the perfect rebuttal to the double assault against him. Against Marcion, it affirms Paul's full cooperation with the believers in Jerusalem, and thus the historical continuity of the church with Israel—with the proviso of course that the Jews had forfeited their claim to be the true Israel. Against those who repudiated Paul as apostate from the law and alienated from the "mother church" from the outset, Paul appears in Acts as fully recognized and commissioned by the Jerusalem elders. Significantly, these same elders proclaim the full equality of Gentile believers, free of any requirements based on the Mosaic commandments.

As for the Pauline letters (including the pseudonymous inventions and the letter to the Hebrews), they were universally read as confirming both the rejection of the old Israel and the abrogation of the ritual commandments. The end result of this process is what has been called a "domesticated apostle." A price was paid for his return to the orthodox fold.

For our concerns, the results of this domestication are momentous. For the process that led to the canonization of the Pauline letters has also determined an anti-Jewish reading of them in all of subsequent Christianity. In addition to our earlier observations regarding those factors that make for such a reading, we must now recognize that it is precisely Paul's place in the New Testament canon that has made it both possible and inevitable all along. It is indeed Paul who "has provided the theoretical structure for Christian anti-Judaism, from Marcion through Luther and F. C. Baur down to Bultmann. . . ."[39] But now we must ask, Which Paul? Whose apostle? When we remove him from his canonical framework, do we find the same Paul? Is the anti-Judaism truly Paul's own, or does it belong to the interpretative assumptions of his readers?

PART IV

The Case of Paul

So also our beloved brother Paul wrote to you according to the wisdom given him, speaking of this as he does in all his letters. There are some things in them hard to understand, which the ignorant and unstable twist to their own destruction, as they do the other scriptures.

2 Peter 3:15–16

Among Christian scholars seeking to undermine the theological and scriptural bases of Christian anti-Judaism, no figure has been discussed more frequently or proven more controversial than Paul. Catholic exegetes and theologians have concentrated primarily on Romans 9–11. Among certain Catholic radicals great emphasis is placed on Israel's continuing election.[1] According to this view, the contrary belief in Israel's rejection is nothing less than heretical Marcionism. These scholars speak of a single people of God now in schism and of a future reunification. Stressing Paul's deep personal affection for his "fellow Jews" (Rom: 11.14), their predetermined role in bringing salvation to the Gentiles, their convenantal primacy vis-à-vis the Gentiles, these Catholics have argued that Christian anti-Judaism reflects a fundamental misunderstanding of Paul. Paul Démann in particular has drawn attention to Romans 11:1–2: "I ask, then, has God rejected his people? By no means. . . . God has not rejected his people whom he foreknew."

Among Jewish readers, Paul is almost unanimously seen as holding that Christ, as the end of the Law, abrogates the Law as a way of salvation, leaving Jews outside the saved community. More often than not such readers put forward the claim that Paul has fundamentally misunderstood the nature of the Law as presented in the Hebrew Bible, in post-biblical Judaism, *and* in Jesus of Nazareth. Solomon Schechter's remark may be taken as typical: "Either the theology of the Rabbis must be wrong, its conception of God debasing, its leading motives materialistic and coarse, and its teachers lacking in enthusiasm and spirituality, or the Apostle to the Gentiles is quite unintelligible."[2]

We are left in something of a quandary. We face an unpleasant alternative: either Paul correctly understood Judaism in his time as a moralistic form of works righteousness *or* he never did understand the nature and purpose of the Torah in Judaism. Furthermore, revisionist attempts to develop a different reading of Paul are dismissed as "strained exegesis,"[3] or rebutted with the rejoinder that whether or not he thinks the present condition of the Jews is part of the divine plan, for Paul that condition is "essentially one of disbelief."[4]

Faced with these difficulties, two new solutions have been proposed quite recently in order to resolve the dilemma concerning Paul's view of Judaism. E. P. Sanders, in his *Paul and Rabbinic Judaism*, has argued that Paul neither misunderstood the Torah nor presented a distorted view of it. The key lies in his conversion. "It is the Gentile question and the exclusiveness of Paul's soteriology which dethrone the law, not a misunderstanding of it or a view predetermined by his background."[5] Against the traditional claim that Paul's vision of the Torah was distorted by his Hellenism, Sanders contends that Paul's view of the Torah is solely the product of his conversion and of his experience as an apostle to the Gentiles. Thus he presents "an essentially different type of religiousness from any found in Palestinian Jewish literature."[6] His polemic is not directed against the Torah as such but "against the prior fundamentals of Judaism. . . . In short, *this is what Paul finds wrong with Judaism: it is not Christianity*."[7]

At the opposite pole stands the solution of Lloyd Gaston, a solution which insists that no Pauline text speaks of the rejection of Israel as God's chosen people *or* of the Mosaic covenant as outmoded *or* of Christianity as the true Israel. We will have occasion to discuss Gaston's views at length in the following chapters. These lines serve to illustrate the radical character of his interpretation:

> If, as we have claimed, Paul's central theological concern was *not* a negative disparagement of the significance of the Torah for Israel, what,

in that case, did he have against other Jews? If my hypothesis is correct, Paul said nothing against the Torah and Israel, but simply bypassed them as irrelevent to his gospel. Thus, the figures of Adam (negatively) and Abraham (positively) are much more important for his understanding of the significance of Jesus than Moses and David. For Paul, Jesus was neither a new Moses nor the messiah, nor the climax of the history of God's dealing with Israel, but the fulfillment of God's promises concerning the gentiles, and this is what he accused the Jews of not recognizing. Paul never accused the Jews of lacking zeal for Torah, and certainly not of legalism, but rather of disobedience to the new revelation he (Paul) had received.[8]

Using this set of extraordinary proposals as a starting point, the following chapters will consider in detail what Paul says of Israel, the Gentiles, and the Torah.

I 2

On Reinventing Paul

The traditional interpretation of Paul, long established and almost universally held by historians, theologians, and exegetes of the Pauline letters, is that Israel, Judaism, and Torah are no longer valid, if indeed they ever were so, for forgiveness of sins, redemption, salvation, or full membership in the people of God. This interpretation hardly differs from that advanced by Marcion. Thus Marcel Simon can write as follows:

> In truth, we are not far removed from the radicalism of Marcion. As a follower of Paul, Marcion will do little more than push to their logical conclusion those results which his master just managed to avoid.[1]

Rosemary Ruether's *Faith and Fratricide* exemplifies the common and inherited view of Paul on these matters. "The Jew, who has the law, then becomes the lawbreaker par excellence";[2] "Christians, not Jews, are the true offspring of Abraham and heirs of the promise";[3] "In Galatians, Paul argues that circumcision is forbidden under the new covenant";[4] "For Paul, the reign of Torah is equivalent to the reign of these demonic powers and principalities of the finite realm";[5] "He enunciates a doctrine of the rejection of the Jews (rejection of Judaism as the proper religious community of God's people) in the most radical form, seeing it as rejected not only now, through the rejection of Christ, but from the beginning";[6] and finally, "contemporary ecumenists who use Romans 11 to argue that Paul does not believe that God has rejected the people of Mosaic covenant speak out of good intentions, but inaccurate exegesis."[7]

⸗ In a series of recent articles and unpublished papers, Lloyd Gaston has undertaken a sweeping reinterpretation of Paul's view on the status and authenticity of Israel, Judaism, and the Torah after the coming of the Christ.[8] An essential part of his work is the demonstration of the fundamental errors and inadequacies of the inherited tradition. His first assault on the entrenched position appeared in a collection of essays prompted by Ruether's *Faith and Fratricide*. Gaston and Ruether agree on two fundamental issues, yet their conclusions are diametrically opposed. In the first place, both hold that the traditional interpretation of Paul has wreaked enormous damage in Western history wherever Christianity has "celebrated" its triumph over Judaism. As ecumenists they concur in the view that this triumphalist stance must be abandoned before any dialogue between Christians and Jews can take place. In the second place they agree, in Gaston's words, that "Torah and Christ are for Paul mutually exclusive categories. . . ."[9] Beyond these two points, there is no agreement: Gaston attacks the inherited view of Paul as altogether mistaken, where Ruether accepts it as fundamentally correct. For Gaston, Paul can be saved from the charge of anti-Judaism; for Ruether, he stands condemned.

In discussing Gaston's radical reassessment of Paul it seems appropriate to refer to T. S. Kuhn's *The Structure of Scientific Revolutions*. Of course it would be premature to speak of a paradigm shift as an accomplished fact. At the moment one can speak only of the potential for revolution. But certainly the potential is present in Gaston's work. He resolutely refuses to proceed in the manner of what Kuhn calls "normal science." He is not content merely to modify earlier views on specific issues and texts. He does not adhere to the assumptions and results of traditional interpreters. He writes, "I suddenly find that I have great difficulty in reading the standard literature on Paul: why do other interpreters miss the obvious while spending much time on matters not in the text at all? I find that I cannot even trust such 'objective' works as lexica on some points. It's almost paralyzing when it comes to writing, for so little can be assumed and all must be discussed."[10]

This is a striking illustration of the role assigned by Kuhn to paradigms in both normal and revolutionary science. Once established, a paradigm operates as much more than a set of consciously recognized points of agreement about matters of substance and procedure. At the unconscious level, it determines what we see in a text and what we fail to see; what we find meaningful, what we dismiss and what we overlook as peripheral; how we make connections between isolated objects in our intellectual landscape; how it is possible to ignore or devalue the significance of anomalies in that same landscape. In brief, its fundamental and indispensable function is to create the conditions for normal science within a community of scholars.

Once we step outside a paradigm, once we question not specific issues or puzzles within the paradigm but the paradigm itself, all is lost. From that moment none of the actions characteristic of normal science makes sense. Under such conditions, criticisms of the old tend to focus not on particular texts, questions, or results but rather on the paradigm itself, on its underlying assumption, on its failures rather than its achievements, and particularly on the manner in which it came to hold its position of prominence, that is, its growth and development in the history of scholarship and culture. Put differently, the goal of criticism at this point is to bring the existence of the paradigm into conscious awareness and to demonstrate the extent to which it governs the interpretative process.

At present there are others besides Gaston—and quite independent of him[11]—whose work shares a common feature: a sense of disbelief at how the traditional reading of Paul came to be in the first place and how it managed to survive for so long thereafter. Their expressions of disbelief are symptomatic of a revolution in process. In a forceful essay on Rom. 10:4 ("Christ is the end of the law"), Paul Meyer has detailed the degree to which virtually all modern commentaries on Paul are governed by "decision[s] made on grounds extrinsic to the text itself."[12] "What is it," he asks, "that casts this dark Manichaean shadow across the pages of Paul and of his commentators?"[13] Why is it that certain interpretations of Paul "are not only very widely held but also in some quarters, and in the commentary literature generally, firmly opposed, sometimes vehemently?"[14] In a similar vein, Krister Stendahl observes of Gal. 3:24 ("So that the law was our custodian until Christ came.") that its common interpretation in Western Christianity has succeeded in reversing "Paul's argument . . . into saying the opposite to his original intention."[15]

Among those mentioned specifically by Gaston as predecessors, reference may be made to the work of Markus Barth,[16] Krister Stendahl,[17] and E. P. Sanders.[18] Barth has written extensively and searchingly on the question of Paul and Israel. His proposal that the Pauline phrase "works of the law" is never used in Jewish texts to refer to the situation within Judaism but refers instead to the adoption of Jewish practices by Gentiles plays an important role in Gaston's argument. Sanders, who in *Paul and Palestinian Judaism* contends that it is impossible to identify Paul's image of Torah with *any* stream of contemporaneous Judaism, has demonstrated the difficulties attendant on all attempts to read Pauline texts on sin, condemnation, and rejection as bearing on the situation of Judaism.

Stendahl prepared the way in his article, "The Apostle Paul and the Introspective Conscience of the West." More recently, he has drawn attention to Romans 9–11 as the culminating section of Paul's letter to the Romans and insisted that relations between Jews and Gentiles rather than justification by faith is Paul's major preoccupation. Speaking of these chapters, Stendahl notes that Paul never says that Israel will accept Jesus as Messiah at the time of God's Kingdom but that "all Israel will be saved" (11:26). And of the extended discussion in 10:17–11:36, he comments that Paul fails there to mention the name of Jesus Christ. Perhaps most significant is the suggestion, which he does not develop, that Paul's thinking on the relationship of Christianity and Judaism may be seen as anticipating the view of Christianity developed in a line of Jewish thinking stretching from Maimonides to Rosenzweig: "Christianity . . . is seen as the conduit of Torah, for the declaration of both monotheism and the moral order to the Gentiles."[19]

Useful, even indispensable as these contributions have been to Gaston, it is he who has extracted the general principles from arguments about particular texts and transformed them into a new synthesis. A brief summary of his results will make readily apparent the distance between himself and his predecessors:

(1) Paul's central concern was the positive justification of the status of Gentile Christians, not a disparagement of the significance of Torah for Israel.

(2) Jews of Paul's acquaintance resisted him on the mistaken assump-

tion that he urged others Jews to abandon the Torah for allegiance to Christ.

(3) For Paul, Jesus was neither a new Moses nor the Messiah, nor the climax of God's dealings with Israel, but the fulfillment of God's promises concerning the Gentiles.

(4) Paul accused his fellow Jews not of lacking zeal for Torah and certainly not of legalism but of resisting his claim that in Christ God had established the righteousness of Gentiles apart from the Torah. For Paul Christ is the fulfillment of God's promise to Abraham as revealed in the Torah.

(5) Paul's concern for the righteousness and convenantal status of Gentiles is both a resolution and a dissolution of the debate regarding Gentiles and the Torah in the Judaism of Paul's time. Torah and Christ were mutually exclusive categories for Paul both before *and* after his conversion. Before, he adamantly rejected the notion that Gentiles could attain righteousness without assuming full responsibility for the Torah. After, and just as adamantly, he rejected the notion that Gentiles need assume any responsibility for the Torah in order to establish their righteousness.

(6) Given the thoroughly eschatological character of Paul's thinking on all matters, we must see Jewish Christianity (observant Jews loyal to Christ) on the one side and Paul himself (an apostate Jew) on the other side as transitional phenomena, as a "bridge generation" before the end.[20]

How does one assess the adequacy and viability of Gaston's strikingly new interpretation? As to its adequacy, it will not do simply to contrast it with traditional views or to argue that later interpreters of Paul merely rendered explicit what was already there by implication. For it is Gaston's contention that the traditional Pauline texts can and must be read in such a way that Paul and he alone among early Christian writers "had no anti-Jewish left hand." Ruether's response to Gaston is instructive at this point: she cannot believe what she reads, and she insists that certain meanings are implicit in what Paul says.[21] In a general way her comments indicate just how difficult it is to step outside traditional assumptions in assessing radically new points of view. At one point, she offers as an incredulous inference what in fact Gaston states quite explicitly, namely, that Paul did not believe that Jesus was the messiah at all. At other points, she simply reiterates the standard claim that the abrogation of Torah, and thus anti-Judaism, is implicit in Paul's theology. What she fails to recognize is that such a claim is entirely dependent on the traditional view that Paul's treatment of Torah and justification by works is aimed at Jews and Judaism rather than at Christians, whether of Gentile or Jewish origin.

Before proceeding to a consideration of the hermeneutical issues raised by Gaston's analysis, it may be instructive to dwell for a moment or two on the sources or motivating forces behind his reassessment of Paul. Dominating the background is the trauma of the Holocaust and its aftermath. As Christians faced charges that their own religion was touched by anti-Judaism at its very roots and that Christian anti-Judaism had powerfully influenced the anti-Semitism of Nazi Germany, many undertook a painful re-evaluation of their tradition. Similarly, as Christians and Jews sought to discover a common ground as the basis for an ecumenical dialogue between equal religious partners, Christians became increasingly aware of the extent to which historical Christianity and its scriptures have denied the religious legitimacy of Judaism.

Within Christian circles this new awareness has provoked nothing less than a theological crisis. At one extreme, Rosemary Ruether has argued that "possibly anti-Judaism is too deeply embedded in the foundations of Christianity to be rooted out entirely without destroying the whole structure."[22] She then proposes to construct a new model for Christian views of Jews and Judiasm, a model based primarily on the common experience of Jews and Christians in the modern world. At the other extreme, one finds a variety of rescue operations designed to isolate specific documents, chapters, or even sources of New Testament writings from the infection of anti-Judaism. For Gaston and others there is a profound theological urgency behind the exegetical task. No longer is it a case of the illegitmacy of Judaism. Unless they succeed in finding within the New Testament some area which is substantially free of anti-Judaism, the issue becomes the illegitimacy of Christianity.

A second factor in the emergence of this new direction in Pauline studies involves a new appreciation of Judaism and its understanding of the Torah at the time of Christianity's birth. Sanders' *Paul and Palestinian*

Judaism is but the latest in a series of studies marked by a sense of sorrow and repentance at the image of ancient Judaism that has long dominated the study of Christian origins. R. Bultmann's deeply biased presentation of rabbinic Judaism in his *Primitive Christianity* has been typical of Christian scholarship generally. The early exceptions to this rule—G. F. Moore, James Parkes, and R. Travers Herford—were always in the minority. Moore's cautionary remark, made in 1921, that "Christian interest in Jewish literature has always been apologetic or polemic rather than historical," has only recently begun to yield fruit.[23] Sanders has laid bare the apologetic and polemical bases of traditional Christian treatments of ancient Judaism in his observation that "the supposed legalistic Judaism of scholars from Weber to Thyen (and doubtless later) serves a very obvious function . . . as the foil against which superior forms of religion are described."[24]

There can be no doubt that Sanders and others have exposed a mortal flaw in this tradition of scholarship and thereby aided in restoring a lost sense of balance. At the same time, however, it must be noted that in the case of Paul, this new image of ancient Judaism yields a somewhat unexpected result. For his part, Sanders has argued vigorously that Paul's image of Torah and Judaism fails to correspond to any discoverable form of ancient Judaism simply because that image is generated exclusively out of his post-conversion Christian experience. In Sander's terse phrase, "This is what Paul finds wrong in Judaism: it is not Christianity."[25] With one elegant stroke he has severed any direct link between Pauline polemics and all forms of first-century Judaism. In other words, at the very moment when students of Paul have at their disposal a more truly faithful picture of first-century Judaism, that picture turns out to be largely irrelevant for understanding what Paul says about Judaism.

Still, the fact of Paul's polemics remains, and its purpose must be determined. And it is precisely at this point that Gaston and Sanders part company. Sanders holds that for Paul Judaism is completely superseded by Christianity: "*Paul in fact explicitly denies that the Jewish convenant can be effective for salvation, thus consciously denying the basis of Judaism.*"[26] Sanders reads all of Paul's arguments from and about the Torah as directed against Judaism itself. Thus he can speak of Paul's "critique of Judaism."[27] But in a parenthetical aside, introduced as if it bore no consequences, he modifies the crucial phrase to read, "his critique of Judaism (or Judaizing). . . ." For Gaston it is precisely this innocent "or Judaizing" that makes all the difference. If it is the case, as he proposes, that all of Paul's critique emanates from his opposition to efforts by some of his Christian contemporaries, whether Jewish or Gentile, to impose Mosaic observances on Gentile converts to Christianity, that is, to require them to Judaize as an essential element of their faith, then his basic hypothesis that Paul said nothing against the Torah would gain considerable plausibility.

SOME HERMENEUTICAL ISSUES

Sander's innocent aside is more than interesting. It is symptomatic of a range of conscious decisions and unconscious commitments that determine in fundamental ways the interpretation of evidence of all kinds, including written texts. In one sense, this is merely to paraphrase Kuhn's revelations about the role of paradigms in all forms of observation and analysis. Contrary to what many of us have been taught, reading and interpreting texts is never a simple matter of letting the words speak for themselves. In the case of Paul, unspoken heremeneutical commitments have consistently shaped the debate about his understanding of the Torah. Before proceeding to assess and extend Gaston's argument, it may prove useful to isolate and comment on a number of such commitments which may determine the results of interpretation even before it begins.

Where to Begin?

The traditional understanding of the relationship between Christ and Torah has always been embarrassed by Pauline texts like Rom. 2:25: "Circumcision is indeed of value if you obey the law."; 3:1–2: "Then what advantage has the Jew? Or what is the value of circumcision? Much in every way."; 3:31: "Do we then overthrow the law by this faith? By no means!"; and 11:1: "I ask, then, has God rejected his people? By no means!"

But to be embarrassed is not to be defeated. For those who do not simply ignore such texts, the solution lies in choosing not to begin with them, but to begin instead with passages that can be read as speaking of the demise of Israel and the abrogation of the Torah, for example, Rom. 10:4: "For Christ is the end of the law, that every one who has faith may be justified," and treating other passages as anomalous items which must be accounted for within this framework. It is apparent here that the beginning point has determined the final result. The truth is a simple one and does not require elaborate exposition: the end depends on the beginning. What does require explanation is why particular beginning points are consistently preferred over others. Here one can only suggest that the need to develop a view of Paul which is consistent both with other writings in the New Testament and with the dominant rejection-replacement attitude toward Judaism in subsequent Christianity provides a powerful incentive.

Contexts Near and Far

It is an axiom of the interpretative process that settings and contexts become increasingly less illuminating for a given text as distance from the text is magnified. Whether the distance be calculated in terms of geography or time, settings closer to the immediate text will necessarily yield more authoritative guidance to the interpreter.

This issue is decisive for Gaston's interpretation. The immediate context of the Pauline letters points irresistibly to an overwhelming preoccupation on Paul's part with the religious status of Gentiles in relation to the Torah. Gaston notes first that Paul's self-presentation in Galatians, following the meeting with the Jerusalem Christians, clearly casts him as the apostle to the Gentiles: "When they saw that I had been entrusted with the gospel to the uncircumcised . . . they gave to me and Barnabas the right hand of fellowship, that we should go to the Gentiles. . . ." (2:7–9) The issues settled at the conference were at least twofold. In the first place, Paul agreed to aim his Torah-free Gospel exclusively at Gentiles. In the second place, it is equally apparent that Paul's gospel was not merely directed at Gentiles but was principally *about* Gentiles: "Scripture foresaw that God would justify the Gentiles. . . ." (Gal. 3:8) Thus for Gaston it is essential to recognize that Paul's letters were written to congregations overwhelmingly made up of Gentiles. Any interpretation that loses sight of this particular setting is bound to go astray.

From the very outset, then, a consideration of contexts reveals the fact that "Paul writes to gentile Christians, dealing with gentile-Christian problems, foremost among which was the right of gentiles *qua* gentiles, without adopting the Torah of Israel, to full citizenship in the people of God."[28]

There remains one further context, somewhat further removed from the text of Paul but nonetheless fundamental to the argument as a whole, for it shows that Paul's concern with Gentiles in relation to the Torah was widely shared by Jews and Gentiles even before the advent of Christianity. On the Jewish side, there can be no doubt that the question of relations between Jews and Gentiles was a fundamental concern in the first century.[29] From Philo, Josephus, and Jewish literature generally, it is apparent that the Torah-Gentile question was alive in all sectors of first-century Judaism. One form of this question corresponds exactly to the issues attacked by Paul in Romans and Galatians, that is, whether Gentile converts to Judaism needed to be circumcised and to assume full responsibility for the Mosaic commandments. Thus the issue discussed by Paul was widely debated in Paul's Judaism, and its *exclusive* focus was the status of Gentiles. On the Gentile side, the debate about precisely the same issues was equally active. There it was prompted, as we have seen, by the strong appeal of Judaism among Gentiles and by the resultant need to determine the conditions under which such liaisons might be deemed legitimate. For those who chose not to convert fully the alternative was to Judaize, namely, to assume one or more Jewish observances, most often the Sabbath and certain food regulations. As we have seen, the evidence from pagan sources makes it possible to affirm confidently that Judaizers and the debate about them were prominent features of the cultural landscape in the Roman world of the first century.

The consequence of ignoring immediate contexts has been a persistent tendency among interpreters of Paul to move rapidly from specific texts to theological generalizations. Perhaps this tendency is a characteristic of interpreters as such, irrespective of the text in question, but it is certainly more pronounced when the text is scriptural, that is, normative for a religious tradition across temporal, geographic, linguistic, and cultural lines. That this is a proper and indispensable function of scripture in any religious tradition is beyond dispute. Equally certain, however, is the tendency to lose sight of settings immediately relevant to the text as interpreters within the tradition seek meanings beyond the time and place of the original environment. As that environment slips away, so does the possibility of constructing certain interpretations.

In his "The Apostle Paul and the Introspective Conscience of the West," Stendahl demonstrates how this tendency has produced an interpretation which is made possible only by ignoring the immediate context of Paul's words. As a recent example, he cites the following statement from Günther Bornkamm's *Paul*: "In a way the Jew represents man in his highest potentialities; he represents the 'religious man' whom the Law tells what God requires of him . . . who refuses to admit that he has failed to measure up to God's claim on him and is in consequence abandoned to sin and death."[30]

Two further examples may serve to illustrate the precise point at which the focus on immediate contexts tends to slip and thus to yield generalizations which are at odds with the text. I refer to the summary statements that normally conclude close textual analysis. Bornkamm's remarks just cited appear in his summary of Romans. Peter Richardson, whose *Israel in the Apostolic Church* is a valuable contribution just because he carefully delineates the circumstances surrounding the Pauline letters, tends to lose sight of these circumstances in his concluding paragraphs. Thus after demonstrating that Paul's argument in Galatians is that Gentile Christians need not be circumcised in order to become part of Israel, his summary reads like a universal claim: "No more do Law and circumcision enter the picture."[31] But surely, as his own analysis has demonstrated, his sentence should read, "No more do law and circumcision enter the picture *for Gentiles*." The same tendency appears in the summary sections of Sander's *Paul and Palestinian Judaism*. At a point where he is treating the question of Gentile converts to Christianity and their status vis-à-vis the Torah, he comments that "Paul's original contribution lies in the antithetical formulation: by faith and not by works of the law."[32] There is, of course, just such an antithesis in Paul between Christ and Torah. But surely we must at least consider the possibility, since in Sanders' own account the specific issue under discussion is Gentiles, that the antithesis defines the status of the Torah for Gentiles and not for Jews.

Loose Ends

The impulse toward consistency may well be a universal human trait. We strive for it in ourselves and desire it in others. Certainly the history of biblical interpretation bears out this claim. The special status of biblical writings as scripture generates a powerful drive toward discovering a consistent and systematic view in them. Works on the theology of the Bible (Old and New Testaments for Christians), of the New Testament, of the canonical gospels, or of Paul always pay a price for consistency. The price, as our earlier discussion of paradigms had led us to anticipate, comes in the form of loose ends, namely, those texts that do not conform and must be either ignored or distorted. This aptly characterizes the traditional interpretation of Paul on Gentiles and Torah, for as we have noted earlier, there is no convenient way to bring a substantial number of texts into conformity with that interpretation.

The issue at stake here is not so much whether Paul is a coherent or systematic thinker but whether interpretations of any text or thinker derive their legitimacy from an ability to tie down every loose end. There is no doubt that legitimacy has often been seen to depend on this ability. But our perception of what constitutes legitimacy will necessarily change if we moderate our demand for consistency.

Beyond these general considerations about the criteria of legitimacy, we must also ask whether there are reasons for expecting—quite apart from what we find—something less than total consistency from Paul himself. Of course the answer is that his circumstances were such as to defeat even the most determined efforts to achieve complete consistency. First, he lacked one of the essential prerequisites for any coherent system of thought, to wit, a body of literature and a sense of extended tradition. So far as we know, Paul had no written Christian texts before him and only a limited amount—the extent is much debated—of pre-Pauline oral tradition. Second, the literary form of his writings as occasional letters, as well as their contents, suggests that Paul's thinking and writing were fundamentally occasioned and shaped by local circumstances. Finally, his eschatological orientation, the fact that he expected Christ's coming in the proximate future, was hardly conducive to systematic reflection or formulation.

This is not to say that there are no common themes, concerns, and commitments running through his letters. Nor is it to assert that the interpreter hereby gains license to dispense with the search for Pauline consistencies. What I do assert, however, is that consistency must not be purchased at too high a price. We must not hold it against Paul when there appear to be loose ends in his thinking, and when we find them, we must not treat them as inimical to sound interpretation.

THE CENTRAL ISSUES

At this point I turn from broad hermeneutical questions to an attempt to expand, strengthen, and in some cases modify Gaston's interpretation. My efforts will be guided in part by Gaston's initiative and in part by the hermeneutical principles discussed above. I have chosen particular points of beginning with the full awareness that they are likely to take the discussion in a particular direction. I shall endeavor to pay the closest attention to the immediate and specific settings of individual letters and to allow these settings to determine the referents of important pronouns like "you," "we," and "they." Finally I shall seek to determine whether Paul develops and follows a consistent view on the relationship between Christ, Torah, and Israel and whether, given the interpretation proposed here, there remain significant loose ends. I do not take it as a given that the interpretation proposed here is the new, correct view of Paul on these matters. I do assume, or rather will undertake to demonstrate that it is a good interpretation, a valid one.

Let me begin with certain aspects of Gaston's argument which I take to be problematic and in any case irrelevant to the final results.

(1) Gaston joins Stendahl and others in referring to Paul's dramatic transformation from persecutor to apostle of Christ as a call rather than a conversion. In my view this is an unnecessary dichotomy, a merely verbal dispute. Calling is not at all incompatible with conversion, indeed may even—though in Paul's case we have access to his thoughts only long after the event—constitute a basic element of the conversion and its consequences. Paul himself certainly uses images of radical transformation that suggest what is normally meant by a conversion. In Gal. 1:13 he speaks of his "former life in Judaism" and in Phil. 3:7f. he contrasts past

and present as loss and gain: "But whatever gain I had, I counted as loss for the sake of Christ."

There is an obvious reason for preferring "call" to "conversion." The traditional view of Paul relies on a general theory of conversions, which is that we repudiate our prior allegiances, as a basis for buttressing the view that the post-conversion Paul had negated not only his own Jewish past but Judaism itself. This is surely too broad an inference. But just as surely it is beyond dispute that he did repudiate fundamental elements of his past—his own "former life in Judaism" and, more pertinently, his former understanding of the relationship between Jews, Gentiles, and Torah. Thus the preference for "call" over "conversion" carries a double disadvantage: it is a false choice and it has no bearing on the basic issue. For in speaking of Paul's conversion and of the element of repudiation inevitably implied by this term, we must still determine from the texts what it is that Paul has repudiated. Is it the legitimacy of Judaism itself, as the traditional view maintains, or rather the relevance of the Torah for determining the religious status of Gentiles, as we are asserting here?

(2) In his discussion of various attempts within first-century Judaism to define the status of proselytes, god-fearers, and sympathizers among Gentiles, Gaston uses texts from Paul's letters to locate Paul's place in Judaism before his conversion. One strand of Judaism took the form of a strict, almost sectarian view and held that Gentiles who stood outside the covenant were not righteous and would be condemned by God. Gaston indicates that such views within Pharisaic circles were held by the House of Shammai and proposes to locate Paul the Pharisee in that house.[33]

There are several difficulties here. Sanders has proposed several reasons for not insisting on the identification of Paul as a Shammaite. Among them is the observation that Gal. 3:10 ("For all who rely on the works of the law are under a curse; for it is written, 'Cursed be every one who does not abide by all the things written in the book of the law, and do them.' ") corresponds neither to general Rabbinic nor to specifically Shammaite positions.[34] That Paul was familiar with and made use of a strict point of view in Gal. 3:10 is obvious. At this point, however, we need to recall Sanders' more general warning that everything about Paul's view of Judaism must be read in the light of his conversion and the years of controversy thereafter. Equally important is the immediate context of

Gal. 3—the argument is directed against efforts to require that Gentile Christians observe selected elements of the Torah. To combat these efforts Paul formulates the strongest possible counter-argument: scripture demands all or nothing, not a selection. On the surface at least it makes better sense to see the argument as arising from Paul's clever use of scripture rather than from any prior association with the school of Shammai.

(3) A problem of great importance for any interpretation of Paul's post-conversion view of Judaism and the Torah concerns Jewish opposition to his missionary activities. As Gaston notes, this question is closely related to the issue of Paul's own persecution of Christians before his conversion. Gaston rejects as absurd three possible explanations for the Jewish opposition to Christianity: first, that the persecution was directed at Gentiles because they adopted certain Jewish ideas and practices alongside faith in Jesus; second, that it was directed at Jews (Christians) who taught Gentiles (Christians) to believe in Jesus apart from the Torah; and third, that it was directed at Jews who kept the commandments because of their faith in Jesus as messiah. By contrast, he argues, if Paul were suspected of urging *Jews* to abandon the Torah for Christ, as his accusers charge in the Acts 21:21, there would be ample grounds for direct and active opposition.

The chief difficulty in Gaston's brief treatment of these issues lies in its strict constructionist orientation. On the one hand, those interpreters, and they constitute the large majority, who seek a narrow legal basis for Jewish persecutions of Christians share the common mistake of overvaluing the legal issue, including the question of whether legal doctrines were understood or applied uniformly in different locales, and of undervaluing non-legal matters such as politics, prestige and the like.[35] On this point we need to learn from those studies that have shown that pagan persecutions of Christians in the Roman Empire more often than not arose from popular sentiment and not infrequently in conscious disregard of established legal procedures. On the other hand, it is striking that Gaston did not think to propose his own view of Paul as the basis for Jewish opposition. If Paul's message was that in Christ Gentiles had obtained equal rights with Jews as members of the covenantal people of God, we would have ample reason for understanding a strong Jewish response.

Such an explanation would differ totally from the charge laid against Paul in Acts 21:21, although the charge itself might represent an effort to bring Paul's unprecedented behavior into the sphere of synagogal competence as a case of apostasy from the Torah.

Despite these minor quibbles, there is no doubt that Gaston has raised a number of fundamental questions relevant to Paul's understanding of the relationship between Jews and Gentiles, Christ and Torah:

(1) Has Christ abrogated the Torah as the basis of historical Israel's covenant status? Has God rejected the Jews as his covenant people?

(2) What circumstances gave rise to Paul's extended discussion of Israel and the Torah in relation to Gentiles and Christ?

(3) What was the heart of Paul's quarrel with his brethren, his kinsmen by race?

These questions will occupy us in the next three chapters.

13

Has Christ Abrogated the Torah?
Has God Rejected His People?

The only point of agreement among modern students of Paul is that for him Torah and Christ are mutually exclusive categories. Yet few have paused to ask how or why. The traditional view is that the exclusiveness is chronological or sequential: once Christianity appears on the scene the Torah is either abrogated or appropriated by Christianity at its true, spiritual level. In either case, whether rejected or replaced, Judaism forfeits its privilege as the chosen people of God. The Torah is no longer, if indeed it ever was, the basis for salvation or redemption, whether for Jew or Gentile.

As noted earlier, this view is difficult to reconcile with a number of texts in Paul's letter to the Romans. We will begin with these and examine other texts in light of them. I take the letter as a whole to be a late product, certainly later than Galatians with which it shares numerous concerns, themes, and arguments.[1] Whether or not Paul was familiar with internal difficulties among Roman Christians and addressed them specifically in his letter cannot be determined. It makes good sense, however, to see as its immediate background Paul's recent experience as apostle to the Gentiles and the attendant issues of the Torah which apparently arose at every turn. Thus, not to force the letter into the category of a systematic treatise, it does appear to show Paul in a reflective mood, summarizing and refining his views following a period of turmoil and dispute.

Romans 2–3

Inasmuch as circumcision was the central issue in these disputes, it is not surprising that Paul's first comment on the continued validity of the Torah singles out that question. In 2:25, as if answering an implied question, he asserts that "circumcision indeed is of value if you obey the law; but if you break the law, your circumcision becomes uncircumcision." Apart from the assertion that circumcision remains valid (*ōphelei*) for the Jew who remains faithful to Torah—hardly a radical claim in the setting of first-century Judaism—Paul insists that the validity of circumcision and observance of Torah are linked together. This carries forward the basic argument of chapter 2—that doing the law is superior to hearing it; Jews who hear the law but fail to do it forfeit any advantage. This is but the opening statement in a prolonged assault on boasting. For the only radical element in his preaching will be that Christ now offers to Gentiles what Israel always claimed to be possible only with the Torah, namely, righteousness and knowledge of God. Throughout Romans and Galatians this will be the burden of Paul's polemic. Not that the Torah ceases to be "useful" for Jews, but that its significance for Israel has now been replicated for Gentiles through Christ. From this it follows, of necessity, that boasting, as Paul understands it, must be the central, indeed the only point of disagreement between Paul and other Jews. By contrast, his claim that "doing the law" rather than merely "hearing" it was what mattered was presumably taken for granted by most of Paul's Jewish contemporaries, certainly by those whose background was similar to his own.

Having established his basic position—the Torah remains valid so long as observance continues; righteous Gentiles stand on an equal footing with Jews (2:13–15)—Paul moves next in characteristic fashion to clear away any potential misunderstanding of the preceding arguments. In 3:1, as if aware of the possibility that his words might be taken as denying the "usefulness" of circumcision, he asserts just the contrary, as he had earlier in 2:25: "Then what advantage has the Jew? Or what is the value of circumcision? Much in every way!" And in 3:3–8, addressing once again the issue of disobedient Jews, he asserts that their faithlessness in no way nullifies the faithfulness of God.

What follows in 3:9–26 is *the* crucial Pauline text on the continued validity of Torah.[2] The traditional view, of course, holds that in verses 21–26 Paul replaces Torah with Christ as the manifestation of God's righteousness and that "faith in Jesus" becomes the sole basis for justification.[3] Against this reading let us ask whether it is possible to read this passage as speaking not to the exclusion of Judaism but rather to the inclusion of Gentiles? Is it possible, one critic has queried, that "modern theology . . . has missed this most simple meaning of the text?"[4]

The main theme of 3:9–26 corresponds to the issue first introduced in 2:17 ("if you call yourself a Jew and rely upon the law and boast of your relation to God . . ."). The question of 3:9a ("What then? Are *we* Jews any better off?") is a conscious reprise of the attack on boasting. The answer in 3:9b is fully consistent with the earlier discussion. The statement that Jews are no better off in no way abrogates their allegiance to the Torah. It simply places Jews and Gentiles on an equal footing and prepares the way for the claim that God's righteousness (for Gentiles) has now been made manifest apart from the Torah, that is, it is no longer Israel's exclusive privilege. The catena of citations from the Psalms and Isaiah thus serves a quite specific and double function. On the one side, it sums up the earlier treatment of Gentile sinfulness (1:18–32) and Jewish disobedience (2:1–24); on the other side, it anticipates the discussion of Adam and sin in chapter 5. The phrase "all men, both Jews and Greeks, are under the power of sin" (3:9b) thus introduces no new categories or groups. It simply describes the human situation after Adam as being "under the power of sin" or later (3:20) as "receiving knowledge of sin through the law." All of these statements, like similar ones in Galatians, are to be read as Paul's effort to circumscribe what he takes to be implicit in Jewish claims about the Torah. They are all part of his assault not on the Torah itself but rather on boasting.

The culmination of the passage in 3:21 asserts that God's righteousness has been "manifested apart from the law, although the law and the prophets bear witness to it, the righteousness of God, through the faith of Jesus Christ, for all who believe." Four points concerning these words require special attention. (1) The phrase "without the law" (*choris nomou*) neither asserts nor implies anything in opposition to or against the Torah. If anything we should read it as "alongside and in conformity with the law," for, as Paul clearly states, "the law and the prophets bear witness to it." In short, the detailed scriptural argument in chapter 4 about Abraham as the father of Gentiles as well as Jews—again the issue of boasting—is already anticipated here. (2) As G. Howard notes in his treatment of this passage, the translation of *dia pisteōs Iēsou Christou* as "through the faith/faithfulness *of* Jesus Christ" points again to the figure of Abraham as an expression of divine faithfulness and thus emphasizes his role as the father of all nations.[5] (3) The words "for all who believe" give rise to the question of whether we should read them as suggesting inclusiveness or exclusiveness. As Howard points out in discussing the similar terminology of Romans 10:4f., both passages are dominated by the theme of the inclusion of the Gentiles.[6] Thus "those who believe" either refers exclusively to Gentiles, as a further specification of the new manifestation of divine righteousness apart from the law, or it refers to all—Jews and Gentiles—who believe as a result of this new manifestation. But in neither case does it exclude anyone. (4) Howard's interpretation also takes account of the words "since he has passed over former sins" in 3:25 by showing that they refer quite specifically to the catalog of Gentile sins in 1:18–28. God shows his righteousness in no longer counting these sins against the Gentiles. Thus it is these Gentiles who have faith in Jesus whom God now justifies. They are also those among whom "there is no distinction" (3:22b), for "they have all sinned. . . ." (3:23). It is not at all clear that Paul is thinking here of Jews. The transition to a primary focus on Gentiles comes earlier, certainly in v. 20 and perhaps already in v. 19.[7]

On the other side, even if we persist with the traditional view that "all" in 3:23 includes Gentiles *and* Jews and that both are justified by faith and grace, we must still resist any interpretation which results in a claim that Jews or Torah are thereby invalidated. For Paul makes it amply clear that grace and faith determine not simply the new relationship of Gentiles to God through Christ but also, and from the beginning, the relationship of Jews to God through Torah. Put differently, this reading of 3:23 stresses the full continuity between chapter 3 and Paul's continuing argument against Jewish boasting. The nature of that argument throughout is never that the Torah is invalidated as a result of the

attitude of boasting but rather that the proper and original attitude of
faith must be restored.

In other words, the entire discussion of Romans 3, which reveals
many similarities to Galatians 3, is informed by a single set of issues,
namely, the changed significance of Torah for Gentiles under Christ.
What follows in 3:27–31 provides the best possible clue to the overall
thrust of the discussion in 3:9–26. Once again Paul looks back to what he
has just written in order to remove any basis for possible misunderstanding. The target of Paul's criticism throughout now shows itself to
have been Jewish boasting. He undermines that ground of boasting not
by abrogating the Torah or by rejecting the Jews but by placing Jews
and Gentiles on the same level. That is why Jews can no longer boast.
This is made clear in the rhetorical question of 3:29: "Is God the God
of Jews only? Is he not the God of Gentiles also?" Not the exclusion of
the Jews, but the inclusion of the Gentiles. Thus Paul functions as his
own interpreter by establishing a series of responses to the problem of
boasting:[8] (1) God is the God of Gentiles as well as Jews. (2) Gentiles
are thus no longer justified by "works of the law" (3:28; cf. 3:20), that
is, by observing elements of the Mosaic commandments. (3) Both Jews
and Gentiles stand as equals before God on the basis of their faith. For
Gentiles this faith has Jesus Christ as its focus (so 3:22, 26); for Jews,
as Paul argued in 2:1–29, faith means doing the Torah rather than
merely having it. (4) Paul thus speaks of two separate groups whom God
will justify on the basis of their respective faith (*pistis*) or better faithfulness. (5) And finally, as if to drive the point home, Paul denies cate-
gorically that his treatment of *pistis* in any way dethrones the law. "By
no means. On the contrary, we uphold the law" (3:31). By which he
means that the proper attitude toward the Torah was never boasting but
rather faithfulness.[9]

ROMANS 4

Once again, in typical fashion, Paul uses the lengthy treatment of
Abraham in chapter 4 to buttress his basic message.[10] In this sense, we

may take chapter 4 as a further guide for evaluating our interpretation of chapters 2–3. The issue once again is boasting. Is it not true that the ground of Israel's special position and thus of its boasting lies in the fact that God guaranteed that position in his promise to Abraham? Once again Paul answers with a resounding *no*. Once again he does so not by setting Israel aside but by returning to the formula of 3:29.[11] "Is this blessing pronounced only upon the circumcised or also upon the uncircumcised?" The answer, of course, is that Abraham is the father equally of the circumcised and the uncircumcised (4:11–12). Of the circumcised, because he is the first among the patriarchs of Israel and because he received circumcision as the fundamental sign of the covenant; of the Gentiles, because Paul insists that since God proclaimed Abraham to be justified *before* he was circumcised, on the basis of his *pistis*, he became the forerunner of all who believe without circumcision, "apart from works" (4:6).

At every point, then, Paul uses Abraham to demonstrate the fundamental parity of Jews and Gentiles! David's blessing concerning the forgiveness of sins is said to cover Gentiles ("the ungodly" in 4:5, "the man without works" in 4:6, the uncircumcised in 4:9) as well as Jews. The promise came to Abraham before his circumcision, that it, "not through the law" (4:13), so that it might "rest on grace" (4:16, cf. 4:14) and thus apply "*not only* to the adherents of the law but also to those who share in the faith of Abraham" (4:16). The statement that the promise was guaranteed to all his descendants is further specified by the citation of Gen. 17:5: "I have made you the father of many nations." Finally, Paul interprets Abraham's status as "father of many nations" as a reference to future events, specifically, to the incorporation of the Gentiles within the community of promise (4:17, 23–25). Beyond this, the elaborate exposition of Gen. 15:6 ("Abraham believed God and it was reckoned to him as righteousness") enables Paul to buttress his earlier claim in 3:27–31 that the principle of faith applies not just to Gentiles, whose justification is through Christ, but to Jews whose justification is through the Torah. In this sense, the use of Abraham also confirms Paul's affirmation that he does not overthrow the Torah by faith!

A straightforward reading of Romans 4 indicates that Paul's underlying concern throughout is to argue that the incorporation of the Gentiles is fully consistent with God's promises and righteousness. The text of Gen. 15:6 clearly lies at the heart of this concern. In his essay entitled "Abraham and the Righteousness of God," Gaston has sought to strengthen this reading by proposing a new translation of Gen. 15:6 (LXX) and by showing that Paul's application of it to the Gentiles is in harmony with a long tradition of Jewish interpretation. He proposes that we translate *kai elogizisthē autō eis dikaiosynēn* as "it was counted/reckoned to him [Abraham] as [God's] righteousness!"[12] In favor of this rendering is the overall theme of Romans and the immediate setting of chapter 4, both of which focus on God's righteousness as understood through his faithfulness and his promise (4:14).

In a broader setting, Gaston is able to show a clear connection between God's righteousness, the promise to Abraham, and the salvation of the Gentiles in several pre-Pauline texts. Isa. 51:1–8 (LXX) addresses those "who pursue righteousness, you who seek the Lord" and urges them "to look to Abraham your father and to Sarah who bore you . . ." (51:2). Then in 51:4–6, the coming salvation of God is previewed:[13]

> Listen to me my people, and give ear to me you Kings. For Torah goes out from me and my justice as a light to the Gentiles [*ethnē*]. My righteousness [*dikaiosynē*] draws near speedily and my salvation shall go forth and the Gentiles rely on my arm. . . . My salvation will be forever and my righteousness will not fail.

Among other texts, Sirach 44:19–21 is perhaps the most significant. Here again the promise to Abraham is interpreted to mean the redemption of the Gentiles:

> Abraham was the father of a multitude of
>   nations
> and no one has been found like him in glory.
> He has kept the Torah of the Most High and was
>   taken into covenant with him;
> He established the covenant in his flesh,
> and when he was tested he was found
>   faithful [*pistos*].
> *Therefore* the lord has assured him by an oath
> That the *nations* would be blessed through his
>   posterity [*en spermati autou*].

In short, there exists a series of texts in which, as the result of his faithfulness, Abraham receives the promise of God's righteousness. Among these texts, some see the promise as fulfilled in the salvation of the Gentiles (Isa. 51; Sir 44). Paul stands in this tradition. For as Gaston puts it, Romans 4 is "not about faith but about grace, expressed in the constantly recurring phrase that God 'counts righteosuness' to Abraham's heirs (4:5, 6, 9, 11, 23, 24), and 'that according to grace' (4:4)."[14] I would modify this only to the extent that faith is present not only here, but in chapter 3 as well. In both places, Paul speaks of two groups: in 3:30 he refers to the faith of both, whereas in 4:16 he describes them as separately "adherents of the law" on the one hand and "those who share the faith of Abraham" (tō ek pisteōs Abraam) on the other.

As a final note to Romans 3-4, it is worth emphasizing that the underlying structure of Paul's argument throughout presupposes Israel's election and proceeds through scriptural exegesis to demonstrate that divine election has come finally to include the Gentiles as well. The structure is fully apparent in the series of rhetorical questions that serve as the backbone of his demonstration: 3:29—"Or is God the God of Jews only"; 4:9—"Is this blessing pronounced only upon the circumcised, or also upon the uncircumcised?"; 4:16—"not only to the adherents of the law, but also to those who share the faith of Abraham, for he is the father of us all."

ROMANS 7

Few texts have received more attention than Paul's seemingly autobiographical ruminations about the Torah and sin in Romans 7. And if Krister Stendahl is correct, few texts have been more thoroughly and persistently misinterpreted.[15] The reasons for this are many. The results are clearly visible not only in theological treatises and biblical commentaries but in vernacular translations as well.[16] At its worst, this tradition has succeeded in turning Paul's argument into the very opposite of his original intention.

There are several good reasons for supposing, as Stendahl argues, that Paul is not contesting the Torah's validity or referring to his own pre-conversion experience of frustration and anguish prompted by an inability to observe it faithfully. In the first place, Paul resorts again to his common device of clarifying his point of view *after* first introducing it. Almost always, following an intricate argument, he raises and answers a series of rhetorical questions. In 7:7, he asks, "What shall we say? That the law is sin?" and responds, "By no means!" In 7:13, "Did that which is good then, bring death to me? By no means!" "The law is holy and the commandment is holy and just and good" (7:12). "We know that the law is spiritual," (7:14) "I agree that the law is good" (7:16). In other words, by using Paul as his own interpreter, Stendahl is able to arrive at the insight that "Paul is here involved in an interpretation of the Law, a defense for the holiness and goodness of the Law."[17]

Far from attacking the Torah, Paul here defends it against the charge that it is responsible for sin and disobedience in the world, the very same sin and disobedience introduced in his initial discussion of the Gentiles and Jews in Romans 2. For it is Paul's special contribution, mentioned earlier in 3:20 and 4:15 and developed further in 5:12–21, that sin operating as an independent entity makes use of the commandments to awaken fleshly desires.[18] A second reason for supposing that Paul cannot here be talking about his own failure as a Pharisee to uphold the Torah is that when he addresses his pre-conversion existence directly he betrays no sense whatsoever of doubt or frustration. Indeed, Stendahl speaks of Paul's "robust conscience" as reflected in Phil. 3; Rom. 9:1; 2 Cor. 1:12 and 2 Cor. 5:10f.[19]

If we take it as given that Paul's basic concern in Rom. 7 is to account for the prominent role assigned to sin earlier in the letter (3:9—"For I have *already* charged that all men both Jews and Greeks, are under the power of sin . . .") and that he does so by driving a wedge between sin and the Torah, we may now ask who Paul has in mind not only in chapter 7 but in chapters 5–6 as well.

At this point Gaston suggests that a number of factors point to Gentiles as the primary focus in these chapters.[20] The statement in 6:15 ("We are not under the law (*hypo nomon*), but under grace.") is perhaps the best indicator; the tell-tale phrase "under the law" is virtually a tag for Gentiles.[21] Furthermore, unless we are to take 5:18 ("as one

man's trespass led to condemnation for all men") as the unique instance
where Paul places Jews as well as Gentiles under condemnation—elsewhere he goes no further than to place Jews under the power of sin—
we will do better to understand chapters 5–7 as expanding on the theme
of God's wrath against Gentile sinners, a theme initiated in 1:18 ("For
the wrath of God is revealed from heaven against all ungodliness and
wickedness . . .") and resumed intermittently in 3:20 ("For no human
being will be justified in his sight by *works of the law*, since through
the law comes knowledge of sin") and 4:15 ("For the law brings
wrath!").[22]

The dilemma of Gentiles before Christ, as Paul makes plain in Gal.
3:10, is that any who fail to uphold the entire Torah fall under a curse of
condemnation and death (5:12–14, 20–21; 7:5). As descendants of Adam
they are defenseless against the power of sin. Perhaps with a backward
reference to 2:14–15, where he appears to turn the Gentiles' knowledge
of the Torah into the basis for their just condemnation by God, in 7:15–23
he contrasts "my" knowledge of what is right and good with "my"
inability to perform it. The dilemma described here is uniquely that of
the Gentiles. Unlike Jews, they had always been without recourse. Now
Jesus Christ has done for them what the Torah could not do. Now there
is no condemnation, for Christ has set "me" free from the body of sin and
death. In line with this, it follows that the exhortations in the remainder
of chapter 8, which are based on the contrast between flesh and spirit, are
directed to a primarily Gentile audience, for in Paul's thinking it is
Gentiles who are associated with sins of the flesh (cf. Rom. 1:24–27).

By way of a final observation concerning Rom. 7, it may be useful to
underline the extent to which our interpretation, or any other for that
matter, depends on determining the referents of personal pronouns. One
important implication of Stendahl's argument against reading Romans 7
autobiographically is that the first person pronoun here does *not* refer to
Paul. Conversely, throughout Galatians he regularly uses the first person
plural pronoun in settings where it is obvious that he means Gentiles—
and himself. Thus in Gal. 3:14 ("that in Christ the blessing of Abraham
might come upon the *Gentiles*, that *we* might receive the promise of the
Spirit through faith") Paul identifies himself totally with his Gentile
readers and includes himself in their company. This highly distinctive use

of pronouns lends further weight to the view that Paul is speaking there, and in the Rom. 5–6 as well, of Gentiles, not of Jews or of humanity in general.

ROMANS 9–11

Among proponents of the view that Paul has set aside Judaism and the Torah as no longer valid, Rom. 9–11 must be seen as a digression from his fundamental preoccupation with justification by faith. If we are justified by faith, so the argument goes, what about Israel? One problem with this interpretation is that it makes it impossible to reconcile certain statements in these chapters with the presumed contents of chapters 1–8. Paul's ejaculation in 11:1 ("I ask, then, has God rejected his people? By no means!") does not square with the view that Paul leaves no room for Israel in the matter of salvation.

The contrary view, advocated most strongly by Krister Stendahl, holds that chapters 9–11 are not an appendix but rather the climax of the whole letter. One particular advantage of this position is that it takes seriously Paul's characteristic way of writing and thinking throughout the letter. Whenever he completes a particularly difficult argument, he never fails to take up the issue a second time in order to clear up any possible misunderstanding. Beyond this, if the fundamental affirmation of chapters 9–11 is that God has not rejected his people, then these chapters, far from being inconsistent with the preceding chapters, are utterly at one with them.

To be sure, Paul adds further refinements here. But our analysis of chapters 1–8 has revealed that Paul's basic concern throughout has been to establish that the incorporation of Gentiles into the company of the elect is fully consistent with God's righteousness as expressed in the promise to Abraham. Thus the particular question addressed here is not, "Since we are justified by faith, what remains for Israel?", but "Given the constancy of God's righteousness, what are we to make of Israel's refusal to recognize and accept the obvious continuity between God's promise to Abraham and his act of redemption in Christ?" As in the rest of the letter, and especially chapter 4, the main theme of chapters 9–11 is the unshakable character of God's righteousness. Everything is understood in terms of this central premise: 9:6—"It is not as though the word of God had failed."; 9:14—"Is there injustice on God's part? By no means!"; 11.1: "I ask, then, has God rejected his people? By no means!"; and 11:29 "For the gifts and the call of God are irrevocable." Although the specific language differs here, chapters 9–11 do little more than expand the question raised earlier in 3:3: "What if some were unfaithful? Does their faithlessness nullify the faithfulness of God? By no means!"

At this point we must pause to ask whether this central theme is broken or contradicted by Rom. 10:4—"For Christ is the *telos* of the law so that everyone who believes may have justification."[23] Traditionally *telos* has been translated as "end" or "termination," sometimes as "fulfillment," or "goal," and sometimes as both, "fulfillment" and therefore "termination." Most frequently, however, "Christ is the *telos* of the law" is read in isolation not only from the second half of the sentence but also from the remainder of chapter 10 and the entirety of chapters 9–11. Only so is it possible to read these words as announcing the abrogation of the Torah. Against this, G. E. Howard has shown that by paying attention to the full text of chapter 10 it is possible to arrive at the rather different view that the entire passage is "dominated by the theme of the inclusion of the gentiles."[24] The following particulars may be mentioned: (1) 10:3 speaks not to efforts by individual Jews seeking to establish their own righteousness before God but to the position of Jews who are insisting on their collective claim to righteousness to the exclusion of Gentiles as a group. (2) Christ is thus the *telos*—the aim and goal—of the law in a double sense; first, because from the very beginning God's righteousness and the Torah pointed to the ultimate redemption of the Gentiles (chapters 3–4)[25] and second, because faith was the proper response to the covenant, from the beginning for Jews and in the present for Gentiles (chapters 3–4). (3) In 10:5–13, 18–20 Paul seeks to establish his case by citing a chain of biblical proofs, all of them pointing to the legitimacy of the inclusion of the Gentiles. Thus whether we read 10:5 and 6ff. conjunctively, as referring to Gentiles or humans generally, or disjunctively, so that 10:5 refers to Jews (*tēn dikaiosynēn tēn ek nomov*) and 10:6ff. to Gentiles (*hē de ek pisteōs dikaiosynē*), the result is the same. The inclusion of the Gentiles is foreseen in scripture. (4) With that established, Paul turns to the Gentiles and addresses them in terms

of *their* faith (10:9—"If you confess with your lips that Jesus is Lord
. . . you will be saved"), whose contents Paul insists again are to be found
in scripture. (5) At the end of this section, he returns to familiar themes
of faith (10:10–11) and the unity of God (10:12—"There is no distinction between Greek and Jew. The same Lord is Lord of all. . . .") in
order to establish once again that Gentiles now stand on an equal footing
with Jews.

This is not to deny that Paul expresses great sorrow and puzzlement
at his kinsmen's resistance to his gospel or that he has translated these
feelings into the claim that the Jews have thereby failed to achieve
righteousness (9:30; 11:7), that they have stumbled (9:32), that their
zeal for God is not enlightened (10:2) and that their disobedience has
made them the target of God's wrath (9:22–23). Paul says these things
and many others in chapters 9–11. But as elsewhere in the letter he never
speaks of Israel as rejected by God, he never speaks of the Torah as having
been abrogated, and he never speaks of Gentiles or Christians as assuming
Israel's place. To the contrary, he explicitly denies each one of these
possibilities.

But before we turn to the question of Paul's argument with his
brethren and their present role in God's mysterious plan of salvation
(Rom. 11), we must take a step backward in order to examine the circumstances under which Paul confronted this issue in the first place. For
as Stendahl argues against Bornkamm, it makes all the difference if we
read these chapters as a continuous polemic against the Jews and their
understanding of salvation.

GALATIANS 3:28

The baptismal formula of Galatians 3:28, along with a number of related
texts, has almost unanimously been taken to signify that the previous
distinctions among humans have been eliminated by Christ.[26] According
to this interpretation, Jews no longer have a separate identity apart from
Christ. Together with the other categories mentioned in the formula, they
have been taken up into a new entity which does not so much cancel as
transcend the former distinctions. The result is a version of the replacement theory not unlike that of Eph. 2:11–3:13 according to which "he

has broken down the dividing wall of hostility, by abolishing in his flesh the law of commandments and ordinances, that he might create in himself one new man in place of the law. . . ." (2:14f.).

There are a number of difficulties attendant on this reading. Not least among them is the fact that Paul behaves in ways which suggest that such distinctions have not passed away altogether. In 1 Cor. 11 he insists on different dress and deportment for men and women during worship; and in 1 Cor. 7:17–24 he urges the Corinthians not to press for the abolition of symbols which mark their status in worldly terms, whether those symbols be circumcision or slavery. At issue here is Paul's eschatological orientation.[27] Unlike the Corinthian enthusiasts, for whom the End had already come, bringing with it the final abolition of worldly distinctions, Paul insists everywhere that the End is not yet and that the symbols of this era may not be discounted. He also adds that such symbols no longer hold for Christians their earlier significance with regard to salvation. Still, the distinctions and their symbolic manifestations remain for the short time until the End.

A further difficulty with the traditional view arises from the introductory element of the formula which is usually regarded as of no significance for understanding the formula itself. "As many as have been baptized into Christ, have put on Christ. . . ." There can be little doubt that *hosois* is used here as a limiting pronoun, the conditions of the limitation being determined by what follows. Thus we must see the formula as applying, even in the sense outlined above, exclusively to baptized Christians. It is not a universal formula and is never used as one by Paul.

The presence of essentially the same formula in 1 Cor. 12:13 ("For by one Spirit we were all baptized into one body—Jews or Greeks, slaves or free. . . .") indicates that Paul was accustomed to using it for parenetic purposes with his Gentile congregrations. In Gal. 5:1–12, on the other hand, similar language appears in a polemical setting. There, in his final assault on the Christian Judaizers, he makes use of the formula in order to subvert their logic. Whereas they had no doubt argued that circumcision remained the essential mark of membership in the covenant community, Paul replied with a double retort: first, that what Christ offered to Gentiles was not membership in the covenant community of

Israel, and second, that circumcision was therefore of no significance for those who were "in Christ" (5:6). As in Gal. 3:28 and 1 Cor. 12:13, the *en christo* of 5:6 is a limiting phrase and says nothing about the significance of circumcision for Jews. That issue Paul addresses elsewhere (Rom. 2–4).

One final observation about the origins of this baptismal formula. Several critics have shown that there is a close connection between the formula of Gal. 3:28 and a number of sayings in rabbinic literature.[28] The threefold structure of the formula bears a striking similarity to a prayer attributed to R. Judah bar Ilai in the Tosefta. R. Judah says:

> One ought to say three blessings every day: blessed is he that he did not make me a Gentile; blessed is he that he did not make me a woman; blessed is he that he did not make me a boor.[29]

Perhaps closer to the wording of Gal. 3:28 is a commentary on Lev. 1:11 in the *Seder Eliahu*:

> When Israel offers up the daily sacrifices on the altar and reads this verse, *northward* [ṣpnh] *before the Lord*, the Holy One, blessed be he, remembers the binding of Isaac the son of Abraham. I call heaven and earth to witness that whether Gentile or Israelite, man or woman, slave or handmaid reads this verse, *northward before the Lord*, the Holy One, blessed be he, remembers the binding of Isaac the son of Abraham, *northward before the Lord*.[30]

It seems likely, then, that the version of the Christian baptismal formula in Gal. 3:28 is either a counter-statement to the daily blessing or a borrowing from the formula in the *Seder Eliahu* or possibly both. In either case, and putting aside the question of whether it is any longer appropriate to speak of a "breakthrough" brought about within Christianity,[31] it is apparent that Paul uses the formula in Galatians only against the Christian Judaizers. Neither here nor elsewhere is it a universal statement about the equality of persons, but rather a statement about the irrelevance of social categories for determining status within the community of Christ.[32] At no point is it relevant to the status of Israel, the Torah, or on circumcision.

GALATIANS 6:16

Peter Richardson has shown that Justin Martyr was the first Christian writer to identify Christianity with Israel in explicit terms.[33] This is a sobering discovery. If language provides any clues to reality, we ought now to be more cautious when speaking about rejection-replacement views of Israel in the earliest stages of Christian development. Paul's writings come a full century before the time of Justin. They are certainly the earliest Christian documents to have survived and perhaps even to have been written. If we knew nothing of their contents and were forced to hazard a guess based solely on an extrapolation from Richardson's observation about Justin, would we arrive at anything like the traditional interpretation of Paul on Israel and the Torah?

In fact, Paul nowhere addresses his churches as Israel. Nor does he transfer to them Israel's distinctive attributes. The RSV translation of Philippians 3:3 ("We are the true circumcision. . . .") indicates such a transfer, but the RSV translation at this point must be seen as dependent on the rejection-replacement view of Israel, not the other way around.[34] As several commentators have insisted, Paul's ire here is directed not at Jews but at Christians who held (for example, Acts 15:1, 5) that circumcision was necessary for salvation.

Another passage which has sometimes been taken in a similar fashion is the benediction in Gal. 6:16. The RSV translation—"Peace and mercy be upon all who walk by this rule, upon the Israel of God"—unambiguously intends "the Israel of God" to be read in apposition to "all who walk . . ." and thus to refer to Christians. Behind this translation stands a common exegetical tradition in which the phrase is taken as identifying Israel with either the church[35] in general or in some cases with Jewish Christianity.[36]

Against this tradition stand a number of important considerations. Already in 1920, E. D. Burton noted the unusual order of *eirēnē kai eleos* ("peace and mercy"). Taking this together with his observation that Paul never uses *Israēl* "except of the Jewish nation or a part thereof,"[37] he concludes that the phrase cannot refer to Christians. Instead it designates the Jews, or rather, "the pious Israel, the remnant according to the election of grace (Rom. 11:5)."[38] On slightly different grounds, Richardson reaches much the same result. Commenting on certain similarities between the form of the blessing in Gal. 6:16 and the nineteenth blessing of the *Shemoneh Esreh*, in one version of which *eirēnē* (*shalom*) also precedes *eleos* (*ḥesed*), he concludes that the sentence must be punctuated and translated so that the blessing falls on two separate groups:[39] those who follow Paul's standard *and* the Israel to whom God will show his mercy, namely, "all of Israel." The blessing thus stands, in the concluding words penned by his own hand, as a summary of the Pauline gospel as a whole. God's mercy has been shown to the Gentiles, that is, those for whom circumcision or uncircumcision no longer counts for anything (Gal. 6:15), and will be shown, as he states quite explicitly in Rom. 11:26–32, to all of God's Israel. Finally, if we allow this parallel passage in Romans to determine our reading of Gal. 6:16, *tou theou* ("of God") will no longer be seen as serving to reduce "Israel" to the faithful remnant, as both Burton and Richardson propose, but rather as designating Israel's unshakable standing with God.

14

What Circumstances Gave Rise to
Paul's Extended Discussion of
Israel, the Torah, and the Gentiles?

In approaching Paul's letter to the Romans, which embodies his fullest treatment of Israel and Christianity, we are at a double disadvantage. For Paul was neither the founder of the Christian community in Rome nor had he ever visited there before writing this letter. Thus it is perilous to build an interpretation of Romans on suppositions regarding the origins of Roman Christianity, its makeup, or its circumstances at the time of Paul's planned visit. Certainly it would be a mistake to assume that problems which troubled the Christians of Galatia, Corinth, or Philippi were replicated in Rome. In the final analysis the letter of the Romans must stand by itself and serve as its own guide for any interpretation. This means that in general terms we must accept Stendahl's warning that "Romans must be interpreted in the light of Paul's ministry and not on the basis of guesses about conflicts among Christians in Rome."[1]

These words of caution are a useful reminder that it is impossible to determine how well informed Paul was about the Christian community in Rome. Speaking broadly, however, the significant overlap of terms, themes, illustrations, and arguments in Romans and Galatians should serve as a warning against considering the two letters as completely unrelated. The presence of certain quasi-technical terms such as "works of the law" and "under the law" indicates that the specific circumstances of Paul's earlier difficulties in Galatia and elsewhere are still very much in his thoughts. It may well be that the failure to perceive these continuities is an essential precondition for the traditional reading of Romans. What, however, are the results if we heed these continuities and allow the earlier discussion in Galatians to serve as a test for our interpretation of the later letter to the Romans?

Concerning the circumstances surrounding the composition of Galatians it is enough to note that it precedes Romans and is written to a community founded by Paul and consisting almost entirely of Gentiles (4:8).[2] The letter is occasioned by reports that the community, or at least some of its members, were deserting Paul and turning to a different gospel (1:6). The bearers of this new gospel had urged the Gentile Galatians to Judaize, that is, not to abandon Christianity for Judaism but to incorporate certain elements of Jewish ritual observance, including circumcision (5:6), into their beliefs and practices. The importance of these circumstances for understanding the letter as a whole can scarcely be over-emphasized. Jews and Judaism are nowhere in the picture. Judaizing, not Judaism, is the issue. And in all likelihood those who were advocating the virtues of Judaizing were Gentiles rather than Jews.[3] Paul's sole concern is to defend the status of his Gentile converts as sons of Abraham without first becoming Jews.

By way of addressing the hermeneutical importance of the circumstances surrounding the letter, we must recognize the extent to which the traditional interpretation of Galatians depends on a failure to heed them. What is more, the view that Paul here firmly rejects the Torah and those who follow it yields necessarily one of two results: *either* Paul is guilty of a fundamental misunderstanding of Jewish teaching about the Torah *or* he correctly understands it as a form of works-righteousness and repudiates it, as one recent interpreter has stated, as "the orthodox Jewish (Pharisaic) doctrine of salvation."[4]

Note should be taken of two additional underpinnings to the traditional interpretation—translation and pronouns. Stendahl's complaint regarding the Moffatt translation of Romans 7:25 is a case in point.[5] We will have occasion to comment on other problematic translations in Galatians and elsewhere. The point here is that translations, however apparently objective, are very much a part of specific theological traditions. Or to put it the other way around, those traditions predetermine certain translations. In one sense this is as it should be, for it could hardly be otherwise. But once the tradition itself is called into question,

translations lose their appearance of objectivity. In some cases, they may
even turn out to be altogether indefensible. As for pronouns, their role in
producing particular interpretations of Romans has been made readily
apparent. This will be equally true of Galatians, and it is to be hoped
that the discussion of pronouns in Galatians may shed light on and perhaps
reinforce our analysis of pronouns in Romans.

GALATIANS 2

Following Paul's outburst of anger at the Galatians' precipitate abandonment of his gospel, he proceeds in a seemingly incongruous manner to
recite a series of events dating back at least two full decades. In the light
of the rest of the letter, it would appear that the underlying purpose of
the narrative is to establish two basic positions against the Judaizers: first,
that Paul's gospel to the Gentiles (1:16; 2:2), that is, the uncircumcised
(2:7), came to him from no human source but directly from divine
revelation (1:12, 15; 2:2); and second, that the legitimacy of his work
among Gentiles, including his insistence on their freedom from Jewish
observance (2:3 where Titus is not required to undergo circumcision;
2:6 where the Jerusalem leaders impose no restrictions on Paul's work),
was fully recognized by James, Cephas (Peter), and John, the leaders
of the Christian community in Jerusalem.

The relevance of these affirmations for the situation in Galatia now
becomes obvious. Those "false brethren" who slipped in and sought to
limit the freedom of Paul's gospel by imposing circumcision and other
elements of the Mosaic commandments are shown to be without any
legitimacy. Furthermore, Peter's subsequent behavior in Antioch, where
he capitulated to pressure from "certain men from James', the circumcision party (presumably connected with the "false brethren" of 2:4)
and, perhaps, local Antiochene Jews (*hoi loipoi Ioudaioi*—2:13) and refused again to eat with Gentile Christians, is also shown to be inconsistent
with the agreement reached in Jerusalem. In short, Paul's narrative suc-
ceeds in robbing the Galatian Judaizers of any possible legitimacy: his
own conversion, his revealed gospel and the leaders in Jerusalem—all
stand in support of Paul's position. With this narrative as the first step
in his polemic against the position of the Judaizers, Paul presents his own

position in a series of theses (2:15–3:5) before turning to proofs from scriptures (3:6–4:31).[6]

We begin with Gaston's proposed translation of 2:15–21:

> (15) We who are Jews by birth and not sinners from the Gentiles (16) knowing [therefore] that a [Gentile] human being is not justified from works of law, but (rather) through the faithfulness of Christ Jesus, we too became believers in Christ Jesus, in order that we might be justified from the faithfulness of Christ and not from works of law, because [as it is written:] by works of law "all" flesh "is not justified" (Ps. 143:2). (17) But, since seeking to be justified in Christ we ourselves too have been found to be [Gentile] sinners, is consequently Christ in the service of sin? Of course not! (18) For since I again build up that which I tore down, I commend myself openly as an apostate. (19) For through the law I have died to the law, in order that I might live to God. (20) I have been co-crucified with Christ. I live yet [really] no longer I, but [rather] Christ lives in me. What I now live in the flesh, I live in the faithfulness of the Son of God, who loved me and delivered himself for me. (21) I do not set at nought the grace of God; for since through law is [the] righteousness [of God], consequently Christ has died as a free gift.

The flow of the passage is governed by personal pronouns. In the opening verses Paul uses "we," in apposition to "Gentile sinners," of himself and other Jews who have believed in Jesus Christ. In 2:18–21 he begins to speak of himself as "I," laying emphasis on the fact of his own apostasy or conversion as the basis for his apostleship to *and* identification with the Gentiles. Thus in a remarkably subtle way, the very structure of the passage mirrors Paul's use of his own career as the central argument against the Judaizers. What he tells them is that even he, a Jew by birth and thus in a position to know such things, recognizes now that no Gentile man is justified any longer by "works of the law." That *anthropos* in v. 16 must refer to Gentiles is clear enough from the context, for Paul's sole concern here is the Gentile Judaizers. Beyond this, Markus Barth has argued persuasively that the phrase "works of the law" and the issue of justification "by works of the law" occur in early Christian literature only "in contexts where the imposition of some legal elements upon the Gentiles is discussed."[7] Here, as in the parallel passage of Rom. 3:20, Paul reinforces his case by citing Ps. 143:2.

What follows in 2:18–20 represents an intensification of the "even I" element in the argument against the Judaizers: if I, a Jew, know that Gentiles are no longer justified by works of the law, how can you Gentiles possibly undertake observance of it? From a different perspective 2:18–19 make the same point: v.18 states that Paul would be, in effect, a double transgressor or apostate—having already, so it seems, abandoned observance of the law as part of his apostleship to the Gentiles—if he were now to permit or encourage Gentiles to observe the law. Paul uses a strong term, *kataluō*, to describe his apostasy in order to underline the radical character of his own transformation. But this is no more vehement than "dying to the law" in the same verse or "suffering the loss of all things and counting them as rubbish (*skybala*)" in Phil. 3:8. Thus v. 19a states: (a) that Paul has "died to the law," that is, that he no longer submits to the covenant of Israel or its commandments; (b) that this came about "through the law," meaning either "law" in the sense of the new law of Christ[8] or perhaps more likely, that his apostasy is in accord with the divine will that Paul should preach Christ among the Gentiles (Gal. 1:16); and (c) "so that I might live to God," which, following on the second sense of "through the law," simply expresses Paul's belief in the divine character and origin of his mission. Finally, in v. 19b–20, Paul completes the appeal to his own apostasy by emphasizing his total dependence on Christ. Gaston uses Paul's own language to summarize its bearing on the case of the Judaizers: "I beseech you, become as I am, for I also become as you are!"

Gaston's translation of the final verse in this passage (2:21) uncovers a number of interesting problems. What is it that Paul is concerned not to nullify? Stylistic considerations would indicate that "the grace of God" must refer to the previous verse, that is, to God's gracious act in Christ and to Paul's new life in Christ. Thus any concession to the position of the Judaizers, namely, "if justification (for Gentiles) is through the law," would mean that Christ had died in vain.

The difficulty with this translation, as Gaston points out, is that it requires *dorean* to mean one thing ("as a gift") in Rom. 3:24 and quite another ("in vain") here. Gaston's translation renders *dorean* identically in the two passages and makes that "grace of God" refer instead to the covenant with Israel. In other words, Paul is here defending himself against a possible charge that his own apostasy amounts to a denial of that covenant. Here there are two difficulties: first, v. 21b ("for since through the law . . . ,") does not seem to follow in any reasonable way from v. 21a ("I do not nullify . . ."), and second, the phrase "since through the law is the righteousness of God" appears to stand in contradiction to Gal. 3:21 ("If a law had been given which could make alive, then righteousness would indeed be by the law"). On balance the first reading seems preferable, if only because it raises fewer difficulties. In either case, however, we must not forget that neither reading supports the conclusion that Paul here abrogates the Torah. Or rather he does abrogate it, but only for Gentiles who continue to insist on its significance for them. He does so because, as he has already made clear in his use of the phrase "Gentile sinners," the Torah signified only one thing for Gentiles, namely, condemnation.

GALATIANS 3:1–4:20

According to the literary structure of the letter, 2:15–21 completes the presentation of Paul's case. If we follow this structure, treating the narrative in 1:11–2:14 as the introduction to the formal presentation of the case in 2:15–21, we have no choice but to use both the narrative and the formal presentation as guides in interpreting the third and final stage of the argument, the proofs from scripture in chapters 3–4. These arguments must be in support of what Paul has earlier demonstrated. Any interpretation that fails to meet this test is beside the point. Thus any interpretation that assumes Paul to be addressing anything other than the situation of the Judaizers in Galatia will have little claim to legitimacy.

The key to this reading of Galatians can be said to hang on two phrases, "under the law" and "works of the law." The assumption that Paul uses "works of the law" to describe the situation of Israel in relation to the covenant involves numerous difficulties. We have earlier accepted the conclusion that the phrase most likely refers to the situation of Gentiles, excluding other than proselytes, who sought to obtain religious benefits by attaching themselves to Jewish communities in piecemeal fashion. We have already seen that the phenomenon of Judaizing was widely debated at Paul's time among Jews as well as Gentiles. We are

now able to say that precisely the same set of issues was debated in the
earliest Christian communities—I mention here the Christian communities
in Galatia, Phillippi, Corinth, Philadelphia (Rev. 3:9; Ignatius, *Philadelphians* 6:1), Magnesia (Ignatius, *Magnesians* 8:1; 10:3), and Antioch
(Galatians).

Gaston has argued that Paul uses the phrase "under the law" [*hypo
nomon*] consistently and exclusively to refer to the enslaved situation of
Gentiles under the law.[9] The context of its use in Gal. 3–4 certainly
points in that direction. Impressive testimony is provided by 1 Cor. 9:
20–22, in which Paul outlines his missionary strategy with respect to
four distinct groups:

> To the Jews, I became as a Jew, in order to win Jews; to those
> under the law [*hypo nomon*] I became as one under the law—though
> not being myself under the law—that I might win those under the law.
> To those outside the law [*tois anomois*] I became as one outside the
> law—not being without law toward God [*anomos theou*] but under
> the law [*ennomos*] of Christ—that I might win those outside the law.
> To the weak, I became weak, that I might win the weak.

A survey of commentaries will reveal how little attention has been
brought to bear on this passage. Gaston is certainly among the very few
to have seen its importance for Romans and Galatians.[10] Since Paul
seems to be speaking in general terms of his missionary work, rather than
of the situation in Corinth, I take it that "those under the law" must
stand between "Jews" and "those outside the law." Thus they can be
neither Jews nor those completely unrelated to Judaism. It is unlikely that
they are proselytes, since Jews and Gentiles alike agreed that proselytes
were no longer Gentiles but Jews. For Paul, at any rate, winning Jews
and winning proselytes would have produced the same behavior. Paul
himself, it should be noted, is careful to distinguish himself from "those
under the law" as well as "those outside the law," but not from Jews.
That he was never "outside the law" is obvious; that he feels no need
to distinguish himself from Jews is equally obvious. What other group
is there to which he did not belong? There is but one real possibility,
namely, that "those under the law" refers to those many and widely-
attested Gentiles who undertook to observe selected elements of the

Mosaic commandments but stopped short of full conversion. Finally, we may cite Rom. 3:19, where Paul speaks of "those in the law [*en tō nomō*]": "We know that whatever the laws says, it speaks to those in [the sphere of] the law, so that every mouth may be stopped and the whole world may be liable to judgment by God." As noted earlier, Paul speaks here as in Galatians of the Torah as placing Gentiles under judgment and condemnation.

This final comment brings us to a third premise in Gaston's analysis of the Torah (*nomos*) which deserves attention. He notes that Paul uses *Torah-nomos* in a double sense, "sometimes saying that it is good and has been fulfilled in Christ and sometimes that it is bad and has been abolished in Christ."[11] It is not too much to say that this tension lies at the very heart of the problem. The solution which underlies the traditional view is that Paul is talking in *both* cases about Jews and Judaism. When priority is given to the second category, namely, *nomos* as bad and abolished, the only possible result is that Paul rejects Judaism and abrogates the Torah. Apart from the obvious problem created by the fact that Paul writes none of his letters *to* Jews, but rather to Gentile Christians, and that his discussion of *nomos* ought to be interpreted with reference to them, Gaston has shown that the double sense of *nomos* in Paul's letters also corresponds to a double usage in contemporaneous Jewish texts. In the first instance, *Torah* meant "the revelation of God . . . in his knowability, in his presence, in his electing will, in his covenant for Israel."[12] In the second instance, *Torah* came to be seen as God's revealed wisdom for all the nations who by virtue of knowing God's will are obligated to fulfill the commandments even while not coming under the covenant with Israel. In both cases, Israel's special status was often explained by insisting that of all the nations Israel alone had received the revelation and remained loyal to it. Both of these views leave the Gentiles *qua* Gentiles in a hopeless position with regard to final salvation. Thus in an important stream of pre-Pauline Judaism "*Torah as law functions in an exclusively negative way, to condemn.*"[13] This tradition is fully displayed in the letter to the Ephesians, where the author depicts the situation of Gentiles prior to Christ in the following terms: "dead through trespasses and sins" (2:1); "by nature children of wrath" (2:3); "alienated from the commonwealth of Israel, strangers to the covenants of promise, having no hope and without God in the world" (2:12); and separated by "the dividing wall of hostility," that is, the law of command-ments and ordinances (2:14–15).

At this very point we rejoin Paul's letter to the Galatians where he makes much the same point. For intertwined with his presentation of Abraham as the forefather of "those who believe" is the correlative theme of Christ as the one who has redeemed Gentiles from the curse of the Torah through his faith (3:8, 13–14). The undercurrent through-out chapters 3–5 is thus that the Torah and Christ stand in irreconcilable tension: "under the Torah" the Gentiles stand condemned; "in Christ" they inherit the promise of sonship and freedom. The contrast is readily apparent in the opening words of 3:1–5 where he poses the rhetorical question, "Did you receive the Spirit from works of the law or by hearing my preaching of faith?" The answer is obvious. When the Galatians first heard Paul they received the Spirit through the gospel of Christ and had not yet begun to Judaize. "Thus," he concludes, "your standing in Christ has nothing to do with keeping the Torah." Next, to further emphasize his point and no doubt to refute the belief of the Judaizers that inheritance of the promises was limited to Israel, Paul introduces the figure of Abraham and his scriptural proof from Gen. 15:6. Here, as in Romans, Abraham is understood as the bearer of the promise for and the fore-father of a future people, "those of faith" [hoi ek pisteōs]. Even more clearly here than in Romans, those ek pisteōs, the promised offspring of Abraham, are understood to be the Gentiles.

In this context, Gaston again emphasizes that Abraham functions here not as a model for Christians, that is, that they should believe and be justified in the manner of Abraham, but as a guarantee in scripture for the legitimacy of Paul's gospel to and about the Gentiles. Pistis, again as in Romans, refers not primarily to the response or attitude of Christians but rather to God's faithfulness in announcing the promise to Abraham in the past and fulfilling it in Christ in the present. Paul expresses himself quite unambiguously both here and in the concluding paragraphs (15: 8–12) of his letter to the Romans. "Christ became a servant to the circumcised to show God's faithfulness, in order to confirm the promises given to the patriarchs, in order that the Gentiles might glorify God for his mercy, as it is written . . ." (Ps. 18:49; 2 Sam. 22:50; Deut. 32:43; Ps. 117:1; Isa. 11:10). The fact that 15:9 ("that the Gentiles . . .") must be read in apposition rather than in conjunction with 15:8 ("Christ became a servant . . .") and that there follows an unusually long catena of biblical quotations indicates the importance that Paul attaches to this apposition. As such it provides still further evidence that Christ was not the climax of God's dealings with Israel but rather the fulfillment of his promise to Abraham concerning the redemption of the Gentiles.

At this point in the argument, having justified his claim that in Abraham's seed God would justify the Gentiles *as* Gentiles and having further established that those who have faith [*hoi ek pisteōs*] are legitimate sons of Abraham the faithful (3:9), he advances to the final stage of his case, namely, that those who believe are no longer under a curse and thus no longer under the Torah (3:10ff.). He cites Deut. 27:26 ("Cursed be every one who does not abide by all things . . . and do them") as his scriptural proof. In so doing, he applies it to the situation of Gentiles with regard to the Torah in two senses: first, *before* Christ, in that all Gentiles as Gentiles stood under the curse; and second, *after* Christ, in that any Gentile who fails to obey every commandment, which was clearly not the case with the Galatian Judaizers, remains under the curse. With this as his fundamental premise, Paul is able to draw two important inferences relevant to the case of the Judaizers:

(1) The Torah as curse leads to justification for no one among the Gentiles (cf. 2:16), for they now live from the righteousness which comes from God's faithfulness in Christ (cf. 2:16!). He is the offspring in which the promise comes to fulfillment (3:16);

(2) The sense of the statements that the Torah does not rest on faith (3:12), that the Torah which came 430 years after Abraham does not void the promise made to him (3:17), that inheritance of the promise is not through the Torah (3:18), that the Torah is not against the promises (3:21), that the Torah cannot make alive (3:21) and that righteousness is not through the Torah—the sense of these statements, as applied to Gentiles, is that the Torah as covenant with Israel simply has no bearing on the promise to Abraham. The covenant at Sinai represents neither the fulfillment of that promise nor its cancellation. This second inference

uses Torah in the sense of God's covenant with Israel at Sinai. Far from impugning the validity of this covenant, Paul cites it against the Judaizers to signify its total irrelevance for the earlier covenant with Abraham, the covenant-as-promise which reaches fulfillment in Christ. The Sinai covenant is not against the promise, just irrelevant as regards Gentiles.

As for the first use of Torah, in placing Gentiles under a curse, it appears in 3:2,5,10,11,13,23,24; 4:4,5. By way of bringing home to the Galatians the folly of their situation "under the law" after Christ, Paul paints an even more dismal picture of their situation before Christ. They were children, slaves to the weak and beggarly elemental spirits of the cosmos (4:3,9; 5:1), ignorant of God and in bondage to false gods (4:8). They were consigned to sin (3:22), confined under the Torah (3:23) and kept under restraint until faith should be revealed (3:23). These statements merely fill out the question ("Why, then, the law?") and answer ("It was added because of transgressions") in 3:19, a question that arises naturally from the discussion in 3:15–18: If the promise made earlier to Abraham was not fulfilled in the Torah (as covenant), why was it added (as curse)? In order, as we have seen earlier, that Gentiles might be held responsible for their sins![14] Likewise, the role of the Torah "as a paidagogos" until Christ came must be seen in a negative light only for Gentiles. *Paidagogos* here designates the Torah as a stern disciplinarian, whose task it is to keep watch over the reckless children until the time of their inheritance (4:2).

Finally the full force of Paul's argument comes in 4:4f., although it has been repeatedly anticipated (3:14,22,24,29). "When the time had fully come, God sent forth his Son, born of a woman, born under the law, to redeem those who were under the law, so that *we* might receive adoption as sons." In short, if we are to take these words at face value, Paul presents Jesus Christ, the offspring of Abraham, as the fulfillment of the promised inheritance of sonship for Gentiles. Like Gentiles, he lived "under the law" in order to redeem those "under the law." Exactly as in 3:13, Jesus assumes the Torah only for the purpose of redeeming those who stand under its curse. The significance of these assertions can hardly be overestimated, for this is not the first but the third version of it in the letter (3:8,14). Jesus' sole function, so it would seem, is to bring to fulfillment the promise to Abraham regarding the Gentiles.

In Gaston's words, "Jesus was neither a new Moses nor the messiah, nor the climax of God's dealing with Israel, but the fulfillment of God's promises concerning the gentiles."[15] This startling conclusion derives not simply from a plain reading of Gal. 3:8, 14 and 4:4–5, but just as much from a reading in context of Paul's complete arguments. Those who suppose that he aims his initial comments at Jews or at the Torah and that he systematically depreciates the Torah as such must assume that Paul suddenly neglects the immediate circumstances in Galatia which prompted the letter in the first place. This setting provides the hermeneutical key; for the traditional view it is a stumbling-block.

GALATIANS 4:21–5:12[16]

The ejaculation of 4:21 ("Tell me, you who desire to be under the law . . .") looks like the introduction of a new point which Paul has suddenly remembered. What follows is part of the continuing search for scriptural support by both parties. This entire section is of a piece with his warning to them (3:10; 5:3) that Judaizing is utterly without justification on its own terms for "every man who receives circumcision . . . is forced to keep the whole law."

The substance of Paul's point concerns Abraham's two sons, their different mothers, and an "allegory" based on them. While the general thrust of Paul's thinking is clear, almost every detail, including variants in the Greek manuscripts and traditional translations, remains obscure.[17] At a general level, Burton is surely right in seeing the story of Abraham's sons as intended to induce the Galatians [that is, the Judaizers] to see that they are joining the wrong branch of the family.[18] As for details, this much seems clear: the structure consists of two parallel but antithetical lists, each one consisting of persons and their corresponding allegorical values:

1st Woman = Covenant (v. 24)	2nd Woman = Covenant (v. 24)
Hagar = Slave	[Sara] = free woman
Son [Ishmael] born of flesh	Son [Isaac] born through promise

> From Sinai, bearing
>   children for slavery
>
> The present Jerusalem   Jerusalem above: free
>   and our Mother
>
> in slavery with her   children of promise,
>   children   like Isaac
>
> born of flesh: persecutor   [born of spirit:
>   persecuted]
>
> Cast out   Inherit

From the final warning in 4:30 (quoting Gen. 21:10–12) the lesson is drawn: do not associate yourself with the line of descent through Hagar and Ishmael, for they are cast out as slaves and will not inherit the promises. Only the children of the free woman count as heirs.

If we ask why it occurred to Paul to apply this reading of Abraham's offspring to the Judaizers in Galatia, the answer must lie in its associations with slavery and bondage (*douleia* in 4:24 and 5:1; *paidiskē* in 4:22,23,30,31). The Judaizers, by placing themselves under the Torah, were reverting to a condition of bondage. As a result they, like Ishmael, will be ineligible for the inheritance.

As is frequently the case with Paul, the key to understanding the passage lies in the immediately following verse, 5:1: "For freedom Christ has set us free; stand fast therefore and do not submit again to a yoke of slavery!" Consequently we can only conclude that the Jews are absent from the entire passage. The contrast is not between Christianity (Sarah) and Judaism (Hagar) but between Israel (Isaac) and the nations (Ishmael).[19] The moral which Paul draws from the contrast is that what is right, namely, circumcision, for the one is wrong for the other. Against all probability, the traditional view holds that Paul's intention is to identify Israel with the offspring of Hagar! Not only is such a view utterly at odds with the biblical narrative, where the descendants of Ishmael are manifestly not the Israelites, it is equally incompatible with Paul's stance toward Israel generally.

With this as background, we are now in a better position to understand how it is that Christ and Torah are mutually exclusive categories for Paul. In fact, he addresses the issue directly in the following passage, Gal. 5:2–12. The hallmark of Gentiles in Christ is freedom, that is, freedom from the Torah and its curse. Thus any return to the commandments of that covenant, in this case circumcision, can only be likened to slavery (5:1). To spell this out, Paul dwells on the antithesis of Christ and Torah, for they are indeed antithetical in terms of their effects on Gentiles. The Torah brings condemnation and slavery; Christ brings freedom (from both) and the Spirit. Thus, Paul asserts, "Christ will be of no advantage to you if you receive circumcision." The only possible result would be condemnation and slavery again. As if to underscore his point, he concludes on a note of bitter resentment. Indulging briefly in a medical fantasy, he expresses the wish that those who are circumcising the Galatian Christians might slip while using the knife and mutilate themselves!

PHILIPPIANS 3:1–11

The circumstances of Paul's polemic in Philippians resemble those in Galatia in some respects while differing in others.[20] On the one hand, the issue here involves certain individuals from the outside who are urging circumcision (3:2) on the Gentile Christians of Philippi.[21] The identity of these outsiders is not clear. Among groups known and identified elsewhere in Paul's letters, we may think of Jewish Christians or Gentile Judaizers. Supporting identification of the troublemakers as Christians of Jewish background is Paul's "boasting" in Phil. 3:4–6, where he appears to be outdoing the Jewish credentials of the opposition. In this case we need not think of the Jerusalem leaders but rather of the "false brethren" who caused so much trouble for Paul in Antioch. The same or similar people surface again in Galatia, Philippi, and perhaps Corinth. On the other hand, if the Judaizers in Galatia are to be seen as Gentiles, we cannot rule out a similar possibility for Philippi.

If we assume that the difficulties in Philippi stem from Judaizers, that is, from those who proclaim that Gentile Christians must add at least circumcision to their Christian faith, then Paul's counter-proclamation becomes readily comprehensible. As in Galatians, he cites his own career, namely, his apostolic apostasy, as the proper basis for the Philippians behavior. "Whatever gain I had, I counted as loss for the sake of Christ. Indeed I count everything as loss because of the surpassing worth of knowing Christ Jesus my Lord . . ." (3:7–8). As in Romans and Galatians, he contrasts the righteousness which is through the law (*ek nomou*) with that which is through the faithfulness (*pistis*) of Christ and righteousness of God (3:9). But he nowhere suggests that his own abandonment of the Sinai covenant is normative for anyone beyond himself. Nor does he show any evidence of claiming for Gentiles the attributes of Israel. The RSV translation of 3:3—"For we are the *true* circumcision"— is seriously misleading, for it misconstrues the nature of the argument and lacks any basis in the Greek text.

In sum, as John Koenig rightly argues, "the apostle is not claiming that the church has replaced the Jewish nation as God's elect people; instead, he is polemicizing against *Christians* who insist that physical circumcision is necessary for salvation."[22] Together with the 3:20 ("our citizenship is in heaven"), 3:3 must be seen as a counter-point to the Judaizers' argument that only the circumcised can enjoy full membership in the covenant community. Against them Paul asserts that Christians are members of the covenant community, but not via Israel's path. "Circumcision" is thus used here, as in Rom. 2:25ff., to show that Jews can no longer claim exclusive access to the covenant relationship. In the same vein, the worship of Christians is legitimated not through dependence on the Jewish cult, that is, circumcision, but through the presence of the Spirit (3:3).

2 CORINTHIANS 3

Another favorite text for those who understand Paul to have removed all legitimacy from Israel and the Torah is the polemical passage in 2 Cor. 3:7–16.[23] The strong language in the passage would appear to lend unimpeachable authority to this point of view: v. 7—"the dispensation (*diakonia*) of death"; v. 9—"the dispensation of condemnation"; v. 14f.— "Their minds were hardened; for to this day, when they read the old covenant, the same veil remains unlifted, because only through Christ is it taken away. Yet to this day whenever Moses is read a veil lies over their minds (*noēmata*)."

Yet the traditional interpretation of these verses is purchased at a price. The cost is inattention to the immediate setting and inconsistency with other Pauline texts. At present it is possible to speak of a significantly different trend among interpreters of 2 Corinthians who are inclined to stand the traditional view on its head.

Beginning with Dieter Georgi's extensive study of Paul's opponents in 2 Corinthians,[24] others have begun to draw attention to certain previously neglected aspects of 3:7–14:[25] first, that it was Paul's Christian adversaries who introduced the figure of Moses and the topic of biblical interpretation into the debate; second, that Paul's heated response is directed at *their* treatment of these issues and not at Jews; and third, that in contrast to Galatians and Philippians, the question of the Torah and its observance simply does not arise here.[26]

Briefly, the situation in Corinth at the time when Paul wrote 2 Corinthians was as follows: accompanied by letters of recommendation (3:1), certain Christians of Jewish origin (11:22) sought to undermine both the legitimacy of Paul's gospel and his apostolic status by contrasting him unfavorably with Moses. These interlopers held a view of Moses as a *theios anēr*, an inspired man of God and a miracle worker, whose great power was made manifest in the radiant splendour of his face as he descended Mt. Sinai, a splendor so bright that he placed a veil over his face in order not to overcome the Israelites. This veil, they argued, symbolized Israel's inability to comprehend its own scriptures. With this situation in mind, it becomes apparent that we must read Paul's agitated reply as aimed exclusively at the gospel of these adversaries. Or to put the matter more forcefully, it becomes increasingly difficult to find any basis in the text for the traditional view.

J.-F. Collange has shown that "the letter" in 3:6 ("the written letter/code kills, but the Spirit gives life") refers not to the Torah as such but rather to a particular mode of interpretation.[27] Against this interpretation Paul opposes the Spirit, the sign of the Christian life generally. Thus the statement that "the letter kills" is part of the polemic which Paul constructs around a series of contrasts:[28]

3:6a : letter—spirit
3:6b : kill—make alive
3:7 : dispensation of death—dispensation of the Spirit
3:9 : dispensation of condemnation—dispensation of righteousness

The fundamental contrast is not between Israel of the past and Christianity of the present, but between a particular appropriation of Moses by these Christians and life in the Spirit. When seen together with Rom. 7–8, Paul's replies come into sharper focus. The characteristic terms (Spirit, life, righteousness, Christ, death, condemnation, old covenant, law), in both letters point to the conclusion that in 2 Cor. 3. Paul's language is meant to contrast not Israel and Christianity but the old and the new for Gentiles!

According to Collange, Paul's reply to the opponents in 3:7–11 is based on two premises: first, that Moses was indeed surrounded by glory at Sinai, and second, that Moses' glory pales in comparison with the glory of the dispensation in Christ. As a consequence, Paul answers, any attempt to mix the two is absurd. And 3:12–16 represents the culmination of Paul's counter-attack in that he turns the figure of Moses against his opponents. Thus it is the opponents whose mind has been hardened; it is they who are veiled whenever they read Moses (3:14f.) in the traditional manner, that is, not through Christ, the Lord or the Spirit. The statement in 3:16 that the veil is removed only by turning to the Lord thus refers not, as many have claimed, to an eventual conversion of the Jews, but rather to the position of Paul's opponents. Not Moses, but Christ, the Spirit and the Lord are the ones who enable Christians to read scripture properly.[29]

And what might that proper reading be? In 2 Corinthians as in Galatians and Romans the proper reading of Scripture is that Moses is no longer of any value for Gentiles. In Paul's reading of the scriptures, Abraham (and Christ) are the figures through whom the Gentiles are released from the curse and the condemnation and are brought to new life. Thus the itinerant ecstatics who arrived in Corinth had the great ill fortune to have advocated Moses as the centerpiece of their gospel. This drove them headlong against the very heart of Paul's arsenal, for the basic thrust of his gospel was that Moses no longer mattered for Gentiles.

15

What Was the Heart of
Paul's Argument with the Jews,
His Kinsmen by Race?

Nothing we have discussed thus far has caused us to modify our earlier observation that for Paul Torah and Christ are mutually exclusive categories. But the relationship between the two is such that neither invalidates the other. Torah remains the path of righteousness for Israel; Christ has become the promised way of righteousness for Gentiles.

Paul neither expects Israel to convert to Christ nor does he tolerate observance of the Mosaic rituals among Gentiles. His reasoning is not just that Christ is the expression of God's righteousness for Gentiles but that the meaning of the Torah for Gentiles has always been and remains curse and condemnation. Because Christ has redeemed Gentiles from this curse, any observance of the Torah by Gentiles must now be tantamount to undoing Christ's work. As for Paul's own conversion, there is no hint that he saw it as anomalous with respect to his general position. At least as we encounter him toward the end of his career he betrays no sense that he expects other Jews to emulate his apostasy. Indeed he offers himself as a model only when addressing Gentiles who are engaged in Judaizing: "Brethren, I beseech you, become as I am, for I also have become as you are" (Gal. 4:12).

We cannot, however, ignore Paul's quarrel with Israel. The nature and consequences of that quarrel have been subject to persistent misunderstandings. The traditional interpretation holds that from the very existence of the quarrel we may infer that Paul rejected Israel and the Torah. That there is no substance to the traditional claim has been the burden of our argument thus far. But the fact of the quarrel remains. We must now turn to this quarrel, both by way of confirming our view that Paul does not anticipate a conversion of Israel to Christ and by way of further specifying Paul's understanding of the differences between his and Israel's attitude toward the Gentiles.

BOASTING

We have treated the issue of Israel's boasting already, and there is no need for extensive further discussion here. We may limit ourselves to several general observations.

The substance of Paul's complaint regarding Jewish boasting appears most plainly in Rom. 2:17–24: "You call yourself a Jew and rely upon the law and boast of your relation to God. . . . You who boast in the law!" What Paul objects to here is neither the Torah itself, nor the claim that it expresses God's righteousness, nor, as customarily asserted, that for Jews justification consisted of "doing the law."

The sole point of contention is Israel's claim to exclusive access to God's righteousness and thus to the privileges that flow from it—the sonship, the glory, the covenants, the giving of the Torah, the worship, the promises, and the patriarchs (Rom. 9:4–5). In fact, this claim to exclusivity never meant that Gentiles were denied access to these privileges. The door was always open to proselytes. Many Jewish communities must have held that Gentiles who observed elements of the covenant, namely, Gentile Judaizers, could enjoy at least some of these privileges, and the catch-all category of "the righteous among the Gentiles," to the extent that it designates neither proselytes nor Judaizers, made room for those who were a law unto themselves. The Gentiles *as* Gentiles, however, stood outside the covenant and its privileges. Certainly this is how Paul presents the Jewish position. It is important to recognize, however, that Paul's difficulties with this position do not rest, as the traditional view has consistently maintained, on the assertion that individual Jews sought to establish their own righteousness, but rather on the issue of collective exclusivity for Israel. This is how we must read Rom. 10:3 where, in the midst of a lengthy discussion about Israel's present condition, Paul comments that the Jews are "ignorant of the righteousness that comes from God and seek to establish their own."

This perspective also makes it possible to understand why Paul singles out boasting for special attention in his quarrel with Israel. For if his gospel is as we have presented it, that is, if Christ was not the climax of the history of God's dealings with Israel, but the fulfillment of God's promises concerning the Gentiles, the one major point of controversy would be Israel's claim to enjoy an exclusive relation to God. This boast would collide directly with Paul's gospel that the Gentiles *as* Gentiles have received sonship not through Israel but through Christ. Thus for Paul, Israel's boasting becomes the principal target of his concern because his own legitimacy and that of his gospel were at stake. If he should be unable to disallow Israel's boasting as inappropriate, his gospel would have no standing. If, on the other hand, we hold to the traditional view that Paul has simply rejected Israel, it is more difficult to understand why he should have been concerned about their boasting at all. Since this boasting meant an exclusive relation to God, it would have represented no threat to Paul, since his view would be that Israel had no relation to God at all. But if he was committed to a view that Gentiles now stood on an equal footing in relation to God, then Israel's boast would become the primary danger.

RIGHTEOUSNESS

Rom. 10:3 is an important key to understanding not only the nature of Paul's complaint against Israel but also the context of his own gospel. If we take "boasting of the law" and "being ignorant of the righteousness that comes from God" as expressions of the same idea, we must conclude that "being ignorant of the righteousness that comes from God" has to do with the exclusivity involved in "boasting in the law." In short, Rom. 10:3 states that the Jews have failed to understand the redemption of the Gentiles in Christ as the expression of God's righteousness, a righteousness revealed as promise in Abraham and as fulfillment in Christ. For, as we noted in our analysis of the figure of Abraham (Rom. 4; Gal. 3–4), Paul uses him to establish one basic point: that the salvation of the Gentiles in

Christ is the fulfillment of God's righteousness in the promise, "a righteousness revealed from faith for faith" (Rom. 1:17). Paul's expression of anguish in Rom. 9:1–3 about Israel's current situation leads him directly to Abraham and the Gentiles:

> It is not the children of the flesh who are the only children of God, but the children of the promise are (also) reckoned as descendants (9:8); he has mercy upon whomever he wills (9:18).

And in 9:25–26 he cites two passages from Hosea to demonstrate God's intention to redeem the Gentiles:

> those who are not my people I will call my people" (Hos. 2:23); "and in the very place where it was said to them, 'You are not my people,' they will be called sons of the living God" (Hos. 1:10).

When Paul speaks of the righteousness of God in this context, he is thinking exclusively of Abraham, Christ, and the salvation of the Gentiles. Consequently, after moving from his own anguish for Israel to the cause of Israel's "stumbling," he returns to the righteousness which comes from God (9:30–31), that is, the redemption of the Gentiles. Israel has not arrived at righteousness based on the law (*eis nomon*) because it stumbled over the Gentiles (9:32; cf. 11:11). It is not that they failed to pursue righteousness (9:31) or lacked zeal for God (10:2), but that their zeal was unenlightened and that they did not submit to God's righteousness. How? Again, as the context reveals, by their failure to recognize Paul's gospel to and about the Gentiles as fully at one with God's righteousness.

Faith

When Paul takes up his own question about why Israel failed to attain what it sought, he answers, "Because they did not pursue it through faith, but as if it were based on works" (Rom. 9:32). If our earlier interpretation of 9:31 and 10:3 is correct, the phrase "based on works" cannot mean that Paul here attributes to Israel a notion of works righteousness. More likely, since he has been discussing the Gentiles all along and continues with the same theme in what follows, he is following the same line of thought that first appears in 3:27–31. In both places, Paul addresses the same set of issues: the boasting of the Jews, faith and works, the incorporation of the Gentiles, and the continued validity of the Torah. "Based on works" is thus to be seen as a compressed reference to Paul's underlying rejection of the Jewish insistence that Gentiles must still enter the covenant community through obedience to the commandments of Moses.

Not stopping at the simple assertion that Israel failed to comprehend and thus to achieve righteousness, Paul takes his analysis one final step, to the issue of faith/faithfulness (*pistis*). In 3:27 boasting is denied the Jews not "on the principle of works" but "on the principle of faith." And in 9:32 Israel is said to have failed because it pursued righteousness not through faith (*ek pisteōs*) but as if it were based on work (*hōs ex ergōn*). Does Paul mean to say here that Israel failed because it did not become Christian? Certainly not. For in 3:30 he affirms that "since God is one, he will justify the circumcised on the ground of (*ek*) their *pistis* and the uncircumcised because of (*dia*) their *pistis*."[1] Neither here nor anywhere else does Paul intimate that the failure of the Jews lies in their refusal to become Christians. What he does say is that their boasting and their failure to attain righteousness come from a single cause, lack of *pistis*. And not surprisingly, *pistis*—whether as God's promise to Abraham, as Abraham's response to God, or as the Christians' response to Christ—turns out to be the central concept behind Paul's contention that God has now redeemed the Gentiles.

What is the specific content of this faith, that is, the faith of the circumcised, as Paul sees it? Clearly it bears directly on the status of the Gentiles:

• *pistis* excludes the principle of boasting and so Israel's claim to an exclusive relation to God (3:27f);

• *pistis* means that the promise was given to Abraham *before* circumcision, so that not circumcision but God's righteousness and Abraham's faithfulness establish the standing of the circumcised (3:9ff.);

• *pistis* means that sonship lies in doing the Torah rather than merely hearing it; Israel's possession of the Torah, and many other advantages, neither guarantees salvation nor permits boasting, for "if you break the commandment, your circumcision becomes uncircumcision" (2:24ff.);

• *pistis* means that God's righteousness was expressed to Abraham as a promise, and thus its fulfillment cannot be understood as limited to Israel (4:14); it is made manifest now in the faithfulness (*pistis*) of the Gentiles who believe (*hoi pisteuontes*) in him (4:22ff; cf. 1:17);

· *pistis* means that various scriptural passages (esp. Hab. 2:4 and Ps. 143:1) can be used to show that even the righteousness which is based on the Torah (9:31) is not "from the law" but rather from God's righteousness to Abraham who believed; Abraham received two signs—circumcision as the mark of his faith through which he becomes the father of Israel, and the promise, as the mark of his faith through which he becomes the father of Gentiles.

The chain of thinking, then, in Paul's quarrel with Israel went something like this: Why has Israel stumbled? Because the Jews have not accepted the legitimacy of Paul's gospel to and about the Gentiles. Why have they not accepted? Because they have insisted on righteousness through the Mosaic covenant. Why have they made this error? Because they fail to see that righteousness rests on faith, whether for the circumcised or the uncircumcised.

THE SINS OF THE JEWS

Paul does not often speak about specific instances of Jewish disobedience or failure to uphold the Torah. That he does so in Rom. 2:17–24 requires an explanation, not least because this passage is often taken as an essential part of Paul's case against the Jews, culminating in 3:21–26.: "since all have sinned and fallen short of the glory of God, they [Gentiles *and* Jews] are justified as a gift, through the redemption which is in Christ Jesus" (3:23f). We have already argued that neither these verses nor any other speak of the salvation of the Jews through Jesus Christ. Therefore we must assign some other function to their exposé of Jewish sinfulness.

There is yet another reason for resisting the traditional view of 2:17–24 as part of a blanket indictment of the Torah. Sanders has recently reminded us that most Jews would have agreed that while everyone was required to assume full responsibility for upholding the covenant, perfect obedience was not expected. Furthermore, an elaborate system of atonement was developed to enable forgiveness for almost every transgression.[2] Paul the Pharisee was certainly aware of this. Unless we wish to accuse him of either a faulty memory or deliberate distortion, we cannot take his discussion of Jewish sins as the basis for a repudiation of either the Torah or the Jews. If, however, we remember the main theme of 2:1–16 and 2:25–29—the Gentiles—we realize that this text actually does the very opposite of impugning the Torah, for Torah teaches them God's will and instructs them in what is excellent (*ta diapheronta*). The point, however, is not that Jews know the divine will through the Torah—that is taken for granted by Paul throughout—but that they have in addition undertaken to share the knowledge and truth embodied in the Torah (2:20) with Gentiles—the blind, those in darkness, the foolish, and the children! This is the point at which Paul introduces his concern about Jewish disobedience.[3] Because of their own acts of transgression they fail in their mission to be a "light unto the nations." How can they teach Gentiles that observance of the Mosaic Torah is carried out in order to honor God (2:23), if they fail themselves? The conclusion is thus not that the Torah is invalid but that the "name of God is blasphemed among the Gentiles because of you" (Isa. 52:5). And, since the passage begins on the topic of boasting, the implication is that Jewish disobedience only serves to undermine their claim to exclusive knowledge and faith. In light of this passage it thus becomes possible to appreciate the overwhelming sense of urgency that attends *Paul's* self-understanding as one "under obligation both to Greek and barbarians, both to the wise and to the foolish" (Rom. 1:14), one who was set apart even before his birth and called to preach God's Son among the Gentiles (Gal. 1:15f.).

PERSECUTIONS

We need not belabor the obvious fact that earliest Christianity was the cause of great tension and hostility between Jews and Christians. Jesus' words in Matt. 10:17 ("Beware of men; for they will deliver you up to councils and flog you in their synagogues"), Paul's activity as a persecutor before his conversion (1 Cor. 15:9; Gal. 1:13, 23; Phil. 3:6) and the background of the gospel of John all show that the hostility could on occasion erupt into acts of harassment and violence. By the same token, there is no reason to assume the existence of a coordinated Jewish policy regarding Christianity until late in the first century, and when such a policy finally emerges it takes the form of disengagement rather than active persecution. Within this general framework Paul is certainly a unique figure, having been both persecutor and persecuted, for in 2 Cor. 11:24 he states that "five times I have received of the hands of the Jews (the) forty lashes less one" and in 11:26 he speaks of being in "danger from my own people."

Our purpose in raising the issue of the persecutions is not to investigate either their specific character or their basis in Jewish legal procedure. Instead, I wish to ask how Paul regarded them and whether he makes use of them to demonstrate that God has rejected his people. There is a certain irony—as was no doubt apparent to Paul, for he develops an elaborate theory around it in Rom. 11—in the fact that Paul is able to use his afflictions in general and his punishments by synagogues in particular to demonstrate his apostolic legitimacy. Against the "super-apostles" who sought to undermine his authority by claiming that he could not match their feats of spiritual prowess, he retorts that the marks of the true apostle are to be found in weakness and suffering rather than in glory. Apostles, like all Christians, manifest their faith in the present age by participating in Jesus' suffering and death. Participation in his glory awaits his return in the dawning age to come (Phil. 3:10). Thus Paul is only too happy to turn his affliction to advantages and it is for this purpose only that he cites the forty lashes less one in 2 Corinthians 11:24.

Romans 11:28 provides a further answer to the question of how Paul treats Jewish hostility toward the Christian movement. Two aspects of this verse are of interest. The first is the phrase "in terms of the gospel they are enemies." The RSV offers a seriously misleading translation ("as regards the gospel they are enemies *of God*") for which there is no basis whatever in ancient manuscripts. This translation forces the sentence in a direction utterly at odds with its context. Instead, we should take the words as a straightforward statement of fact: certain Jews of Paul's day, or rather certain of those who were drawn into the vortex of his activity, were opposed to the Christian message. Likewise, the comment in Phil. 3:18 ("For many, of whom I have often told you and now tell you with tears, live as enemies of the cross of Christ"), if it refers to or includes Jews among the enemies, means nothing other than that many Jews opposed Christianity. It is difficult to see how any other meaning could be imagined.

The deeper significance of 11:28, however, lies in the second phrase: "But in terms of election (*eklogē*), they are beloved for the sake of the fathers." In short, in a passage in which the disobedience of the Jews provides the divinely ordained opportunity for God to show his mercy on the Gentiles, Israel nevertheless remains God's elect people. "For the gifts and the call of God are irrevocable" (11:29). In Paul's theological calculus, the disobedience of the Jews guarantees not only the salvation of the Gentiles but eventually their own as well.

We turn our attention briefly, to the much controverted text of 1 Thess. 2:13–16:

> (13) And we also thank God constantly for this, that when you re-
> ceived the word of God which you heard from us, you accepted it not
> as the word of men but as what it really is, the word of God, which
> is at work in you believers. (14) For you, brethren, became imitators
> of the churches of God in Jesus Christ which are in Judea; for you
> suffered the same things from your countrymen as they did from the
> Jews (15), who killed both the Lord Jesus and the prophets, and drove
> us out, and displease God and oppose all men (16) by hindering us
> from speaking to the Gentiles that they may be saved—so as always to
> fill up the measure of their sins. But God's wrath has come upon them
> at last (*eis telos*).

There are at least two ways of dealing with this passage. The more radical path is to dismiss it as a non-Pauline interpretation. Birger A. Pearson has made such a case and in my judgment his arguments are decisive.[4] On virtually every ground—language, ideas, structure, presumed dates—the passage is inconsistent with the Paul of the other letters. Without rehearsing Pearson's careful analysis, we may conclude that 1 Thess. 2:13–16 was not produced by Paul.

Let us suppose, however, despite indications to the contrary, that Paul did write these words. Let us further suppose that *eis telos* in 2:16 is not to be taken as meaning that God's wrath has come upon Israel temporarily, somewhat as in Rom. 11, but that it should be read as "at last" or even "forever." What then? Would our interpretation of Paul need to be modified? Or even abandoned? I think not. Such evidence would be decisive or relevant only under either of two conditions: *if* we begin, as does the traditional view, with the view that early Christianity generally, and therefore Paul, regarded Judaism and the Torah as rendered obsolete by Christ, or *if* we hold that the legitimacy of an interpretation depends on an ability to account for each and every loose end. If, however, as suggested earlier, we accept neither of these conditions, we will be obli-

gated neither to force a discordant piece of evidence into conformity with
a general pattern nor to modify the pattern itself to fit this single piece.
We would be left, in the case of 1 Thess. 2:13–16, with a momentary
expression of Paul's anger, triggered by local resistance to his preaching,
in which he gave voice to feelings nowhere in evidence in the other
letters. In any case such remarks would be sufficiently out of tune with
what Paul says elsewhere that it would be quite unjustifiable to use them
as a starting point for an examination of his views on Jews and Judaism.

Our analysis of Paul's quarrel with Israel has revealed two evident
sources for his preoccupation with the relationship between Israel, the
Torah, and the Gentiles—the gospel of Christian Judaizers *and* direct
confrontation between Paul and Jewish opponents of Christianity. Both
of these concerns must be kept in view when reading Pauline passages on
these subjects, for both played a role in shaping his thoughts. In his letters
to the Galatians, the Phillipians, and the Corinthians, the immediate
situation of the Judaizers is clearly the primary focus. In his letter to the
Romans, he carries over many of the terms, arguments, and scriptural
proofs developed in the earlier letters, but he sometimes deploys them
differently in answering the charges laid before him by earlier adversaries.

Finally, it is worth commenting that there is every reason to believe
that Paul's gospel, as we have interpreted it, would have elicited from
many Jews a far more violent reaction than either Jewish Christianity,
that is, observance of the Mosaic covenant coupled with confession of
Jesus as the expected messiah, or later Gentile Christianity. According to
Paul's brief description of the situation in Antioch, at least some Jews
there were willing to accept even Gentiles provided that they be
circumcised (Gal. 2:13).[5] As for later Gentile Christianity, its triumphant
stance vis-à-vis Israel left the Jews little choice but to regard Christians
as at best deluded sectarians and at worst apostates destined for perdition.

Let there be no misunderstanding about the conclusions reached thus
far. For Paul, the privileges attendant on Israel's status as God's chosen
people had been momentarily suspended. Israel had failed in its pursuit
of righteousness based on the Torah (9:31, 10:3); their zeal for God was
unenlightened (10:2); Israel had been disobedient (11:30–32); and finally,
"a hardening has come upon a part of Israel" (11:25). Furthermore a

fundamental component of Israel's self-understanding, the privileged relation to God provided by the Mosaic covenant, has been permanently
revoked. And yet Paul goes to great lengths to deny certain inferences
that were already being drawn in his own time and which have served as
the foundations of the traditional view of Paul. At three points in chapter
11 he denies that Israel has been rejected by God. In 11:2, he states simply
that God has not rejected the people whom he foreknew. In 11:11, he
denies that their stumbling leads to their fall. "By no means!" is his reply.
And in 11:28, he affirms that "the gifts and the call of God are irrevocable."

Once again, Paul does not rest content with assertions alone, but offers
several elaborations of his view that Israel has stumbled, though not so as
to fall. In 9:27, 11:5ff., and 11:27–29, he resorts to a series of scriptural
texts in order to show that not even in the present has all of Israel failed
to understand.[6] The hardening has come upon only a part (*apo merous*)
of Israel (11:25; cf. 11:7–10). Here Paul makes use of the idea, found in
various forms of Judaism, that a faithful remnant rather than all of Israel
will be redeemed by God at the end. What he has in mind at this point is
certainly the fact that some Jews, including himself, had recognized what
God had accomplished in Christ. In addition, in citing Isa. 10:22f.
("though the numbers of the sons of Israel be as the sand of the sea, only
a remnant of them will be saved"), 1 Kings 19:10 ("Lord, they have killed
thy prophets, they have demolished thy altars, and I alone am left, and
they seek my life") and 1 Kings 19:18 ("I have kept for myself seven
thousand men who have not bowed the knee to Ba'al"), he is seeking to
refute the charge, whether actual or potential, that Israel's refusal to
acknowledge Jesus Christ is in itself sufficient to refute Paul's gospel. No,
says Paul, scripture speaks of the faithful remnant, perhaps no more than
a single soul, and I represent that remnant!

If this first elaboration seems typical of certain streams within
contemporaneous Judaism, especially in its use of scripture to justify the
idea of a faithful remnant, the second elaboration is atypical and quite
astonishing. Paul turns the disobedience of the Jews into the divinely
preordained occasion, foretold in scripture, for God to offer salvation to
the Gentiles. "Through their trespass salvation has come to the Gentiles"
(11.11b). Having previously argued that God has the right to do what he
has done in Christ for the Gentiles (9:6–24), that his action is clearly fore-

cast in scripture (9:25–26; 10:18–20), and that even the disobedience of Israel had been forseen (9:27–33; 15:21), Paul is driven by the logic of his own case to relate these great events to each other. Hence, Israel's disobedience is not only not accidental to God's plan of salvation, it has become an essential part of its fulfillment!

> Through their trespass salvation has come to the Gentiles, so as to make Israel jealous. Now if their trespass means riches for the world, and if their failure means riches for the Gentiles, how much more will their full inclusion mean! [11:11f.]

Precisely how the trespass, failure, and rejection of the Jews has led to salvation for the Gentiles is not made clear. Perhaps Paul has in mind the motif found elsewhere in early Christian literature that the rejection of the Christian message by the Jews left no other audience but Gentiles. At the conclusion of Acts, in a speech attributed to Paul, the apostle quotes the standard prooftext for the hardness of Israel (Isa. 6:9–10) and moves directly to the following inference: "Let it be known to you, then, that the salvation of God has been sent to the Gentiles. They will listen" (Acts 28:28). If Paul shares this point of view, he does so with two important restrictions or modifications: (a) unlike all other early Christian literature, Paul sees the rejection as temporary, limited to the brief period of time before the End, and he lays great emphasis on the speedy return of the Jews; and (b) he does not refer to Christians as the new Israel nor does he put forward the view that the Jews have been replaced by Christians.

Having made the redemption of the Gentiles dependent on the trespass of the Jews, Paul completes this line of reasoning by making the eventual "inclusion" (11:12) and salvation (11:26) of Israel dependent on the redemption of the Gentiles. Making use of the verb "to make jealous" (*parazēlōsai*) in the verse from Deut. 32:21 cited in Rom. 10:19, Paul comes full circle in affirming that Israel will in turn be made jealous and return to its senses when it sees the riches of God poured out on the Gentiles. Indeed, he makes every effort to highlight his ministry to Gentiles, so as "to make my fellow Jews (*tēn sarka mou*) jealous and thus save some of them" (11:13f.).

In an effort to extract still more evidence of divine providence from Israel's opposition to the gospel, Paul contrasts Jews and Gentiles one final time in 11:30–32. Echoing the important Pauline theme that God offers salvation to sinners and shows mercy to the disobedient, he applies it now to the current situation of the Jews as enemies of the gospel:

> Just as you [Gentiles!] were once disobedient to God but now have received mercy because of their disobedience, so they (the Jews) have now been disobedient in order that by the mercy shown to you they also may receive mercy. For God has consigned all men to disobedience that he may have mercy on all.

Special attention must be given to 11.32. Clearly it bears a close similarity to Rom. 3:9–19 and Gal. 3:22. The parallel is especially marked as between our passage and Gal. 3:22. This similarity is of great significance for our entire project inasmuch as it is now clear that Rom. 3:9–19, 23 refers primarily, if not exclusively, to Gentiles and their sinfulness under the Torah and before Christ. If Paul is thinking of Jews at all in Rom. 3, he is doing so proleptically. For it is clear that Paul applies his principle of salvation-for-sinners to the Jews *only* in respect of their opposition to the gospel.

A further modification or specification of his statement that Israel has stumbled without falling concerns the ultimate return of Israel, or, as he puts it in 11:26, Israel's complete salvation (*pas Israēl sōthēsetai*).[7] Whether or not Paul expected all Gentiles to be saved is not certain. He uses *pleroma* ("fullness") to speak both of those Gentiles who are to come in (11:25) and of the Jews who will return (11:12). If we use 1 Cor. 15:28 as a guide, we should probably conclude that Paul looked forward to universal redemption without exception. In any case, for Israel there is no doubt: "All Israel will be saved."

A final modification involves the eschatological framework that determines all of Paul's activity.[8] We need only mention here that Paul certainly expected the final events (Rom. 8:18–25; 1 Cor. 14; 1 Thess. 4:13–18) in his own lifetime. When he speaks of the *pleroma* of the Gentiles who are to come in and of Israel's return, he is thinking in terms of years—not even decades, let alone centuries or millennia. The preconditions for the final events were well underway. On Paul's shrunken globe, the *pleroma* of the Gentiles seems to have been equivalent to what lay between "Arabia" (Gal. 1:17) and Spain (Rom. 15:24). In short, all of these momentous events were well underway and pressing forward to their end as Paul wrote his letters. Thus when we read of Israel's trespass, failure, and rejection, we must remember that for Paul their duration was to continue for 20 years, not 2,000.

In seeking answers to the question, "How does Paul understand Israel's present status and role in the divine plan of salvation?", we have persisted toward our original goal. Nothing in the answers has forced us to modify our image of a Paul whose gospel to and about the Gentiles did not entail repudiation of the legitimacy of Israel or the Torah. His thinking is everywhere dominated by the recurrent motto of the letter to the Romans—to the Jew first and then to the Gentile. Thus far we have been able to determine that he never modifies or deviates from this motto. At one level, its reference is clearly chronological. Jews were the first to receive the privilege of God's righteousness; now it has come also to the Gentiles. The primacy of Israel is a fundamental Pauline presupposition. It applies not just in the past but equally, if in unexpected ways, in Paul's own time.

The theme of Israel's primacy, present at every point as a presupposition without which nothing makes sense, receives concrete expression in the two metaphors of 11:16 and especially in the elaboration of the second of the two in 11:17–24: "If the dough offered as first fruits is holy, so is the whole lump; and if the root is holy, so are the branches." The underlying idea of the two images is that the separation of a small part from the original source does not change the character of that part. Israel of Paul's time was the first-fruits and the branches. Even though both might be for the time being cut off from their original source, their basic nature is nonetheless fully determined by it. Then, undoubtedly in response to a rejection-replacement view of Israel already current in Christian circles, Paul illustrates his view of Israel's primacy in an extended agricultural digression. What gives the olive tree its character is not the branches but the root (11:16). Thus even if some of the branches have been broken off—he does not say replaced—and wild shoots grafted to the trunk, the new shoots have no right to boast. Their status depends on the root; their character derives from its richness. "If God did not spare the natural branches [Israel], neither will he spare you." Indeed, he concludes, compared to the difficult task of grafting wild shoots onto a cultivated tree, how much easier will it be for God to regraft the natural ones.

This development of the root-branches metaphor incorporates virtually every aspect of Paul's thinking about Israel: the primacy of Israel over the Gentiles, Israel's temporary separation from the tree, her continued "holiness" despite this separation, and the assurance of her return. Finally, it may not be pressing the metaphor too far to suggest that it is an apt illustration of another important theme, namely, the primacy of God's righteousness over both Jews and Gentiles. For in the metaphor, Gentiles as well as Jews are likened to branches, not to the trunk or the roots. Quite apart from the primacy of the Jews over Gentiles, both are seen to depend on the prior support or foundation of divine righteousness (Rom. 3–4, Gal. 3).

Stendahl and Gaston have noted that Jesus and christological language are notable by their absence in Rom. 11, where Paul completes his extraordinary treatise on Jews and Gentiles. The concluding doxology in 11:33–36 is, as Stendahl remarks, the only Pauline doxology "without any christological element."[9] I take this to mean that when Paul thinks and speaks of Israel's imminent restoration *he does not construe this to imply conversion to Christianity*. To be sure, he speaks of individual Jews, including himself, whose faithfulness takes the form of loyalty to Christ. It is presumably of such Jews that Paul is thinking in 9:24 when he refers to "us whom he had called, not from the Jews only but also from the Gentiles" and in 11:17 when he indicates that only some of the natural branches have been broken off from the tree.[10] But in reading these passages we must distinguish between Paul's own time, in which some Jews embraced Christianity, and his conception of God's time in the near future when *all* of Israel would be saved. Perhaps Gaston is correct in proposing that Paul anticipated that all Jews would in time become followers of Christ. "But" he continues, "he does not explicitly say so."[11] Against this proposal is not only the negative evidence that Paul never explicitly equates Israel's salvation with conversion to Christianity, but even more the fact that he uses faith (*pistis*) not just of Christians but of Jews as well. Rom.

3:30 asserts that God "will justify the circumcised on the ground of their faith and the circumcised because of their faith." As we have seen earlier, Paul uses faith here not as the equivalent of faith in Christ but as a designation of the proper response to God's righteousness, whether for Israel in the Torah or for Gentiles in Christ.

To those who would point to Christians of Jewish birth, for example, the Jerusalem pillars and others, as evidence against our contention that Paul does not prescribe Christ as the path to righteousness for all Jews, we would respond as follows: first, that while at the meeting in Jerusalem Paul presumably assented to the legitimacy of Peter's gospel to the circumcised, he never mentions it again except in Gal. 2; second, if we reckon with the possibility of an evolution in Paul's thinking on these issues, it may be that the earlier agreement in Jerusalem became increasingly irrelevant as time passed and that his self-understanding as the apostle to the Gentiles gradually moved him toward the position expressed in Galatians and Romans; and third, though he nowhere states this explicitly, the logic of his position would lead us to conclude that Jewish Christians were the exception rather than the rule, that they were a "bridge generation" between the time of Christ and the End. In any case, the only Jews Paul speaks about directly are himself, who became a Gentile, and all of Israel, who will be saved at the End.[12]

Finally, we must dwell for a moment on an irony embedded in the argument of Rom. 9–11. On the one hand, it would be possible to claim that Paul's basic quarrel was with Israel's failure to fulfill its mission to the Gentiles (Rom. 2:17–29). The irony is that Israel has in fact now fulfilled that mission, but through disobedience rather than obedience to the Torah. For, it must be remembered, salvation has come to the Gentiles *through their trespass!* (Rom. 11:11). The irony is then compounded by the fact that the obedience of the formerly disobedient Gentiles will soon provoke jealousy among Jews and lead to their full restoration. Now the Gentiles have become a light unto Israel!

These are bold thoughts, unique in the literature of early—or indeed later—Christianity. Little wonder, then, that at the end of these reflections, he pronounces a doxology on the marvelous workings of divine providence:

O the depth of the riches and wisdom and knowledge of God. How unsearchable are his judgments, how inscrutable his ways. [11:33]

The words of the doxology sound like a muted acknowledgment of the remarkable set of proposals contained not just in chapters 9–11 but in the entire letter to which they provide a fitting climax.

Little wonder also that such proposals have proved so ineffectual in the time after Paul. Like everything else in Paul's letters, his treatment of Israel, the Gentiles, and the Torah is grounded in his apocalyptic expectations. This is more than a factual statement about the character of Paul's mentality in relation to apocalyptic Judaism in the first century. It is also a statement with profound hermeneutical implications. For whenever Paul's apocalyptic orientation is ignored or forgotten, the meaning of his words is transformed. As we know, the anticipated End never materialized and Paul became the herald of Gentile Christianity for all subsequent generations. The embattled apostle to Corinth, Philippi, and Galatia became the triumphant apostle to the ages. And in this process, Paul's battles and enemies were utterly transformed.

As a consequence of this transformation, Christian readers of Paul have retained from his tortured dialogues on Israel and the Torah only the isolated fragment that Israel was cut off from its roots. Even though he never says so, this has been taken to mean that the only path to Israel's salvation leads through Christ. Conversely, and no doubt for many of the same reasons, Jewish readers of Paul have seen in him the enemy of Israel and the Torah. Even though he never says so, this has been taken to mean that he declared the Torah defunct as the expression of God's righteousness for Israel.

Thus Christ and Torah remain for Paul mutually exclusive categories, though not at all as traditionally understood. He simply held that the significance of Christ was that Gentiles no longer needed to become Jews in order to enjoy the advantages once reserved exclusively for Israel. This is not to say that the Gentiles have been incorporated into God's covenant with Israel at Sinai. Rather it is the case—Abraham is the critical figure here—that God's promise of righteousness leads in two separate directions, each according to its own time. The promise to Abraham as the father of the circumcised is fulfilled through Moses at Sinai. That promise contains clear evidence, states Paul, of a promise to Abraham as the father also of the uncircumcised, a promise fulfilled at a later time through Christ. For him, Christianity is neither superior to Judaism nor its fulfillment. Nor are the two one except insofar as God's promises are one.

This is not to say that the interpretation of Paul developed here would have made his Jewish contemporaries any happier with him. On the other hand, it does seem likely that on specific issues—notably the relationship between God's righteousness, the demand of faithfulness (*pistis*), and the giving of the covenant—this reading of Paul brings him closer to traditional Judaism than many have thought. What makes Paul so difficult for Jewish readers is his stance toward Israel on this very cluster of issues. For it is at the heart of his case that Israel's zeal for God was unenlightened. But at the same time it must be stressed that his *only* evidence for the unenlightened nature of their zeal for God was their refusal to recognize that God had now done for the Gentiles what he had already done for Israel! This is not to say that Paul's gospel gains legitimacy from a Jewish perspective as the result of the interpretation proposed here. It is only to say that he never proclaimed his gospel at the expense of Jews or the Torah as such.

CONCLUSION

Our sense of the past is created for us largely by history's winners. The voices of the losers, when heard at all, are transmitted through a carefully tuned network of filters. The final triumph of orthodox Christianity is instructive in this regard.

In this particular struggle, the losers were many. Beyond the enormous variety of heretics, known to us only through the anti-heretical writings of the orthodox victors, we may enumerate certain others as relevant to our present concerns:

Christian Judaizers, including the numerous groups traditionally labelled as Jewish Christians;
the religion of Judaism itself as represented in Christian sources, ancient and modern;
Gentile sympathizers, reaching back to early Hellenistic times and culminating in the early centuries of the Roman empire.

The consequences of the loss of these ancient voices have been far-reaching. From one perspective the course of modern scholarship in this area can be described as a series of efforts to reconstitute the full chorus of Jews, Gentiles, and Christians in the early centuries. Traditional scholarship was founded on a narrow range of speakers. Certain "fundamental truths" apply only if we listen to an orthodox minority: for example, the progressive de-Judaization of Christianity and the "final break" between Judaism and Christianity as occurring between 135 and 150 C.E. Only an

265

orthodox view of the past makes it possible to assert that "after A.D. 70 there are no more direct contacts with contemporary Judaism save hostile ones."[1]

Occasionally we are blessed with extraordinary discoveries that make it possible for the first time to read the original score. The Dead Sea Scrolls and the Nag Hammadi codices were two such finds. They have revolutionized our conception of the Palestinian Jewish setting of early Christianity on the one hand and our understanding of Gnostic Christianity on the other. But they have also taught a painful lesson. The seemingly insuperable difficulties encountered in trying to reconcile these new documents with ancient descriptions of them by their orthodox opponents —whether Jewish or Christian—remind us not only how little we know of history's losers but even more poignantly how consistently "bad" the reports of the winners have been.

For the most part the task of dismantling the orthodox version of the past consists of laborious deconstruction and intelligent guesswork. Frustration is a constant companion. The problem is not merely that sources for the "other voices" are missing. Such sources, after all, belong to the spoils of victory and frequently have been consumed in the celebratory bonfires. An even more persistent frustration lies in the difficulty of altering our habitual ways of thinking. Without knowing it, we perceive the past according to paradigms first created many centuries ago. In the historical religions of Judaism and Christianity, the distant past shapes the present in untold ways. For this reason, efforts to expose our ways of thinking as rooted in ancient controversies, rather than in "the facts," are subject to repeated failure. One example will suffice. The deeply biased and unhistorical image of ancient Judaism that has characterized so much of modern Christian scholarship has shown an almost incredible degree of persistence. The source of this image is not "the facts" but the literature of controversy between Jews and Christians in antiquity, namely, the gospels and other early Christian literature. Even the Dead Sea Scrolls and the Nag Hammadi writings have frequently been treated as though they could be comfortably inserted into the framework and categories of the orthodox past.

What this means is that not all of history's losers are to be found in the past. We too are the losers. Here I have in mind more than distorted presentations of ancient Judaism in works of modern scholarship. More than this, the ultimate loser may be Western culture itself. This is not the place to rehearse the drama of modern anti-Semitism. The results of our study require us, however, to confront again those who have sought to deny or to minimize the contributions of early Christianity. Such efforts have customarily used one of three arguments: first, that modern anti-Semitism is a uniquely modern phenomenon and has nothing to do with pre-modern history in any form; second, that modern anti-Semitism represents paganism in modern dress and is therefore non-Christian in spirit and content; and third, that anti-Semitism/anti-Judaism in early Christianity derives not from Christian sources but from the influence of pagan anti-Semitism.

The foremost proponent of the view that modern anti-Semitism is a uniquely modern phenomenon is Hannah Arendt. She has characterized it as racial in form and anti-Christian in character. Moreover, she asserts that the modern world is separated from antiquity and the middle ages by such a chasm with respect to Jewish affairs that it is utterly wrong to posit any continuity from one side to the other.[2] Thus she is able to conclude that "the charge against Christianity in general, with its two thousand years of history, cannot be proved, and if it could be proved, it would be horrible."[3]

Arendt's position bristles with difficulties. The notion of an unbridgeable chasm between the modern world and antiquity or the middle ages runs against the grain of common sense and sound historiography. For there are, as E. R. Dodds has put it, no periods in history, only in historians.[4] At the least we must admit that the New Testament managed to survive the perilous journey into modernity. And the New Testament is the heart of the matter. Beyond this, Uriel Tal's study of Germany during the Second Reich (1870–1914) has demonstrated the co-existence and mutual impact of two anti-Semitisms at that time—one Christian, the other explicitly anti-Christian. The Christian variety, expressed widely by pastors and theologians, clearly has roots in the Christian tradition. But even the anti-Christian variety borrowed heavily from Christian sources. Tal observes that "the racial anti-Semites appropriated basic Christian ideas even while reprobating them and adapted them for their own purposes."[5]

A second explanation of modern anti-Semitism in strictly modern terms asserts that it consists of little more than a modern revival of ancient pagan anti-Semitism. Beginning with the Enlightenment, if not before, modern secularists simply "discovered" the pervasive anti-Semitism of their ancient heroes. Unfortunately the explanation of the revival of anti-Semitism in the nineteenth century as the unintended by-product of a return to the ideals of classical antiquity does not hold up under examination. The anti-religious ideology of the Enlightenment manifestly owed a heavy debt to Christianity. Moreover, it is naive to suppose that the *philosophes* encountered antiquity in a void. Their canon of classical authors was chosen with every bit as much care as the ancient canon of Christian writings—and often with the same results. Voltaire and his contemporaries returned to ancient writings with a preconception of Judaism fostered by centuries of Christianity. They selected those authors—Cicero, Tacitus, Seneca—whose views coincided with and reinforced their own. That this canon fails signally to reflect the full range of pagan attitudes toward Judaism has been the burden of Part II of this book.

The third method of minimizing the Christian contribution to Western anti-Semitism has been to trace its more violent forms, even in early Christianity, to pagan sources. As we have seen in Part I, this is a futile proceeding. It requires a gross distortion of the true nature of Gentile attitudes toward Judaism, from the first encounters between Greeks and Jews in the third century B.C.E. to the time of late antiquity. Worse yet, this solution ignores the fundamental differences between Christian and pagan approaches to Judaism.

This is not to say that Christian beliefs about Judaism are alone responsible for modern anti-Semitism. Such is not the case. Nor can it any longer be maintained that early Christianity as such, in its fullest manifestations, led to later expressions of anti-Semitism, whether Christian or otherwise. Our study has led to the conclusion that neither in paganism nor in Christianity is there evidence for a consistently negative understanding of Judaism. Those who argue otherwise must offer a deliberately selective reading of antiquity from which one side of a conversation has been systematically excluded.

All of the surviving testimony—including the most vigorously anti-Jewish and anti-Semitic examples—suggests that Judaism provoked among Christians and pagans alike profound *internal* divisions. Certainly for Christianity in its early stages, the real debate was never between Christians and Jews but among Christians. Eventually the anti-Jewish side won. Its ideology became normative, not just for subsequent Christianity and Western culture but, through the formation of the New Testament, for our perception of earlier Christianity as well. The voice of the losing side fell silent.

At the end we return to the beginning. Ultimately this study springs from a desire to reconstruct the ancient conversation about Judaism in all its dimensions. It is now possible to hear other voices in that conversation—the voice of Christians who saw no need to repudiate Judaism even while embracing Christianity as well as the voice of Gentiles who saw in Judaism a religion for all humanity. Whether this ancient conversation will prove relevant to modern ones, no one can predict. But for those whose self-understanding is firmly rooted in an ancient past, these voices can hardly be ignored.

NOTES

INTRODUCTION

1. Krister Stendahl, *Paul Among Jews and Gentiles* (Philadelphia, 1976) pp. 86f.

2. D. R. A. Hare, "The Rejection of the Jews in the Synoptic Gospels and Acts," in A. Davies, ed., *Anti-Semitism and the Foundations of Christianity* (New York, 1979) pp. 28–32.

PART I: ANTI-SEMITISM AND ANTI-JUDAISM: THE MODERN DEBATE

I: FROM JULES ISAAC TO ROSEMARY RUETHER

1. M. Stern, *Greek and Latin Authors on Jews and Judaism,* two volumes with a third projected (Jerusalem, 1974 and 1980); D. Efroymsen on Marcion, Tertullian, and others in "The Patristic Connection," in Davies, *Foundations,* pp. 98–117; J. Neusner, *Aphrahat and Judaism. The Christian-Jewish Argument in Fourth-Century Iran* (Leiden, 1971); R. Wilken, *Judaism and the Early Christian Mind. A Study of Cyril of Alexandria's Exegesis and Theology* (New Haven, 1971); and N. de Lange, *Origen and the Jews. Studies in Jewish-Christian Relations in Third-Century Palestine* (Cambridge, 1976).

2. M. Simon, *Verus Israel. Etude sur les relations entre chrétiens et juifs dans l'empire romain (135–425)* (Paris, 1964); J. Gager, "The Dialogue of Paganism with Judaism: Bar Cochba to Julian," *Hebrew Union College Annual* 44 (1973): 89–118; W. Meeks and R. Wilken, *Jews and Christians in Antioch in the First Four Centuries of the Common Era* (Missoula, Montana, 1978); A. T. Kraabel, "Paganism and Judaism: The Sardis Evidence," in *Paganisme, Judaïsme, Christianisme: Mélanges offerts à Marcel Simon,* ed. A. Benoit, M. Philonenko, C. Vogel (Paris, 1978) pp. 13–33; and E. M. Smallwood, *The Jews under Roman Rule* (Leiden, 1976).

3. J. N. Sevenster, *The Roots of Anti-Semitism in the Ancient World* (Leiden, 1975); S. Applebaum, *Jews and Greeks in Ancient Cyrene* (Leiden, 1979); A. Fuks, V. Tcherikover and M. Stern, *Corpus Papyrorum Judaicarum*, three volumes (Cambridge, Mass., 1957, 1960 and 1964); and H. Leon, *The Jews of Ancient Rome* (Philadelphia, 1960).

4. C. Y. Glock and R. Stark, *Christian Beliefs and Anti-Semitism* (New York, 1969); and R. M. Loewenstein, *Christians and Jews. A Psychoanalytic Study* (New York, 1951).

5. J. Juster, *Les juifs dans l'empire romain* (Paris, 1914).

6. T. Reinach, *Textes d'auteurs grecs et romains relatifs au judaïsme* (1895). Reprint edition: Hildesheim, 1963.

7. See the brief description of Lewy's project in Stern, *Authors*, vol. I, pp. viif.

8. G. F. Moore, "Christian Writers on Judaism," *Harvard Theological Review* 14 (1921): 197–254.

9. J. Parkes, *The Conflict of the Church and the Synagogue. A Study in the Origins of Antisemitism* (Cleveland and Philadelphia, 1961; first published in 1934). For an assessment of Parkes's work, especially after World War II, see the comments of Alan Davies in *Foundations*, pp. xiii–xvii and also in Davies, *Anti-Semitism and the Christian Mind* (New York, 1969) pp. 53f., 138–143.

10. A. L. Williams, *Adversus Judaeos. A Bird's-Eye View of Christian Apologiae until the Renaissance* (Cambridge, 1935).

11. Moore, "Christian Writers," p. 197.

12. The first French edition, *Jésus et Israël*, appeared in 1948, the English edition in New York, 1971.

13. Among studies produced independently of Simon, see the following: R. Wilde, *The Treatment of the Jews in Greek Christian Writers of the First Three Centuries* (Washington, D.C., 1949); and L. Goppelt, *Christentum and Judentum im ersten und zweiten Jahrhundert* (Gütersloh, 1954). The first half of Goppelt's work has been translated into English as *Jesus, Paul and Judaism* (New York, 1964).

14. Simon, *Verus Israel*, p. 274; my translation.

15. F. Lovsky, *Antisémitisme et mystère d'Israël* (Paris, 1955).

16. G. Baum, *The Jews and the Gospel. A Re-Examination of the New Testament* (London, 1961) p. 4; revised edition, *Is the New Testament Anti-Semitic?* (New York, 1965).

17. Baum, *The Jews*, p. 1.

18. Ibid., p. 5.

19. Ibid., p. 7.

20. R. Ruether, *Faith and Fratricide. The Theological Roots of Anti-Semitism* (New York, 1974) pp. 3f.

21. Ibid., p. 24.

22. Ibid., p. 27.

23. Ibid., p. 28.
24. Ibid., p. 30.
25. Ibid., p. 94.
26. Ibid., p. 123.
27. Ibid., p. 116.
28. Ibid., p. 181.
29. Glock and Stark, *Christian Beliefs, passim.*
30. Ibid., p. 130.
31. Ibid., p. 161.
32. Ruether, *Fratricide*, p. 30.
33. L. Coser, *The Functions of Social Conflict* (New York, 1956). Coser's book is based largely on the work of the German sociologist, Georg Simmel.
34. Coser, *Social Conflict*, p. 70.
35. Ibid., p. 69.
36. Subtitled *Religion, Politics, and Ideology in the Second Reich, 1870–1914* (Ithaca and London, 1975) p. 304.
37. P. Berger and T. Luckmann, *The Social Construction of Reality* (New York, 1967).
38. Ibid., p. 108.
39. Ibid., p. 159.
40. Loewenstein, *Christians and Jews*, p. 199.
41. Ruether, *Fraticide*, p. 181.

2: CONSENSUS AND CRISIS IN THE RESPONSE TO RUETHER

1. For a comment on Ruether's critics, see N. Ravitch, "The Problem of Christian Anti-Semitism," *Commentary* (April, 1982): p. 42.
2. So especially K. Stendahl in his article, "Judaism and Christianity: A Plea for a New Relationship," *Cross Currents* 17 (1967): 445–458.
3. So, Hare in "The Rejection of the Jews," pp. 27–47. Davies's volume contains a number of articles by exegetes and theologians, all of them written in response to Ruether's *Faith and Fratricide.*
4. In Ruether's response to the articles in Davies, *Foundations,* "The *Faith and Fratricide* Discussion: Old Problems and New Dimensions," in Davies, *Foundations,* pp. 238f.
5. Hare, "Rejection of Jews," p. 29. On this issue see also P. Richardson, *Israel in the Apostolic Church* (Cambridge, 1969), Appendix C: "The sects of Judaism and 'true Israel'," pp. 217–228.
6. Ruether, "Discussion," p. 235.
7. Ibid., p. 237.
8. For a recent discussion see G. Vermes, *Jesus the Jew. A Historian's Reading of the Gospels* (Philadelphia, 1981).
9. Hare, "Rejection of Jews," pp. 31f.

10. Ruether, "Discussion," p. 240.

11. Hare, "Rejection of Jews," p. 41.

12. Ruether, "Discussion," p. 237. This observation is reminiscent of the view advanced by Loewenstein, *Jews and Christians*, pp. 190f. and A. Roy Eckardt, *Elder and Younger Brothers. The Encounter of Jews and Christians* (New York, 1973) pp. 22–25, that Christian anti-Semitism results from a projection onto Jews of the negative aspect of the ambivalence felt by Christians toward Jesus Christ.

13. Isaac, *Jesus and Israel*, "Proposition 10: Nothing would be more futile than to try to separate from Judaism the gospel that Jesus preached. . . ." (p. 74).

14. Ruether, "Discussion," p. 235.

15. J. Koenig, *Jews and Christians in Dialogue. New Testament Foundations* (Philadelphia, 1979) p. 36.

16. This point is developed by T. A. Idinopulos and R. B. Ward in their article, "Is Christology Inherently Anti-Semitic," *Journal of the American Academy of Religion* 45 (1977): 197f.

17. For a full discussion of "non-cross" christologies in the early gospel traditions, see H. Koester, "One Jesus and Four Primitive Gospels," in J. M. Robinson and H. Koester, *Trajectories through Early Christianity* (Philadelphia, 1970) pp. 158–204.

18. Ruether, "Discussion," p. 236.

19. D. Flusser, "Jesus in the Context of History," in A. Toynbee, ed. *The Crucible of Christianity* (New York, 1969) p. 225.

20. See the extended discussion on pp. 193–212.

21. See also the comments of Idinopulos and Ward, "Christology," p. 198.

22. Meagher, "As the Twig was Bent: Antisemitism in Greco-Roman and Early Christian Times," in Davies, *Foundations*, p. 21.

23. Ibid., pp. 4f.

24. Idinopulos and Ward, "Christology," p. 202.

25. Sevenster, *Roots;* see especially, pp. 89–144. "In this seldom disowned strangeness, emanating from the way of life and thought prescribed by the Torah, lies the profoundest cause for the anti-Semitism of the ancient world" (p. 144).

26. So W. H. C. Frend, *Martyrdom and Persecution in the Early Church* (Garden City, New York, 1967) p. 96.

27. See D. Georgi's treatment of Judaism as a "Menschheitsreligion" in *Die Gegner des Paulus im 2. Korintherbrief* (Neukirchen-Vluyn, 1964) pp. 182–187.

28. Moore "Christian Writers," p. 197.

29. Simon, *Verus Israel*, pp. 474f.

30. C. Klein, *Anti-Judaism in Christian Theology* (Philadelphia, 1978); the book first appeared in German in 1975. For further literature on this issue see

S. Schechter, "Higher Criticism—Higher Anti-Semitism," in *Seminary Addresses and Other Papers* (Cincinnati, 1915) pp. 35–37; and U. Tal, *Christians and Jews*, pp. 191–222.

31. E. P. Sanders, *Paul and Palestinian Judaism. A Comparison of Patterns of Religion* (Philadelphia, 1977); see esp. pp. 35–59.

32. See ibid., p. 34. In *Paul the Apostle. The Triumph of God in Life and Thought* (Philadelphia, 1980), J. C. Beker has proclaimed that Sanders's book has "destroyed this anti-Jewish bias in scholarship once and for all" (p. 340, note).

33. Moore, "Christian Writers," pp. 23f.; cf. Sanders, *Paul*, p. 52.

34. See Stendahl, "Judaism," pp. 450f.; Klein, *Anti-Judaism*, p. 4; and G. Nickelsburg in his review of Klein in *Religious Studies Review* 4 (1978): 164, 167.

35. In Davies, *Foundations*, p. 48.

PART II: JUDAISM AND JUDAIZING AMONG GENTILES

1. John Meagher, "The Twig," in Davies, *Foundations*, p. 21.

2. Sevenster, *Roots*, pp. 180–218.

3: THE GREEK AND ROMAN ENCOUNTER WITH JUDAISM

1. For a discussion of these authors see Stern, *Authors*, vol. I, pp. 8–17 (Theophrastus); pp. 45–52 (Megasthenes, Clearchus); pp. 93–96 (Hermippus), and pp. 131–133 (Ocellus).

2. M. Hengel, *Hellenism and Judaism* (Philadelphia, 1974) p. 255.

3. See the discussion in Stern, *Authors*, vol. I, pp. 157–164.

4. See in particular. V. Tcherikover, *Hellenistic Civilization and the Jews* (Philadelphia, 1961) pp. 175–203; E. Bickerman, *From Ezra to the Last of the Maccabees* (New York, 1962) pp. 93–111; and Hengel, *Hellenism and Judaism*, p. 307.

5. Diodorus, *Bibliotheca Historica*, 34.1.1–5. For text and discussion see Stern, *Authors*, vol. I, pp. 181–184.

6. Stern, *Authors*, vol I, pp. 28–34; see also J. Gager, *Moses in Greco-Roman Paganism* (Nashville, Tennessee, 1972) pp. 26–37.

7. Stern, *Authors*, vol. I, pp. 97–101.

8. Ibid., pp. 141–147.

9. Josephus, *Against Apion*, 2.79.

10. See Tcherikover, *Hellenistic Civilization*, p. 365 and Sevenster, *Roots*, pp. 51f.

11. Stern, *Authors*, vol. I, p. 143.

12. See especially Smallwood, *Roman Rule, passim*.

13. See Stern, *Authors*, vol. I, pp. 207–212.

14. For the period as a whole, see Fuks and Tcherikover, *Corpus*, vol. I, pp. 1–47 and *passim*.

15. Ibid., p. 25.

16. For texts and discussion, see Stern, *Authors*, vol. I, pp. 62–86 and Gager, *Moses*, pp. 113–118.

17. Hengel, *Hellenism and Judaism*, vol. I, p. 258.

18. In general on the period see Fuks and Tcherikover, *Corpus*, *passim* and Smallwood, *Roman Rule*, pp. 220–225, 389–427.

19. Fuks and Tcherikover, *Corpus*, vol. I, p. 48.

20. Smallwood, *Roman Rule*, p. 234.

21. Josephus, *Apion*, 1.288–292. The account bears a close similarity to the version attributed to Manetho in *Apion*, 1.230–251.

22. Ibid., 1.305–311.

23. Ibid., 2.25.

24. Ibid., 2.94f.

25. Ibid., 2.33.

26. Ibid., 2.38.

27. Ibid., 2.49–56.

28. Ibid., 2.56–63.

29. Ibid., 2.65.

30. So Smallwood, *Roman Rule*, p. 234.

31. Philo's extensive and eyewitness account of these events appears in his *Against Flaccus*.

32. Ibid., 53, 59, 73ff.

33. Text, translation and discussion in Fuks and Tcherikover, *Corpus*, vol. II., pp. 36–55.

34. Philo, *Flaccus*, 20.

35. Fuks and Tcherikover, *Corpus*, vol. II, no. 156c; pp. 78f.

36. Philo, *Flaccus*, 128.

37. Fuks and Tcherikover, *Corpus*, vol. II, no. 156b; pp. 74–78.

38. Ibid., vol. II, no. 157; pp. 82–84.

39. Philo, *Flaccus*, 135.

40. Ibid., 137.

41. Josephus, *Antiquities*, 19.278.

42. Fuks and Tcherikover, *Corpus*, vol. II, p. 52.

43. Josephus, *War*, 2.487.

44. Ibid., 2.487–498.

45. On this revolt see Applebaum, *Jews and Greeks*, pp. 201–344.

46. Fuks and Tcherikover, *Corpus*, vol. I, p. 92.

47. *War*, 2.498.

48. Fuks and Tcherikover, *Corpus*, vol. II, no. 157; pp. 82–84.

49. Ibid., no. 158; pp. 87–99.

50. Ibid., vol. I, pp. 43f.

4: THE LATER ROMAN ENCOUNTER WITH JUDAISM

1. Text and discussion in Fuks and Tcherikover, *Corpus*, vol. II, p. 80 (no. 156d).

2. In the legal brief in defense of his client Flaccus (*Pro Flacco*, 28.69).

3. Horace, *Satires*, I. 9, line 30.

4. Persius, *Satires*, 5, line 184 *(recutitaque sabbata)*.

5. Petronius, *Satyricon*, 68.8.

6. Ibid., 102.13f.

7. Petronius, Fragment 37; text and discussion in Stern, *Authors*, vol. I, p. 444.

8. Martial, *Epigrams*, 7.30, line 5; text and discussion in Stern, *Authors*, vol. I, pp. 523–529.

9. Ibid., 7.35, lines 1–8.

10. Ibid., 7.82, lines 4–6.

11. Ibid., 11.94, lines 1–8.

12. See the recent article by R. Goldenberg, "The Jewish Sabbath in the Roman World up to the Time of Constantine the Great," in *Aufstieg und Niedergang der römischen Welt*, vol. II. 19.1, ed. H. Temporini and W. Haase (Berlin, 1979) pp. 414–447.

13. Among them were Strabo, Suetonius, Martial, and Pompeius Trogus. Goldenberg argues that there may actually have been Sabbath fasting among some Jews in antiquity, although the only evidence he can cite is the fact that some Jews in the middle ages fasted toward the close of Sabbath, while others fasted for an entire Sabbath once a year (ibid., 440).

14. For example, Tacitus and Plutarch.

15. On this much discussed phrase, see Stern, *Authors*, vol. I, p. 326 and Goldenberg, "Jewish Sabbath," pp. 436–438.

16. Ovid, *Art of Love*, 1.75–81, 413–416; Ovid, *Remedies*, 217–220.

17. Persius, *Satires*, 5.176–184.

18. *Embassy to Gaius*, 361.

19. Petronius, Fragment 37.

20. Plutarch, *Dinner Conversations*, 4.4–5.3.

21. Juvenal, *Satires*, 3.60–63.

22. Ibid., 3.12–16.

23. Ibid., 3.295f.

24. Juvenal, *Satires*, 6.542–547.

25. Juvenal, *Satires*, 14.96–106.

26. On the techniques and extent of Jewish proselytism, including the question of whether there were Jewish missionaries in an active and public sense, there is a considerable literature. See J. Munck, *Paul and the Salvation of Mankind* (London, 1959) pp. 264–271; D. Georgi, *Gegner*, pp. 83–187; Simon, *Verus Israel*, pp. 316–355, 482–488; B. Bamberger, *Proselytism in the Talmudic*

Period (Cincinnati, 1939); and W. G. Braude, *Jewish Proselytism in the First Five Centuries of the Common Era, the Age of the Tannaim and Amoraim* (Providence, 1940).

27. The first epitomator is Julius Paris (fourth century C.E.?), the second is Nepotianus (fifth century C.E.?); text and discussion in Smallwood, *Roman Rule*, pp. 129f. and Stern, *Authors*, vol. I, pp. 358–360.

28. On Caecilius see Gager, *Moses*, p. 57*n*94.

29. Josephus, *Antiquities*, 18.65–84.

30. Tacitus, *Annals*, 2.85.4.

31. Suetonius, *Tiberius*, 36; cf. *Claudius*, 25.4 where Suetonius reports that the emperor expelled the Jews from Rome because they constantly made disturbances at the instigation of Chrestus.

32. Smallwood, *Roman Rule*, pp. 202–210.

33. Dio Cassius, *History*, 57.18.5a.

34. *Domitian*, 12.2; see the discussion in Smallwood, *Roman Rule*, pp. 376–385.

35. Dio, *History*, 67.14.1–3, according to the epitome of Xiphilinus.

36. Horace, *Satires*, 1.4.142f.

37. The fragment is quoted by Augustine, *City of God*, 6.11.

38. Justinian, *Digest*, 48.8.11.1. On the period as a whole, see Smallwood, *Roman Rule*, pp. 467–486.

39. *Historia Augusta, Antoninus Pius*, 5.4f.

40. Smallwood, *Roman Rule*, p. 472.

41. Justin Martyr, *Dialogue with Trypho*, 8.4; 23.3–5; 123.1.

42. *Historia, Septimius Severus*, 17.

43. Smallwood, *Roman Rule*, p. 501.

44. Josephus, *Apion*, 2.282.

45. See H. Leon, *Ancient Rome*, pp. 253–256. For further references to proselytes on inscriptions see J. B. Frey, ed., *Corpus Inscriptionum Judaicarum*, 2 volumes (Rome, 1936). A new edition of volume one has been produced by B. Lifshitz (New York, 1975).

46. M. Stern, "Sympathy for Judaism in Roman Senatorial Circles in the Period of the Early Empire," (in Hebrew) *Zion* 29 (1964): 155–167.

47. S. Applebaum, "Domitian's Assassination: The Jewish Aspect," *Scripta Classica Israelica* 1 (1974): 116–123.

48. On Sejanus, the only source is Philo, *Embassy*, 159–161. According to Philo, Sejanus's animosity toward the Jews stemmed from his fear that the Jews' loyalty to the emperor might interfere with his own desire to guide Tiberius's career.

49. On Helicon the only source is again Philo, *Embassy*, 166–178, 203–206. It is important to note that Philo calls Helicon an Egyptian.

50. On Seneca, see Stern, *Authors*, vol. I, pp. 429–434. Stern notes that Seneca's dates place him "at the height of the Jewish proselytizing movement

and the diffusion of Jewish customs throughout the Mediterranean world" (p. 429).

51. On Quintilian see ibid., pp. 512–514.

52. See Leon, *Ancient Rome*, pp. 14f.

53. See the discussion in Smallwood, *Roman Rule*, pp. 385–388. A curious passage in the Babylonian Talmud (*Gittin* 57a) mentions a certain Onkelos, the son of Titus's sister, who used necromancy in order to speak with Balaam. Balaam advised Onkelos not to convert to Judaism.

54. Josephus (*Antiquities*, 21.195) says that Poppaea was *theosebēs*.

55. Smallwood in *Roman Rule* (p. 206*n*15; p. 278*n*78) argues that *theosebēs* simply meant that Poppaea was pious, but this is not certain.

56. On Agrippa's life in Rome, see ibid., pp. 181–200.

57. See Leon, *Ancient Rome*, p. 27.

58. Valerius Flaccus, *Argonautica*, 1.1–20.

59. Silius Italicus, *Punica*, 3.597–606.

60. Frontinus, *Strategemata*, 2.1.17.

61. Martial, *Epigrams*, 2.2, lines 1–6.

62. H. Lewy, "Tacitus on the Origin and Manners of the Jews," (in Hebrew) *Zion* 8 (1943): 17–26.

63. So also Applebaum, *Jews and Greeks*, p. 248.

64. Ibid., p. 247.

65. Ibid., p. 248; cf. Applebaum, "Assassination," pp. 121f.

5: AGAINST THE STREAM

1. See Gager, *Moses*, pp. 26–28; and Stern, *Authors*, vol. I, pp. 167–189.

2. On these authors, see the discussion on pp. 39–41.

3. On Nicolaus see the excellent study by B.Z. Wacholder, *Nicolaus of Damascus* (Berkeley and Los Angeles, 1962).

4. The account appears in Josephus, *Antiquities*, 12.125f.

5. Ibid., 16.43. The use of the first person in Nicolaus's speech has led some interpreters to reject it outright as Josephus's invention. More recently Wacholder in *Nicolaus* (pp. 29, 105) has argued for its authenticity on the grounds that the speech is consistent with Herod's desire to curry favor among Jewish communities of the Diaspora. To support this case, Wacholder points to Josephus, *Antiquities*, 14.66–68, where Nicolaus is said to have praised the piety of those priests who remained at the altar rather than fleeing when the temple was overrun by Pompey's forces in 63 B.C.E.

6. Hazael and Hadad are kings mentioned in 1 Kings 11:14, etc.

7. Pompeius Trogus, *Philippic Histories*, 36.2.6–10.

8. Ibid., 36.2.16.

9. Ibid., 36.2.16.

10. Ibid., 36.3.9.

11. Strabo, *Geography* 16; for discussions see Gager, *Moses,* pp. 38–47 and Stern, *Authors,* vol. I, pp. 294–311.

12. Stern, *Authors,* vol. I, p. 266.

13. Josephus, *Apion,* 2.84.

14. G. W. Bowersock, *Augustus and the Greek World* (Oxford, 1965) p. 124.

15. See Leon, *Ancient Rome,* pp. 11f.

16. Suetonius, *Augustus,* 76.

17. See the discussion on pp. 59f.

18. See the discussion on p. 60.

19. Longinus, *On the Sublime,* 9.9; see Gager, *Moses,* pp. 56–63 and Stern, *Authors,* vol. I, pp. 361–365.

20. Stern, *Authors,* vol. I, p. 362.

21. Epictetus, *Discourses,* 1.11.12.

22. Ibid., 1.22.4.

23. Ibid., 2.9.19–20.

24. So Stern, *Authors,* vol. I, pp. 543f.

25. Ibid., pp. 564–576.

26. Plutarch, *On Superstition,* 8 (169C).

27. Plutarch, *On the Contradictions of the Stoics,* 38 (1051E).

28. In Plutarch, *Isis and Osiris,* 31 (363C-D). According to Plutarch, some had attempted to make this connection by identifying Typhon as the father of Hierosolymus and Judaeus, the supposed forebearers of the Jews.

29. This particular identification with Dionysus must have been fairly common inasmuch as Tacitus, writing in Rome, specifically disputes it, claiming that "Father Liber [Dionysus] established festive rites of a joyous nature, while the ways of the Jews are preposterous and mean" (*Hist.* 5.5). On the possibility that elements of Dionysiac iconography or liturgy might have influenced Jewish worship in the Hellenistic period, see E. R. Goodenough, *Jewish Symbols in the Greco-Roman Period* (New York, 1953–68) vol. 4 (1954) pp. 156–158, and vol. 12 (1965) p. 155.

30. Pliny, *Natural History,* 5.66–73.

31. The saying appears in Synesius of Cyrene's, *Life of Dio,* 3.2; cf. Stern, *Authors,* I. pp. 538–540.

32. Solinus's *Encyclopedia of Remarkable Matters,* probably written in the early third century c.e., for the most part paraphrases Pliny and lays heavy emphasis on the remarkable ascetic discipline of the Essenes. Toward the end of his summary, however, he adds that "whoever commits even the slightest error is expelled as if by divine providence, no matter how strenuously he seeks to gain entry." This detail does not appear in Pliny or any other pagan author. On the other hand, Josephus's picture of the Essenes in the *War* (2.119–161) does mention expulsion from the order as a punishment for wrongdoing, though only for serious offenses. In Martianus Capella's, *The Marriage*

of *Philology and Mercury*, written in the early decades of the fifth century C.E., the author provides the briefest possible account of the geography of the eastern Mediterranean. With no preparation for such an observation, he adds the following: "On the west [of the Jordan] are the Essenes, who live without indulging in intercourse or any other pleasures" (par. 679). Throughout this section, Martianus is dependent on Pliny. The translation is from *Martianus Capella and the Seven Liberal Arts*, vol. II: *The Marriage of Philology and Mercury* (New York, 1977) p. 254. Similarly, Porphyry's extensive quotation and paraphrase of Josephus, which draws on all three of his descriptions, mentions punishment by expulsion for wrongdoers (*On Abstinence*, 4.11–13).

33. Philo, *Every Good Man Is Free*, 75–91.

34. Josephus, *Antiquities*, 15.371.

35. Hengel, *Hellenism and Judaism*, p. 247.

36. Josephus, *Apion*, 1.165.

37. Origen's comment appears in his *Celsus*, 1.15.

38. Antonius as quoted by Porphyry, *Life of Pythagoras*, 11.

39. For the possibility that the epistle to the Colossians presupposes a combination of Jewish and Pythagorean elements, see E. Schweizer, "The Background of Matthew and Colossians," *Jews, Greeks and Christians. Religious Cultures in Late Antiquity* (Essays in Honor of William David Davies), ed. R. Hamerton-Kelly and R. Scroggs (Leiden, 1976) pp. 249–255.

40. Stern, *Authors*, vol. I, p. 362.

41. Johannes Lydus, *On Months*, 4.53. Lydus lived and wrote in the sixth century C.E.

42. It is worth nothing that even Tacitus's list includes at least one theory which holds the Jews to be of illustrious origins.

43. Josephus, *Antiquities*, 12.135f.

44. On Timagenes see Stern, *Authors*, vol. I, pp. 222–226.

45. Morton Smith, "Palestinian Judaism in the First Century," in *Israel: Its Role in Civilization*, ed. M. Davis (New York, 1956) p. 79.

46. Ibid.

47. Josephus, *Apion*, 2.282–285.

48. Philo, *Life of Moses*, 2.17–23.

49. Some ancient Christian authors and a number of modern scholars regard Flavius and Flavia as Christians; against this see the arguments in Stern, *Authors*, vol. II, pp. 380–381.

50. In his discussion of the reports concerning Claudius's action, Stern raises serious doubts as to their reliability; cf., Stern, *Authors*, vol. II, pp. 114–117.

51. Smallwood, *Roman Rule*, pp. 201–210.

52. Tacitus, *Annals*, 2.85.4.

53. See the discussion on p. 60.

54. Ibid.

55. It may be noted in passing that this view does not necessarily mean that Gentile sympathizers are to be identified with god-fearers. In this sense, L. H. Feldman is correct in arguing that *theosebēs, metuentes, phoboumenoi* or *sebomenoi ton theon* are not technical terms which designate official gradations of allegiance to Judaism short of full conversion; see "Jewish 'Sympathizers' in Classical Literature and Inscriptions," *Transactions of the American Philological Association* 81 (1950): 200–208. On the other hand, the claim that they are never used to designate Gentile sympathizers or Judaizers is equally indefensible. A lengthy inscription from Aphrodisias includes a list which consists of two parts; the second part, which begins *hosoi theosebis*, appears to contain only Greek names, among them several members of the town council (*boulē*). Unless all of these names belong to full proselytes, we must reckon with the possibility that terms like *theosebēs* were sometimes, perhaps even regularly, used to designate Gentile sympathizers or Judaizers. Feldman, *Ancient Rome*, states that the use of *theosebēs* in inscription no. 228 is used of a pious Jewish woman (p. 253*n1*). But there is nothing on or about the inscription to indicate that the woman was Jewish. As in Acts 13:43, it may also be used of proselytes, unless the phrase there (*sebomenōn prosēlytōn*) designates Judaizers; so E. Haenchen, *Die Apostelgeschichte* (Göttingen, 1961) p. 335*n5*. Other passages in Acts may be used in a similar way. In particular, the phrase *"en tē synagōgē tois Ioudaios kai tois sebomenois"* (17.17) is paralleled in two inscriptions: the first, from the theater at Miletus, reads *"topos eioudeōn tōn kai theosebion [sic]"* (Frey, *Corpus*, vol. II, p. 478); the second, from the Bosporus reads *"epitropeuousēs tēs synagogēs tōn Ioudaiōn kai theon sebōn* (Frey, *Corpus*, I, p. 683a = pp. 65f. in the Prolegomenon by B. Lifschitz). In agreement with the position outlined here is R. Marcus, "The *Sebomenoi* in Josephus," *Jewish Social Studies* 14 (1952): 247–250: "We have every right, I think, to set the passage in Josephus, *Ant.* XIV, 110, beside the passages in Acts and Philo (e.g., *De Virtutibus*, 179) where *sebomenoi* seems clearly to be used as a technical or semi-technical term for Gentile God-fearers" (p. 250). So also B. Lifschitz, "Du nouveau sur les 'sympathisants,'" *Journal for the Study of Judaism* 1 (1970): 77–82. More recently, A. T. Kraabel has sought to demonstrate that there is little evidence for the existence of an official category of Gentiles known as God-fearers. The term itself, he points out, is limited largely to the book of Acts where it is deployed for Luke's own theological purposes. See Kraabel's article, "The Disappearance of the 'God-Fearers,'" *Numen* 28 (1981): 113–126.

6: ROMAN POLICY TOWARD JUDAISM AND THE RISE OF CHRISTIANITY

1. Portions of the material in this and the following chapter first appeared in my article, "The Dialogue of Paganism with Judaism: Bar Cochba to Julian," *Hebrew Union College Annual* 44 (1973): 89–118.

2. Dio, *History*, 69.14.

3. On the office of the patriarch see Juster, *Les juifs*, vol. I, pp. 391–400; the convenient summary of R. Syme, "Ipse Ille Patriarcha," in *Historia-Augusta-Colloquium*: 1966/67 (Bonn, 1968) pp. 123–125; J. Cohen, "Roman Imperial Policy Toward the Jews from Constantine Until the End of the Palestinian Patriarchate (ca. 429)," *Byzantine Studies* 3 (1976): 22–25; and L. Levine, "The Jewish Patriarch (Nasi) in Third Century Palestine," in *Aufstieg und Niedergang* II. 19.2 (Berlin, 1979): 649–688. The duties of the patriarch included the following: declaring fast days for special purposes; declaring and annulling bans; appointing judges; controlling the calendar of festivals; administering communal supervision and taxation; and issuing decrees on a variety of legislative matters.

4. On the subject as a whole see the discussions and literature cited by Simon, *Verus Israel*, p. 130 and Smallwood, *Roman Rule*, pp. 485f. The relevant talmudic passages have been collected and discussed by S. Krauss, *Antoninus und Rabbi* (Frankfurt, 1910). The identity of Antoninus has been a matter of much speculation. For a survey of recent attempts see S. Baron, *A Social and Religious History of the Jews* (New York, 1952) vol. II, p. 100*n*19.

5. M. Avi-Yonah, *Geschichte der Juden im Zeitalter des Talmud* (Berlin, 1962) pp. 38f.

6. See the extensive discussion in M. Schwabe, "The Letters of Libanius to the Patriarch of Palestine," (in Hebrew) *Tarbiz* I, no. 2 (1930): 85–110. Gamaliel enjoyed considerable status with Theodosius I. According to Jerome, the emperor executed Hesychius, a former consul, because he had stolen some of the patriarch's personal papers (*Epistle* 57.3).

7. The last patriarch, Gamaliel VI, held office when Theodosius II reduced the patriarch's powers (*Codex Theodosianus*, 16.8.22). The biography of Bonasus in the *Historia Augusta* mentions *ipse ille patriarcha* who "when he comes to Egypt is forced by some to worship Serapis and by others to worship Christ" (8.4).

8. *Codex Theodosianus*, 16.8.8; 16.8.22. See the discussion in Juster, *Les juifs*, vol. I, pp. 396f. and Cohen, "Roman Imperial Policy," p. 23. Against the traditional view that Theodosius II abolished the patriarchate in 415, Cohen argues that the emperor simply reduced its significance and that the line of patriarchs died out (ibid., pp. 24f.).

9. Dio, *History*, 69.14; cf. also 65.7 where he reports that Titus and Vespasian refused the title *Judaicus* following the war in 66–73.

10. Philostratus, *Life of Apollonius*, 5.33. Similar sentiments are attributed to Apollonius of Tyana in 5.27.

11. Fronto, *On the Parthian War*, 2.

12. Dio, *History*, 37.9–11.

13. On the period in general, see Smallwood, *Roman Rule*, pp. 467–486.

14. Justinian, *Digest*, 48.8.11 (Modestinus).

15. So Smallwood, *Roman Rule*, pp. 500–506.

16. Justinian, *Digest*, 27.1.15.6.

17. Jerome, *Commentary on Daniel*, 11.34. On the period in general, see Smallwood, *Roman Rule*, pp. 487–506.

18. Justinian, *Digest*, 50.2.3 (Ulpian); see the discussion and references to further literature in Baron, *Social History*, vol. II, p. 110, esp. *n*26.

19. *Historia Augusta, Caracalla*, 1.6.

20. Ibid., *Elagabalus*, 3.5.

21. Dio, *History*, 79.11.1–2.

22. *Historia Augusta, Elagabalus*, 28.4: *struthiocamelos exhibuit in cenis aliquotiens, dicens praeceptum Iudaeis ut ederent;* cf. Stern, *Authors*, vol. II, p. 629.

23. *Historia Augusta, Severus Alexander*, 28.7.

24. Ibid., 22.4; see the discussion of A. Momigliano, "Severo Alessandro Archisynagogus," *Athenaeum* 12 (1934): 151–153.

25. Ibid., 29.2

26. Ibid., 45.7.

27. Ibid., 51.6–8.

28. *Historia Augusta, Claudius*, 2.4–5. For a discussion see Stern, *Authors*, vol. II, pp. 635f.

29. See the recent volumes emanating from the *Historia-Augusta-Colloquium;* cf. also R. Syme, *Ammianus and the Historia Augusta* (Oxford, 1968). For a convenient summary of the critical issues and references to recent literature see the article of A. Momigliano in *The Oxford Classical Dictionary* (1970) pp. 520f.

30. On Dio's view of Rome and his relations with the Severans see F. Millar, *A Study of Dio Cassius* (Oxford, 1964) pp. 16–26, 138–160, 174–192.

31. For literature on Julian see M. A. Adler, "The Emperor Julian and the Jews," *Jewish Quarterly Review* 5 (1893): 591–651; Baron, *Social History*, vol. II, pp. 159–161; Simon, *Verus Israel*, pp. 139–144; G. W. Bowersock, *Julian the Apostate* (Cambridge, Massachusetts, 1978); R. Braun and J. Richter, ed., *L'Empereur Julien: De l'histoire à la légende* (Paris, 1978); and the unpublished Ph.D. dissertation (Harvard) of D. B. Levenson, "A Source and Tradition-Critical Study of Julian's Attempt to Rebuild the Jerusalem Temple" (1979). Reference to Julian's letters will give the enumeration of W. C. Wright in the Loeb edition and the Budé edition of J. Bidez and F. Cumont.

32. Sozomen, *Ecclesiastical History*, 5.22 states that Julian summoned the Jewish leaders and asked them why they had not offered sacrifices in accordance with his edicts. They answered that they could sacrifice only in the Jerusalem temple which was no longer standing; cf. similar versions of the meeting in John Chrysostom, *Against the Jews*, 5.11, and Rufinus, *Ecclesiastical History*, 2.58.

33. Ammianus Marcellinus, *History*, 23.1.2–3.

34. Julian's former friend and schoolmate, Gregory of Nazianzus, says that the emperor used the Jews, own writings to demonstrate that "it was now ordained for them to return to their homeland, to rebuild the temple and to renew the full force of their ancient customs" (Gregory, *Oration*, 5.3).

35. These final decisions are attested only by Julian's *Letter to the Jews* (51 in Wright-204 Bidez-Cumont) whose authenticity is rejected by some.

36. *Against the Galileans*, 305f.

37. Ibid., 356C.

38. *Letter to Theodorus*, 453D–454A.

39. *Against the Galileans*, 354B.

40. Ibid., 49A-D, 57B–66A.

41. Ibid., 49E.

42. Ibid., 134D–146B.

43. Ibid., 148C.

44. Julian interprets the injunction of Exodus 22:27 as an indication that Moses enjoined his people to respect pagan deities. He also quotes the story of Babel (Gen. 11: 4–8: "Let *us* go down. . . .") as proof that Moses recognized more than one god (*Against the Galileans*, 146B).

45. Ibid., 176A-B; 178A; 202A; 209D.

46. Cf. the opposite view, expressed by Adler, "The Emperor Julian," pp. 591–651, and Baron, *Social History*, vol. II, p. 160.

47. Lydus, *On Months*, 4.53.

48. *Letter to Theodorus* 295B-D (*Epistle* 89b Bidez-Cumont). Wright, in the Loeb edition, vol. III, p. lxii, regards it as a separate letter. The fragment occurs in a manuscript of his *Letter to Themistius*.

49. Marcellinus, *History*, 23.1.2.

50. *To the Alexandrians*, 433 (*Ep.* 47 Wright = 111 Bidez-Cumont); see also F 2 in Wright where Julian contrasts Jesus with Moses and Elijah. "Moses fasted 40 days and received the law, Elijah fasted for the same length of time and was granted a vision of god, but what did Jesus receive after his fast of the same length?"

51. See the comments of J. Neusner, *A History of the Jews in Babylonia* (Leiden, 1969) vol. IV, pp. 29f.

52. So W. C. Wright in vol. III, p. xxi of the Loeb edition.

53. See the discussion in Cohen, "Roman Imperial Policy," pp. 1f. In her brief discussion of the issue Smallwood in *Roman Rule* appears to adopt something of a middle position (see pp. 543, 545). Cohen speaks of the traditional view as characteristic of Jewish historians, but as his own references indicate it has been adopted by many non-Jewish historians as well.

54. *Codex Theodosianus*, 16.8.9.

55. On Sardis, see especially A. T. Kraabel, "Sardis Evidence" pp. 13–33; and S. Applebaum, "The Legal Status of the Jewish Communities in the

Diaspora," in *The Jewish People in the First Century* (Assen, 1974) vol. I, pp. 420–463; S. Applebaum, "The Organization of the Jewish Communities in the Diaspora," in *The Jewish People in the First Century*, pp. 464–503; and L. Robert, *Nouvelles Inscriptions de Sardes*, I (Paris, 1964) esp. pp. 41–45. Josephus cites a letter from Antiochus to his governor Zeuxis (*Antiquities*, 12.147–153) ordering the settlement. An inscription discovered at Sardis has preserved a decree of Antiochus which mentions Zeuxis by name. As Kraabel notes (p. 16), while the inscription does not prove that Jews were settled specifically in Sardis, such an inference seems reasonable.

56. Josephus, *Antiquities*, 14.235.

57. Kraabel, "Sardis," p. 17.

58. Josephus, *Antiquities*, 14.259–261; Kraabel, "Sardis, Evidence," pp. 16–18.

59. Kraabel, "Sardis Evidence," pp. 19f.

60. Ibid., p. 19.

61. Ibid., p. 18.

62. Ibid., p. 21 (his emphasis).

63. See Robert, *Nouvelles Inscriptions*, pp. 55–57.

64. Applebaum, "Legal Status," p. 449.

65. On Caesarea see L. Levine, *Caesarea Under Roman Rule* (Leiden, 1975).

66. Levine, *Caesarea*, pp. 11f.

67. Ibid., p. 29, esp. n184.

68. Ibid., pp. 29f.; see Josephus's account in *War*, 2.285–292.

69. On Jews in Caesarea during the second century, see Levine, *Caesarea*, pp. 44f.

70. Ibid., p. 63.

71. Ibid., p. 200n142.

72. See the references in ibid., p. 205nn208–212; references to Origen's consultations with Jewish scholars have been collected by S. Krauss, "The Jews in the Works of the Church Fathers," *Jewish Quarterly Review* 5 (1893): 148–157 and G. Bardy, "Les traditions juives dans l'oeuvre d'Origène," *Revue Biblique* 34 (1925): 217–252.

73. So Levine, *Caesarea*, pp. 81, 83f.

74. Origen, *Homilies on Jeremiah*, 12.13.

75. Origen, *Commentary on Matthew* (23.15), series 16.

76. Levine, *Caesarea*, p. 106.

7: THE DIALOGUE OF PAGANISM WITH JUDAISM IN LATE ANTIQUITY

1. See the important work of R. Walzer, *Galen on Jews and Christians* (London, 1949) and the review of Walzer by A. D. Nock in *Gnomon* 23 (1951): 48–52.

2. The passage comes from a work extant only in Arabic, *On Hippocrates'*
Anatomy; see Walzer, *Galen,* pp. 1of. and 18–23.

3. Galen, *On Differences of Pulse,* 3.3; cf. Walzer, *Galen,* pp. 14f. and
37–48.

4. Galen, *On the Function,* 11.14; cf. Walzer, *Galen,* pp. 11–13 and 23–27.

5. Longinus, *Sublime,* 9.9: "In the same manner what does the lawgiver of
the Jews say—no ordinary man, for he comprehended and brought to light
in worthy fashion the power of the deity when he wrote at the very beginning
of his laws, 'Let there be light' and there was, 'Let there be earth' and there
was."

6. In his review of Walzer in *Gnomon,* Nock notes that Galen's friend,
Flavius Boethus, was governor of Palestine at the time (c. 162–166) when
Galen composed his *On Hippocrates' Anatomy* and must have communicated
with Galen concerning Jewish matters. F. Pfaff, "Rufus aus Samaria, Hippoc-
rates-Commentator und Quelle Galens," *Hermes* 67 (1932): 356–359, states
that Galen relied on Rufus of Samaria's compendium of earlier commentaries
on Hippocrates. Rufus was a wealthy Jewish physician who came to Rome in
Galen's time.

7. Celsus' *True Teaching* has been reconstructed from passages cited in
Origen's *Against Celsus,* written around 248. See especially H. Chadwick,
Origen: Contra Celsum (Cambridge, 1965) whose translation I have followed.

8. Origen, *Celsus,* 1.23; 3.5; 5.41.

9. Ibid., 1.23.

10. Ibid., 1.24; 6.49; 6.50.

11. Ibid., 4.40; 6.61.

12. Ibid., 4.21; 4.41.

13. Cf. Aristobulus (in Eusebius, *Preparation for the Gospel,* 13.12.1 and
13.13.13–16) who claimed that Plato borrowed his legislation from Moses and
that Homer and Hesiod took the idea of a sacred sabbath day from the same
source.

14. The standard edition of his fragments is E. des Places, ed. and tr.,
Numénius. Fragments (Paris, 1973). See also E. R. Dodds, "Numenius and
Ammonius," in *Les sources de Plotin* (Geneva, 1960) pp. 3–32; and J. H.
Waszink, "Porphyrios und Numenios," in *Porphyre* (Geneva, 1966) pp. 35–78.

15. Fragment 1a = Eusebius, *Preparation,* 9.7.1.

16. Fragment 1b = Origen, *Celsus,* 1.15.

17. Fragment 56 = Lydus, *On Months,* 4.53; cf. Exodus 20:3—"You shall
have no other gods before me" and 20.5—"For I the lord your God am a
jealous God."

18. Testimony 30 = Porphyry, *On the Cave of the Nymphs,* 10.

19. Fragment 27 = Origen, *Celsus,* 4.51.

20. Fragment 9 = Eusebius, *Preparation,* 9.8.1–2.

21. Fragment 8 = Clement of Alexandria, *Stromateis,* 1.150.4. The saying

is repeated by Eusebius, *Preparation*, 9.6.9.; Theodoret, (c. 430 C.E.) *Grae-carum Affectionum Curatio*, 2.114f.; the sixth century historian, Hesychius of Miletus (C. Muller, *Fragmenta Historicorum Graecorum*, vol. IV, p. 171); and finally by the *Suda*, s.v. Numenius.

22. Dodds, "Numenius," p. 6; the emphasis is his.

23. Text in Stern, *Authors*, vol. II, pp. 429f. = Eusebius, *Preparation*, 9.10.4; cf. also Eusebius, *Preparation*, 9.10.2., where the oracle of Apollo reports that the Hebrews along with the Phoenicians, the Assyrians, and the Lydians had learned the many paths to heaven.

24. Text in Stern, *Authors*, vol. II, pp. 430–432 = Augustine, *City of God*, 19.23 and Lactantius, *On the Wrath of God*, 23.12.

25. Porphyry, *Life of Pythagoras*, 11.

26. In 4.11 he introduces the Jews as "well-known to us" and mentions three sects—Pharisees, Sadducees, and Essenes. In 4.11–13 he copies out Josephus's account of the Essenes from *War* 2.120–160. Finally, in 4.14, he cites a passage from *Apion* (2.313 with variations).

27. Lydus, *On Months*, 4.53.

28. See H. Lewy, *Chaldaen Oracles and Theurgy* (Paris, 1978) ch. I, notes 32–37 and pp. 162f.

29. See the lengthy discussion in C. H. Dodd, *The Bible and the Greeks* (London, 1935) pp. 99–248.

30. Note the comments of O. Murray in his review of R. MacMullen, *Enemies of the Roman Order*, in *Journal of Roman Studies* 59 (1969): 261–265 and A. A. Barb, "The Survival of Magic Arts," in *Paganism and Christianity in the Fourth Century*, ed. A. Momigliano (Oxford, 1963) pp. 100–125. Both emphasize that magic and astrology moved up the social ladder in the later Empire and that both changed character in the process, that is, they became more systematized and less "popular." The explanation for their increased respectability lies not only in their increased intellectual content but also in the changed make-up of the social classes themselves.

31. Juvenal, *Satires*, 6.544–547.

32. Trogus, *Histories*, 36.2.8.

33. *Historia Augusta*, *Firmus* 8.3; cf. also Apuleius, *Apologia* 90 and Lucian, *Alexander*, 32.13.

34. On Jewish magic in general see J. Trachtenberg, *Jewish Magic and Superstition* (Cleveland and New York, 1939) and Simon, *Verus Israel*, pp. 394–431.

35. See C. Bonner, *Studies in Magical Amulets* (Ann Arbor, Michigan, 1950) p. 28, and E. R. Goodenough, *Jewish Symbols*, vol. II, p. 206.

36. See T. Hopfner, "Mageia," *Paulys Realencyclopädie der klassischen Altertumswissenschaft* 27 (1928): 307, who remarks that after the first century C.E. in Egypt it is best to speak of syncretistic magic and religion. All references to the magical papyri will be according to the edition of K. Preisendanz

et al., *Papyri Graecae Magicae* (*PGM*) I (Leipzig, 1928), II (1931), and III (1941). For volume III, I have used a photographic copy, presumably made from page proofs, in the library of the Warburg Institute, University of London.

37. See the indices in Preisendanz, *PGM*, vol. III, pp. 235–238.

38. Preisendanz, *PGM* V lines 108–118; cf. also *PGM* II lines 12–128; III lines 158f. and XII lines 92–94.

39. See also the tenth treatise of the *Corpus Hermeticum* which is called the *Key* of Hermes. *PGM* XII line 14 accuses Hermes of plagiarizing the names of sacrificial fumes from the *Eighth Book* of Moses. It should also be noted that the Jewish apologist Artapanus says that Moses was called Hermes by the Egyptian priests because he provided an interpretation (*hermeneia*) of their sacred writings (in Eusebius, *Preparation*, 9.27.3–5).

40. In general on alchemy see M. Berthelot, *Les origines de l'alchimie* (Paris, 1885); W. Gundel, "Alchemie," *Reallexicon für Antike und Christentum* I (1950): 239–260; and Jack Lindsay, *The Origins of Alchemy in Graeco-Roman Egypt* (New York, 1970).

41. M. Berthelot and C. E. Ruelle, *Collection des anciens alchimistes grecs* I (Paris, 1887), II-III (1888). See also the series, *Catalogue des manuscrits alchimiques grecs*, published by the Union Académique Internationale (1924–   ).

42. Berthelot and Ruelle, *Collection*, vol. I, Introduction, pp. 110f.

43. Berthelot and Ruelle, *Collection*, vol. I, pp. 38f. (text); Gundel, "Alchemie," pp. 245, 249.

44. Berthelot and Ruelle, *Collection*, vol. II, pp. 300–315 (text).

45. Berthelot and Ruelle, *Collection*, vol. II, pp. 182f. (text).

46. On Zosimus, see Gundel, "Alchemie," pp. 246f.

47. Berthelot and Ruelle, *Collection*, vol. II, p. 245.

48. Ibid., pp. 211, 213.

49. Cf. Berthelot and Ruelle's index, vol. III, pp. 463f.

50. Cf. the parallel passage where the sixth-century Neo-Platonist Olympiodorus quotes our text with occasional variants; Berthelot and Ruelle, *Collection*, vol. II, p. 90.

51. Berthelot and Ruelle, *Collection*, vol. II, p. 240 and Gundel, "Alchemie," pp. 241, 245. It is not clear whether the "Hebrew prophetess" mentioned in a writing attributed to "the Christian" (Berthelot and Ruelle, *Collection*, II, p. 404) is to be identified with Maria.

52. Cf. C. H. Dodd, *The Bible*, pp. 99–248.

53. See the discussion in R. Reitzenstein, *Poimandres* (Leipsiz, 1904) pp. 271f. The manuscript is described in *Catalogus Codicum Astrologorum Graecorum* (Brussels, 1901) vol. III, pp. 32–40. The date of the manuscript is the thirteenth century, but Reitzenstein places the original much earlier.

54. Vettius Valens, 2.28f.

55. Firmicus Maternus, *Mathesis*, 4.17.2; 4.18.1; 4., pr. 5.

56. E. R. Dodds, *Pagan and Christian in an Age of Anxiety* (Cambridge, 1965) ch. 4.

57. M. D. Herr, "Anti-Semitism in Imperial Rome in the Light of Rabbinic Literature," (in Hebrew) in the *Benjamin DeVries Memorial Volume*, ed. E. Z. Melamed (1968) pp. 149–159, has discussed the problem as reflected in Jewish sources. Herr identifies two levels or types of material, one literate and the other popular (as reflected in Roman satirists). The literate level simply reflects the common motifs of Greek and Roman authors prior to about 150 C.E. As for the popular level, most of the evidence appears in later sources, especially midrashim to Esther, that is, precisely where one would expect to find collections of anti-Jewish materials from diverse periods. Thus, without wishing to deny the existence of a popular dialogue, I hesitate to accept the midrashic evidence cited by Herr as firm evidence for pagan attitudes in the period from 150–300. Furthermore, we must reckon with the possibility that most or all of the passages cited by Herr point not to pagans but to Christians as the source of this anti-semitic material! See A. Marmorstein, "Judaism and Christianity in the Middle of the Third Century," in *Studies in Jewish Theology* (London, 1950) pp. 193–221.

58. *Against the Galileans*, 319D.

PART III: CHRISTIANITY, ISRAEL, AND THE TORAH

8: JUDAIZING AND ANTI-JUDAISM IN THE CHRISTIAN TRADITION

1. On Chrysostom, see Simon, *Verus Israel*, pp. 256–263, and Meeks and Wilken, *Jews and Christians*, pp. 25–52, 83–126. The lack of critical editions and reliable translations of Chrysostom's sermons remains a serious problem; see the comments in Meeks and Wilken, pp. 83f.

2. See ibid., p. 31.

3. See R. L. Wilken, *Judaism and the Early Christian Mind. A Study of Cyril of Alexandria's Exegesis and Theology* (New Haven, 1971) pp. 54–58.

4. See Cohen, "Roman Imperial Policy," p. 5, esp. n26 and Parkes, pp. 166–168.

5. Simon, *Verus Israel*, p. 262 (my translation).

6. See J. Neusner, *Aphrahat*. I have depended on Neusner's discussion of Aphraat's texts throughout. Especially useful are the tables in which Neusner shows the similarities and differences between Aphraat, the New Testament, other Christian writers and the rabbis in their use of biblical quotations. On Syrian Christianity generally, see R. Murray, *Symbols of Church and Kingdom. A Study in Early Syriac Tradition* (Cambridge, 1975).

7. See the discussion in Neusner, *Aphrahat*, pp. 127–129.

8. Ibid., p. 136.

9. Simon, *Verus Israel*, p. 121.

10. Murray, *Symbols*, p. 7.

11. Ibid., p. 19.

12. So S. Kazan, "Isaac of Antioch's Homily Against the Jews," *Oriens Christianus* 49 (1965): 74. Kazan locates the origins of this tradition well before the time of Ephrem.

13. See the discussion in Murray, *Symbols*, pp. 41–68.

14. Ibid., pp. 56–60.

15. Ibid. p. 68.

16. Ibid., p. 41.

17. Kazan, "Isaac," *Oriens Christianus* 47 (1963): 89. Kazan notes much the same situation in the somewhat later writings attributed to Isaac of Antioch. In his case the warnings are directed at Christians who were resorting to Jewish magicians.

18. Kazan, "Isaac," ibid., p. 97.

19. On early Syrian Christianity see also W. Bauer, *Orthodoxy and Heresy in Earliest Christianity*, ed. R. Kraft and G. Krodel (Philadelphia, 1971; originally published in German, 1934) pp. 1–43. Murray, *Symbols*, pp. 4–23 reviews more recent discussions and gives a generally positive assessment of Bauer.

20. See G. Strecker, "On the Problem of Jewish Christianity," in Bauer, *Orthodoxy*, pp. 241–285, esp. pp. 257–271; "The Kerygmata Petrou," in *New Testament Apocrypha*, ed. E. Hennecke and W. Schneemelcher (Philadelphia, 1965), vol. II, pp. 102–127; *Das Judenchristentum in den Pseudoklementinen* (Berlin, 1958); and W. A. Meeks, ed., *The Writings of St. Paul* (New York, 1972) pp. 176–184.

21. *Epistle of Peter*, 1:3 (Meeks's translation; *Writings*, p. 179).

22. Ibid., 2:5 (Meeks's translation; ibid.).

23. Ibid., 2:3 (Meeks's translation; ibid.).

24. See Meeks, *Writings*, p. 178, note.

25. *Epistle*, 2.3 and 7.

26. *Homilies of Peter*, 2.16.

27. Ibid., 17.13–19.

28. *Epistle*, 2:3.

29. See Strecker, "Problem," p. 262.

30. So Simon, *Verus Israel*, pp. 362–369 and Strecker, "Problem," pp. 248–251. On the Didascalia see also *Disdascalia Apostolorum*, ed. R. H. Connolly (Oxford, 1929); Connolly presents a lengthy introduction and a translation of the Syriac text.

31. See Strecker, "Problem," pp. 245–251.

32. Simon, *Verus Israel*, pp. 361–367.

33. Ibid., p. 365.

34. Murray, *Symbols*, p. 7.

35. So C. K. Barrett, "Jews and Judaizers in the Epistles of Ignatius," in *Jews, Greeks and Christians*, p. 240. Barrett provides a useful survey of recent scholarship on the Judaizers in Ignatius's letters.

36. In an unpublished essay, "Judaism of the Uncircumcised in Ignatius and Related Writers," Lloyd Gaston argues persuasively that the Judaizers in question must be seen as Gentiles.

37. See Meeks and Wilken, *Jews and Christians*, pp. 20f.

38. Josephus, *War*, 7.45.

39. See the discussion in Meeks and Wilken, *Jews and Christians*, p. 17.

40. So Barrett, "Jews and Judaism," pp. 241f.

41. See Simon, *Verus Israel*, pp. 356–393, on Christian Judaizers generally.

42. See the discussion in ibid., pp. 382–384.

43. Origen, *Celsus*, 2.3.

44. See de Lange, *Origen*, pp. 36, 86.

45. In addition to Simon, *Verus Israel*, see R. E. Taylor, "Attitudes of the Fathers toward Practices of Jewish Christians," *Studia Patristica* IV, Part II (Berlin, 1961): 504–511.

46. Meeks and Wilken, *Jews and Christians*, p. 35.

9: CONTROVERSIES AND DEBATES BETWEEN JEWS AND CHRISTIANS

1. See R. Travers Herford, *Christianity in Talmud and Midrash* (London, 1903); A. B. Hulen, "The 'Dialogues with the Jews' As Sources for the Early Jewish Argument Against Christianity," *Journal of Biblical Literature* 51 (1932): 58–70; and Simon, *Verus Israel*, pp. 214–238.

2. Ruether, *Fratricide*, p. 181.

3. See M. Smith, *Jesus the Magician* (San Francisco, 1978) pp. 158–164.

4. See my article, "The Gospels and Jesus: Some Doubts about Method," *Journal of Religion* 54 (1974): 244–272.

5. A classic study of such modifications is J. Jeremias, *The Parables of Jesus* (New York, 1955).

6. For a discussion of the Q hypothesis by one of its defenders, see W. G. Kümmel, *Introduction to the New Testament* (Nashville, 1975) pp. 56–80; see also J. M. Robinson, "Logoi Sophon: On the Gattung of Q," pp. 71–113 and K. Koester, "One Jesus and Four Primitive Gospels," pp. 158–204; both in Robinson and Koester, *Trajectories through Early Christianity*.

7. I have followed the reconstruction of Q as presented by H. C. Kee, *Jesus in History. An Approach to the Study of the Gospels* (New York, 1970) pp. 62–73.

8. The passion story of Jesus' death and resurrection plays no role in Q. Koester in "One Jesus" argues that in this regard Q represents not just pre-gospel traditions but an altogether different conception of Jesus as the eschatological prophet of the last days and the teacher of divine wisdom.

9. See Gager, *Kingdom and Community. The Social World of Early*

Christianity (Englewood Cliffs, N.J., 1975) pp. 22–28.

10. Altogether different, I would argue, are other Q passages which speak of opponents in general terms, without naming individuals or groups, but are turned against the Pharisees by the gospel writers themselves. By adding a line at the beginning, sometimes in the midst of such sayings, sayings originally directed against unnamed groups suddenly become, in the context of the gospels as a whole, both anti-Pharisaic and anti-Jewish in a broader sense. Thus in Matthew 3:7, as an introduction to Jesus' warning, "You brood of vipers!," Matthew adds, "But when he saw many of the Pharisees and Sadducees . . . ," where Luke has Jesus simply addressing "the multitudes." A similar case occurs at Luke 7:30 where the author introduces an anti-Pharisaic line ("but the Pharisees and lawyers rejected the purpose of God for themselves, not having been baptized by him [John]") into a passage which clearly had nothing at all to do with Pharisees in its original form. Luke follows the same procedure in the non-Q passage of 16:14–15; cf. also 15:1–2 and Matthew 12:38.

11. In typical fashion, Matthew redirects this saying against the Pharisees through the introductory words, "Then some of the scribes and Pharisees said to him. . . ." (Matt: 12.38).

12. See the discussion of these and similar passages in Hare, "Rejection," p. 35.

13. L. Gaston, *No Stone on Another. Studies in the Significance of the Fall of Jerusalem in the Synoptic Gospels* (Leiden, 1970) pp. 244–369.

14. Ibid., p. 275.

15. Ibid., p. 298.

16. Hare, "Rejection," p. 35.

17. Ibid., pp. 34f.

18. S. G. F. Brandon, *Jesus and the Zealots* (New York, 1967) p. 274.

19. Ibid., pp. 3f.; cf. also pp. 248, 260–264.

20. P. Richardson, *Apostolic Church*, p. 167.

21. Ibid.

22. See the discussion of Mark by Donald Juel, *Messiah and Temple* (Missoula, Montana, 1977).

23. Richardson, *Apostolic Church*, p. 167.

24. Ibid., pp. 169f.

25. Ibid., p. 170.

26. Ibid., p. 38.

27. Hare, "Rejection," p. 40.

28. See ibid., pp. 38f.

29. This line is absent in Luke's version (14:15–24) of the parable.

30. So Richardson, *Apostolic Church*, pp. 188f.

31. So Hare, "Rejection," pp. 39f.

32. For a rather different treatment of this inconsistency, see ibid., pp. 43–46.

33. Ibid., p. 40.

34. Ibid., p. 41.

35. Ibid.

36. Ibid., p. 35.

37. Richardson, in his *Apostolic Church*, also draws attention to the growing sense of discontinuity between Christians and Jews and the complementary emphasis on continuity between "Israel" and the church (pp. 162, 165).

38. E. J. Epp, "The 'Ignorance Motif' in Acts and Antijudaic Tendencies in Codex Bezae," *Harvard Theological Review* 55 (1962): 51–62, has demonstrated that Codex Bezae consistently modified the text of Acts so as to heighten rather than diminish Jewish responsibility for the death of Jesus.

39. J. Jervell, *Luke and the People of God* (Minneapolis, 1972). For a similar interpretation, see Koenig, *Jews and Christians*, pp. 119–121.

40. In his unpublished paper, entitled "Anti-Judaism and the Passion Narrative in Luke-Acts," L. Gaston has shown that the enemies of the church in Acts 1–5 are always identified with the temple and its leaders (4:1, 5–6, 8, 15, 23; 5:17, 21, 22, 24, 26, 27, 34, 41). By contrast, the friends of the church are presented as standing in some tension with these same leaders (4:1–2, 17, 21; 5:13, 26). The same pattern appears in the gospel, where the people are seen as friends of Jesus before the passion narrative but as enemies thereafter.

41. Ruether, *Fratricide*, p. 76. See also J. Neusner, *From Politics to Piety. The Emergence of Pharisaic Judaism* (Englewood Cliffs, N.J., 1973), who notes the distinctive character of Luke's view of the Pharisees: "They appear as allies of the Christians and friends of Jesus" (p. 71). On the other hand, this does not tell the full story of Luke and the Pharisees. In Luke 11:40 Jesus calls the Pharisees fools for insisting on ritual purity. He utters woes against them for requiring tithes while neglecting justice (11:42) and for their ostentatious piety (11:43), and so forth in 11:44, 46, 47, 52. The passage concludes with a warning: "Beware of the leaven of the Pharisees, which is hypocrisy" (12:1). It is worth noting that the final phrase, "which is hypocrisy" does not appear in Matthew or Mark. Only in Acts do we find the Pharisees consistently presented in a favorable light.

42. Ruether, *Fratricide*, p. 83.

43. Gaston, *No Stone*, pp. 368f.

44. Ruether, *Fratricide*, pp. 111–116; J. Townsend provides an extensive listing of similar views in "The Gospel of John and the Jews," in Davies, *Foundations*, p. 88n2. See also W. A. Meeks, " 'Am I a Jew?'—Johannine Christianity and Judaism," in *Christianity, Judaism and Other Greco-Roman Cults. Studies for Morton Smith at Sixty*, Part One: New Testament, ed. J. Neusner (Leiden, 1975) pp. 163–186.

45. Townsend, "Gospel of John," p. 74.

46. So. J. L. Martyn, *History and Theology in the Fourth Gospel* (New

York, 1968) and W. Meeks, "The Man from Heaven in Johannine Sectarianism," *Journal of Biblical Literature* 91 (1972): 44–72.

47. J. L. Martyn, "Source Criticism and *Religionsgeschichte* in the Fourth Gospel," in *Jesus and Man's Hope*, vol. I (Pittsburgh, 1971) pp. 254–256.

48. R. Leistner, *Antijudaismus im Johannesevangelium? Darstellung des Problems in der neueren Auslegungsgeschichte und Untersuchung der Leidensgeschichte* (Bern and Frankfurt, 1974).

49. Townsend, "Gospel of John," pp. 74f.

50. John's "assaults on the Law" are not comparable to those of Paul. (p. 75)

51. Meeks, "Johannine Christianity," p. 172.

52. For general discussions of this literature see Juster, *Les juifs*, vol. I, pp. 43–76; Williams, *Adversus Judaeos;* and B. Blumenkranz, *Les auteurs chrétiens latins du moyen âge sur les juifs et le judaïsme* (Paris, 1963).

53. Williams, *Adversus, Judaeos*, pp. 67f.

54. Origen, *Celsus*, 1.45.

55. Origen, *Letter to Africanus*, 5.

56. *Commentary on the Epistle to Titus*, 3.9 (Migne, *Patrologia Latina*, 26, 595b).

57. On the question of *testimonia* see the early study of Rendel Harris, *Testimonies*, vol. I (Cambridge, 1916) and vol. II (Cambridge, 1920); Williams, *Adversus Judaeos*, pp. 3–13; B. Lindars, *New Testament Apologetic. The Doctrinal Significance of the Old Testament Quotations* (Philadelphia, 1961); and J. A. Fitzmyer, *Essays on the Semitic Background of the New Testament* (Missoula, Montana, 1974) pp. 59–89.

58. See the discussion in Williams, *Adversus Judaeos*, pp. 56–64.

59. See Marmorstein, "Judaism and Christianity in the Middle of the Third Century," pp. 179–224.

60. Ibid., p. 193.

61. Philo, *Migration of Abraham*, 89–93. Philo's view, like that of the early Jewish writing, *Letter of Aristeas* (esp. 128–171), is that while the true meaning of the commandments is moral and spiritual, Jews must also observe them literally.

62. Jerome, *Catechesis*, 13.7 (Migne, *Patrologia Latina*, 33, 779–782).

10: ANTI-JUDAISM IN THE THEOLOGICAL RESPONSE
TO MARCION AND THE CHRISTIAN GNOSTICS

1. On the formation of the New Testament canon see Kümmel, *New Testament*, pp. 475–510 and Hans von Campenhausen, *The Formation of the Christian Bible* (Philadelphia, 1972).

2. D. Efroymsen, "The Patristic Connection," in Davies, *Foundations*, pp. 98–117.

3. Ibid., p. 101.

4. In general on Marcion and his influence, see A. von Harnack, *Marcion. Das Evangelium vom fremden Gott* (Leipzig, 1921), p. 215; E. C. Blackman, *Marcion and his Influence* (London, 1948); J. Gager, "Marcion and Philosophy," *Vigiliae Christianae* 26 (1972): 53–59; and B. Aland, "Marcion. Versuch einer neuen Interpretation," *Zeitschrift für Theologie und Kirche* 70 (1973): 426–447.

5. Efroymsen, "Patristic Connection."

6. Ibid., p. 100.

7. Ibid.

8. Ibid., p. 101.

9. Ibid.

10. Ibid., p. 105.

11. See Efroymsen's unpublished Ph.D. dissertation, "Tertullian's Anti-Judaism and its Role in his Theology" (Temple University, 1975).

12. Ibid., chapter I.

13. Whether or not the well-known passage in *To the Nations* (I. 13), where Tertullian appears to speak of Judaizing practices among pagans, can be used as evidence in this regard is not clear. Simon in *Verus Israel* (pp. 332, 385), with many others, has used it in this manner. Their reading of the text has now been questioned by J. Nolland, "Do Romans Observe Jewish Customs (Tertullian, *Ad. Nat.* 1.13; *Apol.* 16)," *Vigiliae Christianae* 33 (1979): 1–11.

14. Whether or not Tertullian had much firsthand knowledge of Jews or Judaism is uncertain. Efroymsen in "Patristic Connection" argues in the negative. C. Aziza, *Tertullien et le judaïsme* (Nice, 1977), argues in the positive. Aziza is even willing to propose, with no textual support, that Tertullian was a Jewish proselyte before becoming a Christian and that he left Judaism because he was not satisfied with it (pp. 220–224)! What attracted him to Judaism in the first place? His agitated and combative personality (p. 221), his love of order and his legalism (p. 221). What all of this amounts to is not evidence but unbridled speculation.

15. L. W. Barnard, *Justin Martyr. His Life and Thought* (Cambridge, 1967) p. 40.

16. Ibid., p. 52.

17. Ibid., p. 40.

18. T. Stylianopoulos, *Justin Martyr and the Mosaic Law* (Missoula, Montana, 1975).

19. Ibid., p. 36.

20. Ibid., p. 39.

21. See Efroymsen, "Patristic Connection," p. 105.

22. So de Lange, *Origen*, p. 28.

23. See above, p. 133.

24. de Lange, *Origen*, p. 87.

25. On the development of this theme in Origen and his predecessors see ibid., pp. 77–82.

26. Origen, *Celsus*, 2.8.

27. See the full discussion in de Lange, *Origen*, pp. 66–68.

28. Efroymsen, "Patristic Connection," p. 99.

29. I prefer this designation to Coptic-Gnostic or Christian-Gnostic; references to individual writings will use the designation CG. A number of the documents discovered at Nag Hammadi are not Gnostic at all; others are not Christian; and none of them was written originally in Coptic. As to their original date and provenience, the individual writings vary greatly. One of the many unsolved puzzles of this "library" is how this assortment of writings came to be bound as a set of thirteen codices and stored, so it seems, in a single jar. For a review of this problem see M. Krause, "Die Texte von Nag Hammadi," in *Gnosis. Festschift für Hans Jonas*, ed. B. Aland (Göttingen, 1978) pp. 216–243.

30. The complete set of writings is available in an English translation, with brief introductions to individual writings and a general introduction; *The Nag Hammadi Library*, ed. J. M. Robinson (San Francisco, 1977).

31. H. Jonas, "Response to G. Quispel's 'Gnosticism and the New Testament'," in *The Bible in Modern Scholarship*, ed. J. P. Hyatt (Nashville and New York, 1965) p. 286.

32. For a review of this position and its variants, see W. C. van Unnik, "Gnosis und Judentum," in *Gnosis*, ed. Aland, pp. 65–86.

33. R. Grant, *Gnosticism and Early Christianity* (New York, 1966) esp. pp. 98f.

34. G. Macrae, "The Jewish Background of the Gnostic Sophia Myth," *Novum Testamentum* 12 (1970): 86–100.

35. K. Rudolph in many writings; most recently in *Die Gnosis. Wesen und Geschichte einer spätantiken Religion* (Göttingen, 1978) esp. pp. 297f.

36. So G. Quispel, "Gnosticism and the New Testament," in *The Bible in Modern Scholarship*, p. 269.

37. Ibid.

38. B. Pearson, "Jewish Haggadic Traditions in *The Testimony of Truth* from Nag Hammadi (CG IX, 3)" in *Ex Orbe Religionum. Studia Geo Widengren . . .* (Leiden, 1972) p. 470.

39. Jonas, "Response," p. 287.

40. Ibid., p. 288.

41. Ibid.

42. Ibid., p. 293.

43. Ibid., p. 291.

44. Jeremiah 3:1–4; Hosea 2:2–7; Ezekiel 16:23–26; Psalm 103:1–5; Isaiah 30:15, 19–20; Psalm 6:6–9.

45. H. Jonas, *The Gnostic Religion* (Boston, 1963) p. 306.
46. *Tripartite Tractate* (CG I. 5), 111.5ff.; cf. 113.5ff.
47. *Gospel of Philip* (CG II. 3), 55.30.
48. See also the comments of A. H. Armstrong, in *Gnosis*, ed. Aland, "Gnosis and Greek Philosophy," p. 92*n*. 7.
49. A. Segal, *Two Powers in Heaven. Early Rabbinic Reports about Christianity and Gnosticism* (Leiden, 1977) p. 264.
50. Ibid., p. 266.
51. Tertullian, *Against Marcion*, 1.11.9; 2.26.1, etc.
52. Gen. 1:26: Tertullian, *Against Marcion*, 2.5.1 = *Hypostasis of the Archons* (CG II. 4), 87.23ff.; Gen. 2:7: Tertullian, *Against Marcion*, 2.9.1 = *Hypostasis of the Archons*, 88.3ff.; Gen. 3:22: Tertullian, *Against Marcion*, 2.25.4 = *Origin of the World* (CG II. 5), 120.25ff.
53. Irenaeus, *Against Heresies*, 1.27.3 = *Second Treatise of the Great Seth* (CG VII. 2), 62.26ff (biblical heroes as laughingstocks).
54. In general see E. Pagels, *The Gnostic Paul. Gnostic Exegesis of the Pauline Letters* (Philadelphia, 1975).
55. As reported by Clement of Alexandria, *Stromateis*, 7.106.
56. *Excerpts of Theodotus*, 23.

11: PAUL'S FRIENDS AND ENEMIES

1. So, among others, W. Bauer, *Orthodoxy and Heresy*, p. 225. For a re-evaluation of this traditional view, see A. Lindemann, *Paulus im ältesten Christentum. Das Bild des Apostels und die Rezeption der paulinischen Theologie in der frühchristlichen Literatur bis Marcion* (Tübingen, 1979).
2. See Pagels, *Gnostic Paul*, p. 161.
3. According to Irenaeus, *Against Heresies*, 1.27.
4. For the text, see D. J. Theron, *Evidence of Tradition* (Grand Rapids, Michigan, 1958) pp. 110f.
5. Tertullian, *On Baptism*, 17.
6. Markus Barth, *Ephesians* (Garden City, New York, 1974) pp. 244f. and others interpret 2:8b ("this is not your own doing, it is the gift of God—not because of works, lest any man should boast. . . .") as a polemical thrust against Gentile Christian Judaizers like those cited in Col. 2:16.
7. So Richardson, *Apostolic Church*, pp. 150–156.
8. So Barth, *Ephesians*, p. 291: "Christ has abrogated the divisive function of the law—and therefore not God's holy law itself. . . ."
9. Richardson, *Apostolic Church*, pp. 150–156.
10. Barth in *Ephesians*, p. 310, comments that the author never intended "that the Gentiles must become Jews, or the Jews Gentiles."
11. For a discussion of authorship, date and related matters see Kümmel, *New Testament*, pp. 392–394.

12. The citation and exegesis of Psalm 95:7–11 in ch. 3 is not evidence to the contrary. The psalm is cited only to warn the readers not to be rebellious like the Israelites in the desert. In 3:16, the author specifically limits the rebels to those who left Egypt under Moses' leadership.

13. See especially the lengthy passage in the Philo, *Migration of Abraham*, 89–93. "There are some who, regarding the written laws as symbols of spiritual realities, pay too much attention to the latter while disregarding the former" (89). Philo concludes with the following statement: "Why, we shall be ignoring the sanctity of the temple and a thousand other things, if we pay heed only to what is revealed in the inner meaning of things" (92). This statement should serve as a warning to those who seek to show significant parallels between Philo and Hebrews. What they share is the cultural environment of Hellenized Judaism. This should not obscure the fact that on the issue of the Torah and its true meaning, Hebrews stand far closer to the extreme Jewish allegorists whom Philo resists than to Philo himself.

14. See P. Vielhauer, "On the 'Paulinism' of Acts," in Meeks, *Writings*, pp. 166–175.

15. So Meeks and Wilkens, *Jews and Christians*, p. 16.

16. J. Knox, *Marcion and the New Testament* (Chicago, 1942), p. 139.

17. Gaston, "Anti-Judaism," p. 23.

18. Ibid., p. 21 (emphasis added).

19. See the discussion on pp. 124f.

20. Epiphanius, *Panarion*, 28.5. 1–3; cf. Meeks, *Writings*, p. 178.

21. Epiphanius, *Panarion*, 30.16. 6–9; cf. Meeks, pp. 177f.

22. Hippolytus, *Refutation*, 8.20.1.

23. The passage appears in Origen's commentary on Psalm 82 as reported by Eusebius, *Ecclesiastical History*, 6.38.

24. Irenaeus, *Against Heresies*, 3.15.1.

25. Justin, *Dialogue*, 47.

26. Origen, *Celsus*, 2.3.

27. Epiphanius, *Panarion*, 29.9.1.

28. Origen, *Celsus*, 2.1.

29. See the discussion by Taylor, "Attitudes of the Fathers," pp. 509–511.

30. Jerome, *Commentary on Galatians* (*Patrologia Latina*, 26, 342).

31. Augustine, *Epistle* 40.

32. Jerome, *Epistle* 112.13.

33. Augustine, *Epistle* 82.

34. Ibid., *Epistle* 196.

35. Knox, *Marcion*, p. 117. Compare the comment of von Campenhausen, *Christian Bible*, p. 181: "Only when combined with these inauthentic letters could the genuine legacy of the apostle be tolerated by the Church and made 'canonical.' "

36. See the discussion in von Campenhausen, *Christian Bible*, pp. 177ff.

37. See M. Wiles, *The Divine Apostle: The Interpretation of St. Paul's Epistles in the Early Church* (Cambridge, 1967) pp. 132–134; reprinted under the title, "The Domesticated Apostle," in Meeks, *Writings*, pp. 207–213.

38. So E. J. Goodspeed, *The Formation of the New Testament* (Chicago, 1926) p. 75.

39. Gaston, "Paul," in Davies, *Foundations*, p. 48.

PART IV: THE CASE OF PAUL

1. The phrase, "Catholic radicals," is used by Davies, *Anti-Semitism*, p. 91.

2. S. Schechter, *Aspects of Rabbinic Theology. Major Concepts of The Talmud* (New York, 1909) p. 18.

3. So Eckardt, *Brothers*, p. 56.

4. Davies, *Anti-Semitism*, p. 102.

5. E. P. Sanders, *Paul*, p. 497.

6. Ibid., p. 543.

7. Ibid., p. 552 (his emphasis).

8. Gaston, "Paul," p. 66.

12: ON REINVENTING PAUL

1. Simon, *Verus Israel*, p. 98 (my translation).

2. Ruether, *Fratricide*, p. 96.

3. Ibid., p. 98.

4. Ibid., p. 100.

5. Ibid., p. 102.

6. Ibid., p. 107.

7. Ibid., p. 106.

8. Gaston, "Paul," in Davies, *Foundations*, pp. 48–71; Gaston, "Abraham and the Righteousness of God," *Horizons in Biblical Theology* 2 (1980): 39–68; and Gaston, "Israel's Enemies in Pauline Theology," *New Testament Studies* 28 (1982): 400–423.

9. Gaston, "Paul," p. 54.

10. Quotation from personal correspondence.

11. See especially Koenig, *Jews and Christians*. Koenig appears to have arrived at his conclusions independently of Gaston. His treatment of Paul (esp. pp. 37–59) is in certain respects less far-reaching than Gaston's.

12. P. Meyer, "Romans 10:4 and the 'End' of the Law," in *The Divine Helmsman. Studies on God's Control of Human Events*, ed. J. L. Crenshaw and S. Sandmel (New York, 1980) p. 64.

13. Ibid., p. 72.

14. Ibid., p. 69.

15. Stendahl, *Paul*, pp. 86f.

16. Barth has written extensively on the subject of Paul and Judaism. Gaston gives particular credit to Barth's commentary, *Ephesians*, especially pp. 242–252 where he discusses the meaning of the phrase "works of the law" in Paul's letters. See also, Barth, "Was Paul an Anti-Semite?," *Journal of Ecumenical Studies* 5 (1968): 78–104; and Barth, "Das Volk Gottes. Juden und Christen in der Botschaft des Paulus," in *Paulus. Apostat oder Apostel? Jüdische und Christliche Antworten* (Regensburg, 1977) pp. 45–134.

17. Stendhal, *Paul Among Jews*, where his influential article, "The Apostle Paul and the Introspective Conscience of the West," first published in 1963, is reprinted.

18. Sanders, *Paul*.

19. Stendahl, *Paul Among Jews*, p. 4.

20. For the idea of a bridge generation see Eckardt, *Brothers*, pp. 137–140.

21. See Ruether's response to Gaston in Davies, *Foundations*, pp. 240–242.

22. Ruether, *Fratricide*, p. 228.

23. Moore, "Christian Writers," p. 197.

24. Sanders, *Paul*, p. 57.

25. Ibid., p. 552.

26. Ibid., p. 551 (author's emphasis).

27. Ibid.

28. Gaston, "Paul," p. 56. Compare the similar statement in Idinopulos and Ward, "Christology," p. 198.

29. So W. D. Davies, "From Schweitzer to Scholem: Reflections on Sabbatai Svi," *Journal of Biblical Literature* 95 (1976): "*The* crucial question which it [Judaism] confronted was that posed by the Gentile world" (p. 547).

30. G. Bornkamm, *Paul* (New York, 1971) p. 95; Stendahl refers to this passage in his *Paul Among Jews*, p. 133. Compare Gaston's comment in "Paul," p. 52, that "most of the great interpreters of Paul identified Paul's opponents with their own." As an example he cites E. Käsemann's *Commentary on Romans* (Grand Rapids, Michigan, 1980) in which Käsemann repeatedly speaks of the Jews as exemplifying the universal type of the *homo religiosus*.

31. Richardson, *Apostolic Church*, p. 101.

32. Sanders, *Paul*, p. 519.

33. Gaston, "Paul," pp. 61f.

34. Sanders, *Paul*, p. 138n61.

35. See the useful discussion in Richardson, *Apostolic Church*, pp. 45–47.

13: HAS CHRIST ABROGATED THE TORAH?
HAS GOD REJECTED HIS PEOPLE?

1. On introductory matters generally, see Richardson, *Apostolic Church*, pp. 126f.; Bornkamm, *Paul*, pp. 88–96; and Kümmel, *New Testament*, pp. 305–320.

2. On this passage see R. B. Hays, "Psalm 143 and the Logic of Romans 3," *Journal of Biblical Literature* 99 (1980): 107–115. Hays argues as follows: (1) Psalm 143 enables Paul to argue that it is God's righteousness, his *pistis* and *dikaiosynē*, that establishes the standing of Jews; (2) 3:9–20 is thus a rebuttal of any suggestion that God is unfair in declaring that Israel has no advantage; (3) there is no break between 3:20 and 3:21; and (4) throughout chapter 3 the issue is not "justification by faith" or "works righteousness" but the primacy of God's righteousness.

3. So Käsemann, pp. 93f.: "the law actually reaches people only in this religious perversion, so that only Christian faith can give it back its character as promise by putting an end to pious achievement. . . . The obedience of faith abrogates the law as a mediator of salvation, sees through the perversion of understanding it as a principle of achievement. . . ."

4. G. Howard, "Romans 3:21–31 and the Inclusion of the Gentiles," *Harvard Theological Review* 63 (1970): 233.

5. Ibid., pp. 223–233, esp. 229.

6. G. Howard, "Christ and End of the Law: The Meaning of Romans 10:4ff.," *Journal of Biblical Literature* 88 (1969): 336. J. Koenig offers a similar reading of Rom. 3:22 and 10:4ff. as pointing to the inclusion of the Gentiles rather than to the exclusion of Israel. Christ was indeed the "end of the law" but *only* for those who believed, namely, Gentile Christians (*Jews and Christians*, pp. 43f. and 46).

7. So Gaston, "Paul," pp. 63f., especially note 63.

8. So Howard, "Romans 3.21–31," p. 230: "Since Paul opens and closes with the theme of universalism, it is logical to look to it as the key to his theology in the present passage."

9. So Gaston, "Paul," pp. 63f.

10. See Gaston, "Abraham," p. 57: "Rom. 4 is not about Christian faith. . . ."

11. The reference is to Ps. 32:1–2 regarding the forgiveness of sins.

12. Gaston, "Abraham," p. 41.

13. The translation is based on the Greek text of the Septuagint.

14. Gaston, "Abraham," p. 57.

15. Stendahl, *Paul Among Jews*, pp. 86f. and 92–94.

16. See ibid., p. 94 about the Moffatt translation of Romans 7:25b.

17. Ibid., p. 92; cf. p. 94.

18. Clearly the story of the serpent and its seduction of Eve in Genesis 3 lies in the background of Paul's thought.

19. Stendahl, *Paul Among Jews*, p. 80.

20. Gaston, "Paul," pp. 62–64.

21. See the discussion on p. 233.

22. See Gaston, "Paul," p. 64, where he shows that the early chapters of Romans are dominated by a view of Gentiles as descendants of Adam and thus subject to his sinfulness.

23. On this verse and its place in the overall setting of Rom. 9–11, see Meyer, "Romans 10:4," pp. 59–78.

24. Howard, "Christ," p. 336.

25. Koenig, *Jews and Christians*, offers a somewhat different reading of 10:4, based on his view that "every one who has faith" is Paul's typical way of referring to Gentiles (pp. 43, 46).

26. So, for instance, W. Meeks, "The Image of the Androgyne: Some Uses of a Symbol in Earliest Christianity," *History of Religions* 13 (1973–74): 165–208, esp. 207f.

27. So also ibid., p. 208.

28. See D. Kaufmann, "Das Alter der drei Benedictionen von Israel vom Freien und vom Mann," *Monatsschrift für Geschichte und Wissenschaft des Judentums* 37 (1893): 14–18; and Madeleine Boucher, "Some Unexplored Parallels to 1 Cor 11, 11–21 and Gal 3, 28: The NT on the Role of Women," *Catholic Biblical Quarterly* 31 (1969): 50–58.

29. Tosefta, *Berakhot* 7.18; see Boucher, "Parallels," pp. 53f.

30. *Seder Eliahu* 7; see Boucher, "Parallels." The saying depends on the double meaning of *spnh*: (1) "northward" and (2) "hidden, treasured up."

31. See Boucher's remarks in "Parallels," pp. 51, 55.

32. Typical of the contrary view is H. Schlier, *Der Brief an die Galater* (Göttingen, 1965): the formula "betont sehr stark die Wirklichkeit der Gleichheit aller in Christus Jesus" (p. 175).

33. Richardson, *Apostolic Church*, pp. 9–14, 74.

34. There is no counterpart for "true" in the Greek text.

35. See the authors cited in Schlier, *Galater*, p. 283*n*2.

36. See the authors cited in ibid., p. 283*n*3.

37. E. D. Burton, *The Epistle to the Galatians* (New York, 1920) p. 358.

38. Ibid.

39. Richardson, *Apostolic Church*, pp. 79–80.

14: WHAT CIRCUMSTANCES GAVE RISE TO PAUL'S EXTENDED
DISCUSSION OF ISRAEL, THE TORAH, AND THE GENTILES?

1. Stendahl, *Paul Among Jews*, pp. 127f.

2. On introductory matters, see Kümmel, *New Testament*, pp. 294–304.

3. So J. Munck, *Paul*, pp. 87–134.

4. H. D. Betz, *Galatians* (Philadelphia, 1979) p. 116.

5. Stendahl, *Paul Among Jews*, p. 94.

6. For an analysis of the overall literary structure of Galatians as consisting of *narratio, propositio,* and *probatio,* see Betz, *Galatians*, pp. 113f.

7. Barth, *Ephesians*, p. 246.

8. Cf. Rom. 7:4: "You Gentiles have died to the law through the body of Christ."

9. See especially Gaston, "Paul," pp. 62–64.

10. Ibid., pp. 63f.

11. Ibid., p. 62.

12. Ibid., p. 59.

13. Ibid., p. 61 (author's emphasis).

14. On this meaning of *paidagogos*, see Stendahl, *Paul Among Jews*, p. 86. In an unpublished essay entitled "Angels and Gentiles in early Judaism and Paul," Gaston dismantles the traditionally anti-Jewish reading of Galatians 3:19b ("and it [the Torah] was ordained by angels through an intermediary"). The force of this traditional, and virtually unanimous reading is that Paul is here seeking to diminish the status of the Torah by having it transmitted by angels rather than by God himself. Against the frequent claim that Paul relies on a common Jewish tradition concerning the role of angels in transmitting the Torah, Gaston demonstrates that there is no such tradition. What we find instead is a number of texts which speak of God's angels ruling over "the nations" as administrators of his law. This proposal has several important advantages: it is fully consistent with the status of Gentiles elsewhere in Galatians, where they are as being "under the law"; and it takes seriously the fact that the letter as a whole is directed to Gentiles and deals exclusively with the question of Gentiles and the Torah.

15. Gaston, "Paul," p. 66.

16. On this passage see Gaston's essay, "Israel's Enemies in Pauline Theology," 400–423.

17. There is good reason for supposing that verse 25a is a marginal gloss (so Burton, *Galatians*, p. 259). Verse 25b, which presupposes a situation of Jerusalem in slavery, looks very much as though it had been written after 70 C.E. or even after 135, when Jerusalem was converted into a pagan city. The most radical treatment of the passage from a textual perspective is to be found in J. C. O'Neill, *The Recovery of Paul's Letter to the Galatians* (London, 1972). He concludes that "if 4.21–24a, 28, 29, 31 cannot be isolated, all 4.21–31 is not Paul" (p. 64).

18. Burton, *Galatians*, p. 251.

19. Gaston in "Israel's Enemies," has shown that Isaac and Ishmael were often used in post-biblical Judaism to illustrate God's dealings with Israel and the Gentiles. He cites a midrash on Deut. 33:2 (Mekilta, *Baḥodesh* 5), a portion of the book of Jubilees (15.28–32), and the Targum of Pseudo-Jonathan at Gen. 22:1. The third text depicts a controversy between Isaac and Ishmael in which the latter boasts of his greater righteousness on the basis of having been circumcised as an adult. But here, as in the other passages, God elects Isaac and turns away Ishmael, the father of the nations. Jubilees adds that God appointed spirits over Ishmael and his descendants "to lead them astray from Him." Gaston comments that if "the troublemakers in Galatia were not only boastful but specifically were boasting of being circumcised as adults (Gal.

6.13–14), then Paul must have immediately thought about Ishmael when he heard of them" (p. 407).

20. On the background to the letter see Kümmel, *New Testament*, pp. 320–335 and Richardson, *Apostolic Church*, pp. 111–117.

21. Richardson, *Apostolic Church*, pp. 112f., is inclined to see the threat as potential rather than actual. This makes no difference to the argument.

22. So Koenig, *Jews and Christians*, p. 163n7 (author's emphasis).

23. On the background of the letter, see Kümmel, *New Testament*, pp. 279–293; Georgi, *Die Gegner des Paulus*, passim; and J.-F. Collange, *Enigmes de la deuxième Epitre de Paul aux Corinthiens* (Cambridge, 1972) pp. 1–20.

24. Georgi, *Die Gegner des Paulus*.

25. See especially, H. Ulonska, "Die Doxa des Mose. Zum Problem des Alten Testaments in 2. Kor. 3, 1–16," *Evangelische Theologie* 26 (1966): 378–388; and Collange, *Enigmes, passim.*

26. So also Kümmel, *New Testament*, p. 285.

27. Collange, *Enigmes*, p. 64.

28. So Ulonska, "Doxa des Mose," p. 382.

29. Collange notes that the term "lord" in 3:16 is used consistently by Paul in this way with reference to God, not Christ.

15: WHAT WAS THE HEART OF PAUL'S ARGUMENT WITH THE JEWS, HIS KINSMEN BY RACE?

1. In both places, 3:30 and 9:32, Paul uses the preposition *ek* to describe the situation of Jews and the preposition *dia* to describe the situation of Gentiles.

2. Sanders, *Paul*, p. 157.

3. It may be noted here that Paul's position presupposes that covenant status and salvation are not identical concepts.

4. B. A. Pearson, "1 Thessalonians 2:13–16: A Deutero-Pauline Interpolation," *Harvard Theological Review* 64 (1971): 79–94.

5. The statement in Gal. 6:12 ("It is only those who want to make a good showing in the flesh that would compel you to be circumcised, and only in order that they may not be persecuted for the cross of Christ.") suggests that Gentile Christians were acceptable at least to some Jews provided that they underwent circumcision.

6. The passage in Rom. 9:6f. may be taken as referring not to the faithful remnant within Israel but to Gentiles.

7. We should probably understand the "some" (Jews) of 11:14 as those who will be brought around as the result of Paul's activity, and the "all Israel" of 11:26 as those who will be saved by God at the end.

8. On the eschatological character of Paul's missionary activity see most recently Richardson, *Apostolic Church*, pp. 102–111.

9. Stendahl, *Paul Among Jews*, p. 4.

10. Paul's remark in Romans 11:14 that he hopes to make "my fellow Jews jealous, and thus save some of them," is certainly not a program for the conversion of the Jews. At most it means that some Jews might follow in his tracks.

11. Gaston, "Paul," p. 67.

12. Eckardt, *Brothers*, p. 156.

CONCLUSION

1. G. Dix, "The Ministry in the Early Church," in *The Apostolic Ministry*, ed. K. E. Kirk (London, 1946) p. 228.

2. H. Arendt, *The Origins of Totalitarianism* (New York, 1966) p. xi. See the discussion of Davies, "On Religious Myths and Their Secular Translation: Some Historical Reflections," in Davies, *Foundations*, pp. 188–207.

3. H. Arendt, *Eichmann in Jerusalem: A Report on the Banality of Evil* (New York, 1963) p. 297.

4. E. R. Dodds, *Pagan and Christian*, p. 3.

5. Tal, *Christians and Jews*, p. 304.

GENERAL INDEX

Aaron, 70
Abel, 110
Abraham, 70, 93, 95, 110, 121, 151, 197, 217, 219f., 238f., 241f., 246, 249, 250f., 263f.
Acts, 156, 184–86, 190f.
Acts of Paul and Thecla, 174, 176
Acts of the Alexandrian Martyrs, 49, 53
Acts of the Pagan Martyrs, 110
Adam, 110, 124
Adler, M. A., 284
Adonai, 103
Adversus Ioudaeos: type of Christian literature, 153
Agatharchides of Cnidus, 39
Agathos Daimon, 68
Aland, B., 296
alchemy, 54, 109f.
Alexander Polyhistor, 39
Alexander Severus, 93
Alexandria, 19, 36; anti-Semitic clubs, 48, 50; synagogue, 52; Christians, 54
allegory, 104, 158
Alypius of Antioch, 94
Ambrose, 97, 120, 160
Ammianus Marcellinus, 92, 96
anti-Judaism (Christian), 6, 8, 20, 114; Christian sources, 20, 24–27, 117; in New Testament, 33f.; intrinsic to Christianity, 20; pagan sources, 19f.; types of, 8, 25, 140f., 144, 147–49, 169–73, 183; unlike pagan anti-Semitism, 29
anti-Romanism, in Egypt, 43–54
anti-Semitism (ancient pagan), 6–8, 166; extent of, 9, 59, 112
anti-Semitism (Christian): perversion of true Chris-

tianity, 17f.; present in New Testament, 18
anti-Semitism (modern), 13, 202, 267; Christian sources, 19, 20–22, 202, 267
Antioch, 129, 131
Antiochus IV Epiphanes, 39f., 46
Antiochus VII Sidetes, 40, 62, 70
Antoninus Pius, 61, 91f.
Antonius Diogenes, 81, 106
Aphraat, 121–25; references to Jewish "debater of the people," 121
Apion, 31, 36, 43, 45–47, 49, 71, 82
Apollonius Molon, 41, 56
Apollonius of Tyana, 93, 283
Applebaum, S., 36, 62, 66, 272, 278, 285f.
Aptus, 189
Arabia, 260
Arendt, Hannah, 267, 306
Armstrong, A. H., 298
Artapanus, 54
Ascellicus, 189
Asia Minor, 132
ass-worship: attributed to Jews, 40, 46
astrology, 54, 109f.
Athenagoras, 175
Attis, 77
Augustine, 133, 160, 188f., 278
Augustus, 43, 62, 75, 86f.
Avi-Yonah, M., 89, 283
Aziza, C., 296

Bamberger, B., 277f.
Barb, A. A., 288
barbara superstitio (term applied to Judaism), 58
Bardy, G., 286
Barnabas: letter of, 130f., 158, 183
Barnard, L. W., 164, 296
Baron, S., 283

Barrett, C. K., 292
Barth, M., 200, 233, 301
Basileides, 175
Bauer, W., 291
Baum, G., 17–19, 33, 272
Baur, F. C., 11, 191
Beker, J. C., 275
Berenice, 62
Berger, P. and Luckmann, T., 22, 273
Berthelot, M., 289
Berthelot, M. and Ruelle, C., 109, 289
Betz, H. D., 303
Bible: Hebrew/Jewish, 21f., 26, 121; pagan knowledge of, 46, 76, 111, 171
Bickerman, E., 275
Blumenkranz, B., 33, 295
boasting: as Pauline idea, 248f.
Bonner, C., 288
Bornkamm, G., 32, 207, 225, 301
Boucher, M., 303
Bousset, W., 32
Bowersock, G. W., 74, 280, 284
Brandon, S. G. F., 144
Braude, W. G., 278
Braun, R. and Richter, J., 284
bridge-generation: term applied to Jewish Christianity, 201
Bultmann, R., 32, 191, 203

Caecilius of Calacte, 59f., 75
Caesarea, 98–101
Caligula, 45, 48f., 57, 62
Callinicum, 120
Campenhausen, H. v., 295
Caracalla, 93
Celsus, 69, 103, 111
Cerinthus, 187
Chadwick, H., 287
Chaeremon, 43, 45, 49, 82
Chaldean Oracles, 107

INDEX OF BIBLICAL PASSAGES